A Southern Woman
OF *Letters*

Women's Diaries and Letters of the South
Carol Bleser, Series Editor

A Woman Doctor's Civil War: Esther Hill Hawks' Diary
Edited by Gerald Schwartz

A Rebel Came Home:
The Diary and Letters of Floride Clemson, 1863–1866
Edited by Ernest McPherson Lander, Jr., and Charles M. McGee, Jr.

The Shattered Dream: The Day Book of Margaret Sloan, 1900–1902
Edited by Harold Woodell

The Letters of a Victorian Madwoman
Edited by John S. Hughes

A Confederate Nurse: The Diary of Ada W. Bacot, 1860–1863
Edited by Jean V. Berlin

A Plantation Mistress on the Eve of the Civil War:
The Diary of Keziah Goodwyn Hopkins Brevard, 1860–1861
Edited by John Hammond Moore

Lucy Breckinridge of Grove Hill: The Journal of a Virginia Girl, 1862–1864
Edited by Mary D. Robertson

George Washington's Beautiful Nelly: The Letters of
Eleanor Parke Curtis Lewis to Elizabeth Bordley Gibson, 1794–1851
Edited by Patricia Brady

A Confederate Lady Comes of Age:
The Journal of Pauline DeCaradeuc Heyward, 1863–1888
Edited by Mary D. Robertson

A Northern Woman in the Plantation South:
Letters of Tryphena Blanche Holder Fox, 1856–1876
Edited by Wilma King

Best Companions: Letters of Eliza Middleton Fisher and Her Mother, Mary
Hering Middleton, from Charleston, Philadelphia, and Newport, 1839–1846
Edited by Eliza Cope Harrison

Stateside Soldier: Life in the Women's Army Corps, 1944–1945
Aileen Kilgore Henderson

From the Pen of a She-Rebel: The Civil War Diary of Emilie Riley McKinley
Edited by Gordon A. Cotton

Between North and South: The Letters of Emily Wharton Sinkler, 1842–1865
Edited by Anne Sinkler Whaley LeClercq

A Southern Woman of Letters:
The Correspondence of Augusta Jane Evans Wilson
Edited by Rebecca Grant Sexton

A Southern Woman
OF *Letters*

THE CORRESPONDENCE OF
AUGUSTA JANE EVANS WILSON

Edited by Rebecca Grant Sexton

University of South Carolina Press

© 2002 University of South Carolina

Published in Columbia, South Carolina, by the
University of South Carolina Press

Manufactured in the United States of America

06   05   04   03   02   5   4   3   2   1

Library of Congress Cataloging-in-Publication Data

Evans, Augusta J. (Augusta Jane), 1835–1909.
  A Southern woman of letters : the correspondence of Augusta Jane
Evans Wilson / edited by Rebecca Grant Sexton.
    p. cm. — (Women's diaries and letters of the South)
  ISBN 1-57003-440-0 (cloth : alk. paper)
    1. Evans, Augusta J. (Augusta Jane), 1835–1909—Correspondence.
  2. Novelists, American—19th century—Correspondence. 3. Women—
Southern States—Correspondence. 4. Women and literature—Southern
States. I. Sexton, Rebecca Grant, 1945– II. Title. III. Series.
PS3333 .A44 2002
813'.3—dc21   2002003437

For Ken and Helen

Contents

Illustrations

Series Editor's Preface

A Southern Woman of Letters: The Correspondence of Augusta Jane Evans Wilson is the latest volume in what had been the Women's Diaries and Letters of the Nineteenth-Century South series. This series has been redefined and is now titled Women's Diaries and Letters of the South, enabling us to include some remarkably fine works from the twentieth century. This series includes a number of never-before-published diaries, some collections of unpublished correspondence, and a few reprints of published diaries—a potpourri of nineteenth-century and, now, twentieth-century Southern women's writings.

The series enables women to speak for themselves, providing readers with a rarely opened window into Southern society before, during, and after the American Civil War and into the twentieth century. The significance of these letters and journals lies not only in the personal revelations and the writing talent of these women authors but also in the range and versatility of the documents' contents. Taken together, these publications will tell us much about the heyday and the fall of the Cotton Kingdom, the mature years of the "peculiar institution," the war years, the adjustment of the South to a new social order following the defeat of the Confederacy, and the New South of the twentieth century. Through these writings, the reader will also be presented with firsthand accounts of everyday life and social events, courtships and marriages, family life and travels, religion and education, and the life-and-death matters that made up the ordinary and extraordinary world of the American South.

Carol Bleser

Acknowledgments

This book could not have been written without the assistance and encouragement of Dr. Rosemary F. Franklin, professor at the University of Georgia and excellent teacher, scholar, and mentor. I am also indebted to Dr. James E. Kibler, who introduced me to Augusta Evans Wilson and whose scholarship and teaching remain an inspiration.

I am grateful to the librarians and researchers who assisted me in locating and photocopying Augusta Evans Wilson's letters: Andrea Watson, special collections librarian, William Stanley Hoole Special Collections Library, University of Alabama; Debbie Pendleton, assistant director for public services, Alabama Department of Archives and History; Cindy Bolling, University of Alabama Press; Karen Dobrusky, reference librarian, Barnard College Library, Columbia University; William H. Loos, curator, Rare Book Room, Buffalo and Erie County Public Library; M. N. Brown, curator of manuscripts, Special Collections, Brown University; Jean Ashton, director, Rare Book and Manuscript Library, Columbia University; Craig Lloyd, director of archives, Simon Schwob Memorial Library, Columbus State University; Philip N. Cronenwett, curator of manuscripts and chief of special collections, Dartmouth College Library; Noel VanGorden, manager, Burton Historical Collection, Detroit Public Library; William R. Erwin, Jr., senior reference librarian, Special Collections Library, Duke University; Beverly B. Allen, reference archivist, Special Collections, Robert W. Woodruff Library, Emory University; Mary Ellen Brooks, head of Hargrett Rare Book and Manuscript Library, University of Georgia; Diana Franzusoff Peterson, manuscripts cataloger, Special Collections, Haverford College; Jean Getchell, archives chairman, Historic Mobile Preservation Society Archives; Linda Stanley, curator of manuscripts and archives, The Historical Society of Pennsylvania; the staff in the Manuscript Division of the Library of Congress; Charles J. Torrey, museum researcher, City of Mobile Museum Department; Richard A. Shrader, Public Services, Manuscripts Department and Southern Historical Collection, Wilson Library, University of North Carolina, Chapel Hill; Leon C. Miller, manuscripts librarian, Howard-Tilton Memorial Library, Tulane University; Michael Plunkett, director of special collections and curator of manuscripts, Clifton Waller Barrett Library of American Literature, University of Virginia Library; and Stephen Jones, researcher, Beinecke Rare Book and Manuscript Library, Yale University.

Grateful acknowledgment is made to the University of Alabama Press for permission to quote at length from the letter of AJEW, 4 August 1862, previously published in *The Alabama Confederate Reader* (1992).

I am very grateful for the able help I received from the editors at the University of South Carolina Press. Barbara A. Brannon, the managing editor, and Jennifer Hynes, the copyeditor, worked meticulously to polish my manuscript. I am also indebted to Alexander Moore, acquisitions editor, for his patience and assistance during the acceptance process. Series editor Carol Bleser also provided guidance. It is an honor to have this work included among the books in her Women's Diaries and Letters of the South series.

I would also like to express appreciation to my mother, Helen Grant, who patiently spent many hours helping me research poetry quotations. Finally, I would like to honor my husband, Ken Sexton, who set aside his own projects to give me the encouragement and support to finish mine.

Prefatory Note

In collecting Wilson's letters, I have faithfully reproduced her spelling, punctuation, and format. She, for example, frequently omitted periods after abbreviations such as Dr, Mrs, and Mr. She also did not observe paragraphing in
her letters.

For the sake of consistency and convenience, in all my notes on the letters I refer to Augusta Evans Wilson by her married initials, AEW, although
she was Augusta Evans until 1868.

At the beginning of each letter on the left of the page is an italicized
manuscript number that I have assigned the letter for convenience. Next to
this number, also in italics, is an abbreviated title of the library in which the
letter is housed. Please see the Abbreviations of Source Libraries on page xvii
for complete information on each library.

Abbreviations of Source Libraries

Alabama
Augusta Evans Wilson Papers
William Stanley Hoole Special
  Collections Library
University of Alabama
Tuscaloosa, Alabama

Alabama Archives
Alabama Department of Archives
  and History
Montgomery, Alabama

Alabama Press
Malcolm C. McMillan,
  The Alabama Confederate Reader
(Tuscaloosa: University of Alabama Press,
  1992). Used by permission.

Barnard College Library
Barnard College Library
Overbury Collection
Columbia University
New York, New York

Buffalo Public Library
Buffalo and Erie County Public Library
Buffalo, New York

Brown
Brown University Library
Providence, Rhode Island

Columbia
E. C. Stedman Papers
Harper Brothers Papers
Rare Book and Manuscript Library
Columbia University
New York, New York

Columbus
Louise Jones DuBose Papers
Chattahoochee Valley Historical
  Collections, The Archives

	Simon Schwob Memorial Library
	Columbus State University
	Columbus, Georgia
Dartmouth	Dartmouth College Library
	Hanover, New Hampshire
Detroit Public Library	Burton Historical Collection
	Detroit Public Library
	Detroit, Michigan
Duke	Rare Book, Manuscript, and Special Collections Library
	Duke University
	Durham, North Carolina
Emory	Special Collections
	Robert W. Woodruff Library
	Emory University
	Atlanta, Georgia
	Letter to Dr. W. S. Wyman, Dec. 12 [n.y.] in Miscellaneous Collections
	(E) — Literary Manuscripts. Also see the Pierre Gustave Toutant Beauregard Papers, the Mildred Seydell Papers, the Alexander Hamilton Stephens Papers, and the Warren A. Candler Papers.
Georgia	Hargrett Rare Book and Manuscript Library
	University of Georgia Libraries
	Athens, Georgia
Haverford	Charles Roberts Autograph Letters Collection
	Haverford College Library
	Haverford, Pennsylvania
Historic Mobile Society	Historic Mobile Preservation Society Archives
	Mobile, Alabama

Historical Society of Pennsylvania	The Historical Society of Pennsylvania Philadelphia, Pennsylvania

Library of Congress	The John Esten Cooke Collection
	    (MMC-853)
	The Jabez L. Curry Papers
	    (Series two, volume one)
	Manuscript Division
	The Library of Congress
	Washington, D.C.

Mobile Museum	City of Mobile Museum Department Mobile, Alabama
North Carolina	Southern Historical Collection The Rachel Lyons Heustis Papers, #1200 Wilson Library University of North Carolina at Chapel Hill Chapel Hill, North Carolina
Tulane	Townsend-Stanton Family Papers Special Collections Tulane University Library New Orleans, Louisiana

Virginia	Correspondence of Augusta Evans Wilson
	    (MSS 8293)
	Clifton Waller Barrett Library of
	    American Literature
	Special Collections Department
	University of Virginia Library
	Charlottesville, Virginia

Yale, Beinecke Library	Yale Collection of American Literature Beinecke Rare Book and Manuscript Library Yale University New Haven, Connecticut

Introduction

The name Augusta Evans Wilson does not appear in most literary histories of American literature. Her novels are not analyzed in collections of critical essays, and excerpts from her writings are not found in anthologies. Yet she was one of the most popular authors of the nineteenth century, with most of her novels becoming national best-sellers. Her fourth book, *St. Elmo,* sold more copies than any other novel of the nineteenth century except *Uncle Tom's Cabin.* More than a best-seller, *St. Elmo* became something of a cultural phenomenon. As Wilson's biographer, William Perry Fidler, reports, steamboats, railway coaches, hotels, two villages, a punch, a cigar, several "blue-ribboned dogs," and "one of Mobile's finest camellias" were all named St. Elmo. All across the United States, numerous baby girls were christened Edna Earl after the novel's heroine and baby boys were named St. Elmo after the hero. Many estates were dubbed "La Bocage" after St. Elmo's home (Fidler, *A Biography,* 128–29).

Wilson wrote a total of nine novels, and all but the first were very successful, making her name a household word across the United States. Who was this woman whose novels brought her fame and fortune while male writers such as Nathaniel Hawthorne and Herman Melville were struggling to find an audience?

Augusta Jane Evans was born on May 8, 1835, in the frontier town of Columbus, Georgia. Her parents, Matthew Evans and the former Sarah Howard, were both from prominent, wealthy, old Southern families. Columbus was experiencing a boom period, and Matthew Evans prospered along with the town. He built a grand mansion—later known as "Matt's folly"—for his family and opened a store with his brother. When Columbus's boom period was followed inevitably by depression, Augusta's father went bankrupt and lost his home, his business, and his wife's $30,000 dowry (Fidler 11–19).

Attempting to repair his fortune, Matthew Evans moved his family, now consisting of Augusta (age ten) and five younger children, to San Antonio, Texas, and then to Mobile, Alabama. The family, however, remained in poverty until Augusta Evans began earning money from her novels.

Augusta Evans thus spent her first ten years amid wealth and luxury, only to learn the deprivation and humiliation of poverty. Her childhood experiences left her with such fear of poverty—and its attendant powerlessness—that later, as a wealthy adult, she always carried $100 in her pocket (Fidler 20).

As a young woman, Evans missed the usual youthful period of courtship and marriage, perhaps because of her father's financial situation. Helen Papashvily speculates that because of her family's aristocratic background, Evans would have expected to make a good match; her father's straitened circumstances, however, made this impossible (*All the Happy Endings,* 154).

Although Evans always claimed that it was a great joy to make her father financially secure, she must surely have felt ambivalent about the man who lost his wife's fortune and had to be supported by his daughter. Perhaps it was wish fulfillment that caused Evans to write about heroines such as Beulah Benton and Edna Earl who, like Evans herself, had been powerless and poor in their youth but who, unlike Evans, were nevertheless ardently pursued by a succession of wealthy, extremely desirable suitors. In all Evans's novels, her heroines marry men who are strong, dominant, powerful, wealthy, and twenty to thirty years older than their brides, thus serving as combined husband–father figures. In fact, Evans herself, at the age of thirty-three, married a wealthy man who was twenty-seven years her senior.

Evans's first novel, *Inez: A Tale of the Alamo* (1855), was written to help her financially troubled family. This immature work is set in San Antonio and is concerned primarily with the heroine's successful efforts to refute the evil doctrines of Catholicism. Evans supposedly began the novel when she was fifteen and, at the age of twenty, presented the manuscript to her father as a Christmas present. Fidler explains that this gift was not an act of filial devotion but rather an attempt to win her father's approval of her writing a novel. Happily, she was successful in her strategy to overcome his reservations (40–41).

Anne Goodwyn Jones also discusses Evans's presentation of her first manuscript to her father and links it to an event from Evans's childhood. Shopping with her mother as a young child, Augusta stole a pair of red shoes. When her mother discovered the theft, Augusta insisted that taking the shoes was not stealing because she intended to give them to her baby brother. Later, as a young woman, Evans used the same strategy to overcome her father's possible disapproval of her writing a novel by implying that she had done it for him. Jones claims that these two incidents reflect Evans's "lifelong habit of explaining her controversial acts as really sacrificial" (*Tomorrow Is Another Day,* 70).

Evans applied the same reasoning to her career. Although she wrote her first two novels because she and her family needed money, Evans continued to write long after she had become wealthy. Never would she admit that she wrote as a means of self-fulfillment. Instead, she insisted all her life that she wrote to provide guidance and moral instruction for others. According to Jay

Hubbell, she "took immense satisfaction in the letters she received from reclaimed infidels and from culture-hungry young people who asked her what books they ought to read" (*South in American Literature,* 613).

The publication in 1859 of her second novel, *Beulah,* secured Evans's place as a popular author and made her financially comfortable. Also, with the publication of *Beulah, Macaria* (1864), and *St. Elmo* (1866), Evans entered the ranks of the domestic novelists. The traditional definition of the domestic novel, according to Nina Baym's *Woman's Fiction,* is a novel that takes place mostly within a home setting and that is based on the "cult of domesticity," the idea that a woman is most fulfilled through marriage and family. Baym, however, argues that the domestic novel has a broader definition: it is simply a novel about social relations. Far from presenting the woman as isolated at home, the domestic novel presents everyone as being based in a home setting. The woman, as the dominant figure in the home, can teach the virtues of love, cooperation, and support to counterpoint the marketplace values of the world. By shaping the values of her family, the woman can, indirectly at least, influence the values of society (26–27).

In addition, Baym argues that domestic novels present the idea that the heroine and, by extension, women in general, have the power to shape their own lives. The plot always involves what Baym calls a "trials and triumph" (17) theme. The heroine is left to fend for herself in some way. She is usually an orphan but might have a sickly widowed mother to support. Sometimes, though, she is an heiress who, due to some misfortune, loses her wealth and position. At any rate, she has to learn to develop her own capabilities and inner strength and to make her way in the world. The novel usually concludes with a happy marriage that, as Baym explains, is the "symbol of the successful accomplishment of the required task and resolutions of the basic problems in the story, which is in most primitive terms the story of the formation and assertion of a feminine ego" (12).

It is interesting to note that in domestic novels the heroine, while she is still in a weak, dependent state, cannot (either due to her choice or outside factors) marry the hero who is wealthy and powerful and who could solve all of her problems for her. Instead, she has to be somehow raised to a position of strength; only from there can she marry the man she has loved all along. Charlotte Brontë's Jane Eyre is lifted from her lowly state by a deus ex machina: an uncle she never knew dies and leaves her all of his money. (Of course Brontë goes a step further and has Mr. Rochester blinded and crippled so that he, not Jane, is in a weak position for their wedding.) Evans's novels *Beulah* and *St. Elmo* are similar to *Jane Eyre* but with an important difference: Evans's heroines must rise out of dependency and poverty by their own efforts. They reject marriage as an easy way out and instead develop careers as successful artists, teachers, or writers. Having established themselves in the world, they can then marry.

Most domestic novels conclude with a happy marriage. Evans's novels, however, here again have a twist, this time an ironic one. Her heroines, after having worked hard throughout the novel to establish their independence, frequently marry domineering men who demand their submission. (Portraying her heroes as strong, powerful, and domineering was perhaps Evans's reaction to growing up with a weak father.) In *Beulah,* when Guy Hartwell proposes to the title character, he addresses her as "child" and she calls him "sir." He asks her to choose between the "tyrant Ambition" (her career as a successful writer) and "that tyrant Guy Hartwell." She meekly replies, "Well, if I am to have a tyrant, I believe I prefer belonging to you?" (*Beulah,* 500), ending with an uncertain question mark.

This resolution, however, violates the integrity of the plot since Beulah's growth throughout the story has been toward independence and autonomy. Because several of Evans's novels end with the heroine submitting to a husband and/or to God's will, Drew Gilpin Faust claims that the heroines' independence is "safely contained" by the conclusion. Her verdict is that "Evans in the end subverts her own subversion" (*Mothers of Invention,* 175).

Beulah, however, actually ends with juxtaposed—and conflicting—scenes of power: Hartwell's proposal to Beulah, in which he assumes the dominant role, and Beulah's efforts to convert him to Christianity, a scene in which she is his spiritual superior. The novel thus ends with a tension of unresolved conflicts.

Nina Baym believes that the domestic novel represents a "moderate or pragmatic feminism," which is to say a feminism existing within the constraints of the values and mores of the time (*Woman's Fiction,* 18). Baym also points out that "Augusta Evans' heroines are the strongest, most brilliant, and most accomplished in the long line of women's heroines." They become independent not because they *have* to but because they *choose* to; they scorn dependency. Baym asserts that Evans "represents something that the plots of necessity had largely concealed: that a woman might *wish* to struggle and strive, that she might find the protected and pampered ideal life (assuming it were attainable) frustrating and dull" (278).

For example, early in the novel Beulah makes a strong feminist statement to her friend Clara, a conventional, weak-willed young woman who advocates a life of dependency for women. Beulah exclaims:

> Don't talk to me about woman's clinging, dependent nature. You are opening your lips to repeat that senseless simile of oaks and vines; I

don't want to hear it; there are no creeping tendencies about me. You can wind, and lean, and hang on somebody else if you like; but I feel more like one of those old pine trees yonder. I can stand up. (*Beulah,* 141)

Again and again Beulah refuses the help and financial support of Dr. Hartwell and insists on making her own way in the world, first as a struggling teacher and later as a very successful writer.

The domestic novels served somewhat as "how-to" books, giving young women instructions and examples of how to make their way in the world. In addition to urging women to follow a path toward independence, the novels also stressed the importance of a good education. Here again Evans went further than her contemporary authors. As Baym points out, Evans wanted to prove that women were capable of receiving the same education as men. Other novelists such as Susan Warner and Maria Cummins showed their heroines mastering difficult subjects, but Evans goes beyond them and presents heroines such as Beulah and Edna Earl who are true scholars (*Woman's Fiction,* 280). Edna even masters such esoteric languages as Hebrew and Chaldee. Evans has other heroines studying advanced mathematics, astronomy, theology, and, of course, Greek and Latin.

Evans wrote with a pedantic, erudite style and a heavy-handed use of classical allusions and quotations. Critics repeatedly attacked her novels for their stilted language, but she refused to change, believing that she wrote to uplift and educate her readers. Baym compares her to the nouveau riche who want to show off their wealth; Evans was proud of her education and wanted to display it (280). In addition, she wanted to prove that women were capable of being well educated. (She also frequently used this pedantic style of writing in her letters—particularly when writing to powerful men.)

The domestic novels also encouraged young women to use their reason and not allow their emotions to sway them into making a bad marriage. In this respect, the domestic novel was a major advance over its predecessor, the seduction novel, which portrayed women as the passive victims of men, victims who could be emotionally manipulated into making bad choices. In the domestic novels, however, as Baym points out, the heroines used good judgment to select a suitable husband. They never allowed themselves to be deceived by a man's promise to reform after marriage and, more important, they refused to be the agents of his reformation.

In *St. Elmo,* the suitor by that name, who is a rake and Byronic hero, begs Edna Earl to save him by marrying him. He asks her to do what only a good wife can do and "save her erring, sinful husband. . . . Edna, as you value my soul, my eternal welfare, give yourself to me! Give your pure, sinless life to purify mine." Refusing to be swayed by his emotional appeal, Edna sends him away to find his own salvation: "No! no! I am no viceregent of an outraged and insulted God! I put no faith in any man whose conscience another keeps. Go yonder to Jesus. He only can save and purify you" (*St. Elmo*, 263).

St. Elmo follows Edna's advice; by the end of the novel he has become a minister and he and Edna marry. Through his conversion to Christianity, he has acquired the feminine qualities of nurturing and caring for others. Edna's heart ailment, on the other hand, literally indicates a broken heart, for she has long loved St. Elmo but had at first rejected him because of his unrepentant nature.

These changes in both characters indicate not a dominance of one over the other but a mutual need for each other. St. Elmo's position as minister is also significant in that this is work Edna can share with him. Edna will thus have a more egalitarian marriage than most nineteenth-century women, real or fictional (see Baym, *Woman's Fiction*, 41).

In *Macaria*, published in 1864, Evans pleads the cause of the Confederacy so effectively that Union General George H. Thomas, in Tennessee at the time with his army, called the book "dangerous" and ordered that all copies found among his troops be confiscated and burned (Hubbell, *South in American Literature*, 611). In addition to being an apology for the Confederacy, *Macaria* is also a domestic novel with a twist: after overcoming trials and adversity, the two heroines are rewarded at the end not with marriage but with careers and the opportunity to be of service to others. As Faust explains, in 1864 almost half of Southern white males were either wounded or dead. As a result, many women could look forward to a single life. Continuing the didactic purpose of the domestic novel, Evans sought in *Macaria* to show these women how to live a productive life. While admitting that married women might be happier in a superficial way, Evans claimed that the single woman could be more useful, having a greater opportunity for service and achievement (*Mothers of Invention*, 172–73).

Also in this novel Evans creates a role reversal between the heroine, Irene, and the man who loves her, Russell Aubrey (Faust, *Mothers of Invention*, 171). It is Russell who emphasizes the importance of love and romance as he begs Irene to marry him. Irene refuses on the grounds that she and Russell must be free to carry out their respective life's work.

On December 2, 1868, Augusta Evans married Lorenzo Madison Wilson, a wealthy, older neighbor. Six months after their wedding, Evans, now Mrs. Wilson, published her fifth novel, *Vashti*. (Most of the writing had been done before the wedding.) This novel is quite different from her previous ones and marks a radical departure from the plot of the domestic novel.

While the heroines of Wilson's earlier works triumphed over all obstacles, the women characters in *Vashti* are all victims. One young woman, Salome, gifted with a beautiful voice, goes to Paris to pursue a career in opera. When her former suitor discovers her years later, he learns that an illness has destroyed her voice and she now lives a quiet life as a lacemaker. Although Beulah and Edna were handsomely rewarded for pursuing careers and independent lives, Salome is punished for having these same goals. The title character fares no better. She marries a man she loves dearly, only to discover that he is inter-ested solely in her money. Refusing divorce on the grounds that marriage is a sacrament, Vashti leaves her husband to live the rest of her life in limbo—neither married nor single. Perhaps Wilson's bitter disappointment over the defeat of the Confederacy, evident in her letters, caused her to write a novel about loss and endurance rather than triumph over obstacles.

Baym uses *Vashti* to illustrate the demise of the domestic novel, arguing that from this point on women's fiction split into children's literature (*Little Women*) or, for adults, the gothic romance. Baym offers no definitive answer as to why this change occurred, but one possibility is that social changes may have made the concerns of the domestic novel seem dated (*Woman's Fiction,* 296–97). The fact, however, that Baym would use Wilson's novels to illustrate the rise and fall of the domestic novel in America is indicative of Wilson's popularity and importance in nineteenth-century literature.

After the publication of *Vashti* in 1869, Wilson became more of a wife and less of a writer. By all accounts, the Wilsons seem to have had a happy marriage. After the publication of *St. Elmo,* she was a wealthy woman and he, having wisely invested money outside the South before the Civil War began, was a wealthy man. They settled into a tranquil life at Ashland, their estate in Mobile. Lorenzo Wilson had three grown children and a thirteen-year-old daughter, Fannie, still at home. Augusta Wilson assumed the role of step-mother and formed a close relationship with Fannie.

Wilson also took seriously her new role as mistress of Ashland. She trans-formed the house, with its elaborate gardens, into a showplace. Enjoying the estate's five greenhouses, Wilson grew many flowers and even developed some new varieties of camellia-japonicas. She supervised the housekeeping carefully and kept the servants on such a strict schedule that neighbors swore they could tell the time of day by the chores the Wilsons' servants were doing (Fidler, *A Biography,* 152–55).

In addition to her household duties, Wilson also found time each day to work on her correspondence and novels. She had always supported "digni-fied careers" for women as long as they did not interfere with the women's domestic duties. In almost all of her novels, she attacked the society matrons and self-centered women who failed to care properly for their families and homes (Fidler 156).

Fidler claims that Wilson had time to pursue both careers—home and writing (156). The fact remains, however, that her writing slowed considerably after her marriage. Before marriage, she produced a novel every three to four years: *Inez* in 1855, *Beulah* in 1859, *Macaria* in 1864, and *St. Elmo* in 1866. During the twenty-three years of her marriage, from 1868 until her husband's death in 1891, she produced only three novels, one of which, *Vashti* (1869), was almost completed before her wedding took place. *Infelice* was published in 1875 and *At the Mercy of Tiberius* in 1887. Perhaps she was merely busy with new interests, or perhaps her creativity diminished with age.

Hubbell offers another explanation for this decline in Wilson's productivity: Her husband "tried to prevent her from working too hard at writing. . . . Perhaps, impressed though he was by the success of her novels, Mr. Wilson did not quite approve of his wife's writing novels" (*South in American Literature,* 612).

Fidler also relates that by 1870 Augusta Wilson's health began to suffer from the strain of her many interests. "Writing, study, housekeeping, singing —any one of which was a career in itself—were pursued simultaneously, until Mr. Wilson spoke his mind. . . . She acceded to his wishes and spent fewer hours at her writing desk and in the library" (*A Biography,* 173). It is interesting to note, however, that of all Wilson's interests (and Fidler mentions only a few here) her husband asked her to reduce her involvement in only two: studying and writing.

At any rate the marriage appears to have been a happy one and lasted for twenty-three years until Lorenzo Wilson's death in 1891. After her husband died, Wilson sold the Ashland estate and bought a house in town. Her brother Howard, who had never fully recovered from wounds sustained in the Civil War, lived with her for nine years until his death in 1908.

In 1902, fifteen years after her last novel, Wilson published *A Speckled Bird,* an "old-fashioned romance." Despite the fact that this was now the age of realism and naturalism, her name on the title page was enough to generate a demand for the novel, which was in its third printing within a month of publication (Fidler 204–5). In addition to being a love story, the book also expresses Wilson's conservative views that women should not be involved in politics or business.

In 1907, at the age of seventy-two, Wilson dictated a short story to her niece. She had planned to publish the story in a magazine, but her publisher persuaded her to allow him to publish it as a book. *Devota* was a thin volume, printed with wide margins that were filled with a floral design. This novel, like the previous one, was a combination of love story and the author's conservative views.

In 1909, the day after her seventy-fourth birthday, Augusta Wilson died of a heart attack. Her funeral was the largest ever held in Mobile, and articles and obituaries were printed in newspapers across the United States. A remarkable career had ended. Fidler points out that Wilson's success is difficult to measure in precise terms due to the lack of reliable records and sales indexes before 1895. However, writing in 1951 Fidler claimed that *St. Elmo* would easily be in the top three best-selling novels of all time, next to *Uncle Tom's Cabin* and *Ben Hur*. Within four months of publication, a million people had supposedly read *St. Elmo,* and its popularity continued for almost a hundred years. Thirteen editions of the book were published in 1912, six in 1928, and four in 1949 (Fidler, *A Biography,* 129–30). Although not nearly as successful as *St. Elmo,* all of Wilson's novels were best-sellers—except the first, *Inez,* written when she was fifteen. Wilson's career spanned five decades and made her name a household word throughout the United States.

Through her letters, Wilson reveals much about her life, relationships, writing, and the time in which she lived. She had long-term epistolary relationships with two powerful men: Confederate General P. G. T. Beauregard and Confederate Congressman J. L. M. Curry. She met Beauregard in 1862 in Mobile, where he had gone to recuperate from an illness. While there, he was entertained by Mobile society and met Augusta Jane Evans, already a famous author (after the publication of *Beulah* in 1859). Evans met Curry when both attended the Convention of Seceding States in Montgomery, Alabama, in February 1861, she as an onlooker and he as a delegate from Georgia.

In corresponding with these two men, Evans reveals herself to be well informed about current events, and she freely and confidently gives both men advice concerning everything from battle plans to government politics. Perhaps the fact that she was a famous author caused both men to receive her opinions and advice with more respect than they might have another woman's. Beauregard, at any rate, certainly knew that she had the ability, through her writing, to do important public relations work for him, as she did in writing her novel *Macaria*. He shared his battle plans with her concerning the Battle of Manassas, and she wrote back to verify a few details before including an account of the battle in her novel (AEW to Beauregard, March 17, 1863). The result was a very favorable portrayal of Beauregard, neatly glossing over a few of his mistakes. Beauregard continued to share military information with her, including such things as his detailed battle plans that were rejected (unfairly) in favor of another's and a manual that he wrote on military policy (AEW to Beauregard, March 17, 1863; April 29, 1863; August 19, 1863). The implication, of course, was that she would not only understand these matters but would even be interested in them.

In corresponding with Curry, Evans advised him on which subjects to use for his speeches (AEW to Curry, July 15, 1863) and offered to do some research for him. She also knew quite well the problems facing the Confederacy and urged him to repeal the Exemption Bill, which allowed men to avoid military service by paying a substitute to join the army on their behalf, among other provisions, and to take measures to deal with inflation and the low morale of the Confederate soldiers (AEW to Curry, December 20, 1862).

Other men besides Beauregard and Curry sometimes consulted Evans about problems in the government and military. When Admiral Buchanan spoke to her about the difficulties he had encountered in obtaining recruits for the Confederate navy, she passed his complaint along to Curry, who, as a Confederate congressman, was in a position to initiate action (AEW to Curry, January 27, 1864). Admiral Buchanan no doubt knew that Evans had the ear of men in high places. On another occasion, after Beauregard had sent her information about problems with the Confederate gunboats, she wrote him to ask if *she* could forward the information to Admiral Buchanan (AEW to Beauregard, December 14, 1863).

On one hand, Evans writes to these men on equal terms, presenting herself as a well-informed and confident woman. At other times, however, in these relationships she reveals the same conflicts and contradictions about the role of women that were portrayed in her novels. In 1862 she wrote Beauregard that she regretted that she, as a woman, could not play a more direct and active part in the war but that she would use her writing to support the Confederate cause. Her writing gave her a powerful voice, yet she wrote of "my feeble, womanly pen" (AEW to Beauregard, August 4, 1862).

On another occasion, when Beauregard complimented her on an article she had published anonymously, she explained why she had not signed her name: "To animadvert upon national grievances, and to attempt to institute reforms in any department of State, is regarded as unsuitable work for womanly hands." Furthermore, she claimed that she was always "reluctant to transcend the proper sphere of womanhood, and always fearful of encroaching upon the prerogatives of your sex." Nevertheless, she excused herself by claiming that her patriotic *duty* sometimes compelled her to step out of the feminine role. Then she retreated again by refusing to sign her name, a woman's name, to the article in order to avoid "unnecessary notoriety" (AEW to Beauregard, August 19, 1863).

Once, when writing Curry, Evans skillfully refuted the subject that Curry had proposed for a speech. She then gave him another subject, which he developed and successfully presented in several cities (AEW to Curry, July 15, 1863). Later, when he wrote to thank her for her help, she replied that her ideas were merely "crude, waif-like suggestions." In the same letter she confidently delivered her opinion of John Stuart Mill's book, *Political Economy*, but then meekly asked Curry to tell her if her "criteria" were not correct (AEW to Curry, October 16, 1863).

An especially painful conflict for Evans, concerning the proper sphere for a woman, occurred after the war ended in 1865. She determined to write the definitive history of the Confederacy and wrote to Alexander Stephens, the former vice president of the Confederate states, to ask for his assistance in obtaining information. She began the letter stating a fear that she lacked the "intellectual credentials" for the task and that "*no woman* is capable of the rare critical acumen in military matters,—and of the broad and lofty generalizations" needed by someone who would be the "historic custodian of our national honor." Having made the requisite deference, she went on to say that she planned to undertake the work anyway—as a tribute to the Confederacy (AEW to Stephens, November 29, 1865). Later she sorrowfully abandoned the project when she learned that Stephens planned to write his own history.

Like the heroines in her novels, Evans would step out of the feminine role only, ostensibly at least, to retreat back into it. Perhaps her "retreat" was merely a superficial gesture toward the proprieties of the time. At any rate, her self-deprecating moments were infrequent and were in marked contrast to the confident, forceful tone with which she usually delivered her opinions, as evident in her letters.

In addition to her correspondence with Beauregard and Curry, Evans conducted a third major epistolary relationship with Rachel Lyons Heustis. The two young women met in New York City in 1859 while Evans was there to supervise the publication of *Beulah* and Rachel was visiting friends. When they returned to their respective homes in Mobile and Columbia, South Carolina, they began a lifelong friendship and correspondence, sometimes visiting in each other's homes, but always writing.

In her article, "The Female World of Love and Ritual: Relations between Women in Nineteenth-Century America," Carroll Smith-Rosenberg explores the emotionally intense, long-lasting relationships between women in Evans's era. Smith-Rosenberg bases her analysis on a study of numerous letters and diaries written by nineteenth-century American women. This material, never intended to be made public, sheds light on the private emotional lives of women (3).

One reason for the development of such close relationships between women, Smith-Rosenberg theorizes, is that relationships between young women and men were so restricted and proscribed. Consequently, women developed intense love and devotion for each other, and their relationships had the spontaneity and intimacy that were not permissible between the sexes (9, 20–21). The relationships between women were not only emotionally deep but also both platonic and sensual. Such relationships were entirely socially acceptable and "fully compatible with heterosexual marriage" (8).

Although Evans frequently addresses Lyons as "My darling" and repeatedly expresses affection for her, Evans's letters to her friend do not reach the degree of emotional intensity and fondness of most of the letters in Smith-Rosenberg's study. Perhaps this is merely due to individual differences in personality and taste. There was, however, another major difference between Evans and Lyons that could have colored the emotional tone of their relationship: soon after the two met, Evans became a well-known author (with the publication of *Beulah*) while Lyons, like most women of the day, did not have a career. Also, Evans's career created many demands on her time and made it difficult for her to correspond with Lyons as often as she would have liked. Her letters are filled with apologies for not writing sooner or more often. Nevertheless, the two women were lifelong friends and wrote to each other about the dreams and hopes of young women, about the war that enveloped them, and later about marriage and family.

In addition to these personal relationships, Evans's business as a writer is also revealed through her letters. During the Civil War years, Evans encountered some problems that hampered her writing and the publication of her novels. For example, the publishers of *Macaria,* West and Johnston of Richmond, Virginia, had contracted with Evans and Cogswell, a company in Charleston, South Carolina, to do the actual printing. When Charleston came under attack, this company moved to Columbia, South Carolina, for safety, a move which delayed the publication of *Macaria* by several months (see AEW to Rachel, November 21, 1863.) Also, because of the scarcity of supplies in the South, *Macaria* had to be printed on coarse brown paper with wallpaper to cover the binding (Fidler, *A Biography,* 106).

Later Evans smuggled a copy of *Macaria* to her publisher in New York City, J. C. Derby. The manuscript traveled on a blockade runner by way of Cuba before reaching New York. While Derby was making arrangements to have the novel published in the North, another publisher, Michael Doolady, had already printed a pirated edition of *Macaria* and, using the war as an excuse, did not intend to pay any royalties to Evans. Derby, along with J. B. Lippincott, visited Doolady and pressured him into paying Evans's royalties into a reserve fund, controlled by Derby, until after the war (see AEW to Beauregard, December 14, 1863, note 4).

Introduction

xxxiii

The war years were dramatic, but Evans's letters also reveal the more routine aspects of a writer's life. She frequently wrote to Rachel Lyons about how little free time she had because of her writing. In one letter she spoke of spending weeks at her desk, some days from 8:00 A.M. until after midnight, recopying the manuscript of *Macaria* before sending it to the publisher (see AEW to Rachel, March 20, 1863). Later, she had to stay in Columbia, South Carolina, for three weeks to proofread the galleys before the novel was printed (see AEW to Rachel, November 21, 1863).

Her position as a famous writer gave her certain responsibilities and problems. She corresponded on several occasions with other writers who wanted biographical information about her to include in their own books or who wanted permission to excerpt passages from her novels in their anthologies (for an example, see AEW to Rutherford, October 12, 1905). She also tried to help new or less famous authors as in the letter she wrote to *Belford's Magazine* endorsing a novel by her friend, Elizabeth Bellamy (AEW to Belford's Magazine, November 14, 1887). On at least one occasion she had to defend herself against a charge of plagiarism when H. T. Peck, editor of *The Bookman,* accused her of plagiarizing an incident in *St. Elmo* (see AEW to Peck, October 31, 1900).

In writing to Lyons, Evans discussed her views on the role of a novelist. Evans believed strongly that writing was a special calling, a means by which one could exert a Christian influence on others by writing uplifting, didactic stories (see AEW to Rachel, July 30, 1860.) Because of this belief, Evans did not agree with the trend toward realism in writing. She felt that novels should reveal spiritual truths and moral examples, not portray life as it was, with all of its sordid aspects.

In a letter to Lyons, she emphasized that a novelist should not reflect life too closely, for to do so was to commit the error of "patronizing coarseness, vulgarity, and ignorance." Evans considered George Eliot's *Adam Bede* (1859) to be an example of this type of writing, probably because of the character Hetty Sorrel, who has a baby out of wedlock. Evans emphasized to Lyons that "the world needs *elevating* and it is the peculiar province of the Novelist to present the very highest *noblest types* of human nature" (see AEW to Rachel, November 15, 1860).

Cathy N. Davidson, in her book *Revolution and the Word: The Rise of the Novel in America,* discusses Evans's theory about the proper role of the novelist. Davidson points out that the early novels in America were regarded with suspicion. Many feared that the popularity of the novel would discourage people from reading good literature such as the Bible: people would read for

amusement rather than for moral instruction. Also, novels might stir unrealistic ambitions in the unprivileged and cause them to be discontented with
their position in life, perhaps to the point of creating social unrest. Worse yet,
novels might give young women unrealistic expectations and cause them to
be unhappy with the drudgery of domestic duties or might make unsavory
activities seem appealing to young women. According to Davidson, the early
American novelists answered this criticism by insisting that their novels had a
moral purpose. Even the authors of seduction novels claimed that their stories
could inform, and thus protect, young women from these situations (39–49).
Evans's claim that her novels provided moral guidance was therefore consistent with a view of the novel that lasted well into the nineteenth century.

Evans corresponded with many others: fans and acquaintances, friends
and relatives. Through all of her correspondence, we can piece together a
glimpse of her life. As the letters, diaries, and journals of other women during this time are discovered and published, more light will be shed on the
thoughts and lives of American women in the nineteenth century. The land-
mark *Mary Chesnut's Civil War* (C. Vann Woodward, ed., New Haven, Conn.:
Yale University Press, 1981) describes the Civil War from a woman's perspec-
tive. Nevertheless, Chesnut's well-known diary is but the tip of the mountain
of women's written work. The letters of Augusta Evans Wilson, in addition
to the letters and diaries of her contemporaries, add greatly to our understanding of the lives of women during this era.

Several collections of letters by nineteenth-century American writers,
artists, and feminists have already been published. These include the letters
of Louisa May Alcott, Anna Julia Cooper (an African-American author),
Emily Dickinson, Mary Wilkins Freeman, Margaret Fuller, Charlotte Perkins
Gilman, Angelina and Sarah Grimké (abolitionists and feminists), Harriet
Hosmer, Sarah Orne Jewett, Caroline Kirkland, Emma Lazarus, Elizabeth
Cady Stanton.

Paul Lauter, in his article "Teaching Nineteenth-Century Women Writers,"
refers to letters as a "private expression of self" (294). Through discovering and
publishing additional letters of nineteenth-century American women, we can
learn more about their lives, the issues that concerned them, and their beginning steps toward autonomy and self-fulfillment. Through these means, we
place these women in context.

In an interesting side note, Lauter sees the letter form as having been
especially useful to women writers of this time because many people still considered writing for publication to be an unsuitable profession for women—
because it was public. Published *letters,* on the other hand, gave the reader the
sense of a *private* communication and gave the author the opportunity to be

both private *and* public. Perhaps for this reason, many nineteenth-century women writers structured their novels as a series of letters. These include Caroline Kirkland's *A New Home—Who'll Follow?* (1839), Lydia Maria Child's *Letters from New York* (1879), and Jane Swisshelm's *Letters to Country Girls* (1853). Nonfiction works were also sometimes structured as letters, such as Sarah Grimké's *Letters on the Equality of the Sexes* (1838) and Margaret Fuller's articles in the *New-York Tribune.* Surprisingly, Lauter even includes Emily Dickinson in this group of authors who used the letter format since Dickinson described one of her poems as "my letter to the World / That never wrote to me" ("Teaching Nineteenth-Century Women Writers," 293–94).

The letters of Augusta Evans Wilson are, of course, not in this category because they are private correspondence not written for publication. Still, Lauter's discussion emphasizes the importance of the letter form as an expression of the self and, when published, as a means for "bridging the private and public worlds." Lauter calls letters, journals, and diaries "discontinuous forms" of literature that are important in the canon of women's writing (293–94).

Emphasizing the importance of discovering and publishing letters from another time, Ben W. Griffith states, "There is an evocative quality about an old letter. By its absorption in its own contemporaneity it can evoke a living picture of an era. And, like Tennyson's flower in the crannied wall, the understanding of each small facet of it leads to an understanding of a people, a culture, a way of life" ("The Lady Novelist and the General," 97). In the following letters, Augusta Evans Wilson speaks with her own voice to tell us about her life as a Southern patriot, a woman, and a woman writer in nineteenth-century America.

A Southern Woman
OF Letters

CHAPTER 1

"Our glorious spring time"

1 / MS Virginia   Georgia Cottage[1] May 27th [1859][2]

My dear Rachel[3]

Allow me to introduce to your acquaintance my friend Dr Taylor, the distinguished Chinese Missionary, whom you doubtless know by reputation. Dr Taylor is a resident of your city and I trust the acquaintance will prove mutually agreeable; nay I feel assured that it will.

Your affectionate friend
Augusta J. Evans

1. The Evans family rented Georgia Cottage, a house on the outskirts of Mobile, for a year. In 1860, after the early success of *Beulah,* AEW purchased the house for herself and her parents and siblings. In providing her family with a home of their own, she accomplished what her father had been unable to do; nevertheless, she registered the house in her father's name. It was called Georgia Cottage because the first owner built the house with slave labor from Georgia.

2. The year was added in darker ink and in what appears to be a different handwriting. The year could not be correct because AEW did not meet Rachel until the autumn of 1859.

3. Rachel Lyons, of Columbia, South Carolina, was a beautiful young debutante when she met AEW while both were visiting in New York City in the autumn of 1859. AEW was visiting with her publisher, J. C. Derby, and his family while her second novel, *Beulah,* was being published. Later letters indicate that Rachel also knew the Derbys. The two young women became lifelong friends.

❧ ❧ ❧

2 / MS Alabama   Mobile Oct 17 1859

My own dear Sister Rachel

Thank you again and again for your kind, welcome, but undeserved letter, which I received yesterday, and hasten to express my gratitude for. Let me premise, however, that I write very hastily, and under extremely disadvantaged circumstances. My dear Mother has been quite sick since my return, and though she is now much better, I am still too anxious about her, to give my undivided attention to my epistolary duties, or spend more than five minutes at my desk. Your letter dear Rachel gave me sincere, heartfelt pleasure; again I thank you for remembering me so kindly. Most especially do I appreciate and prize the affectionate candor which impels you to acquaint me with the various objections urged against my book. Verily, there are numbers to flatter me, but <u>very few</u>, sufficiently <u>my friend</u> to tell me honestly of my faults. Regretting extremely that I have not leisure at this juncture to enter fully into an explanation of my views, I must content myself for the present, with a brief allusion to that portion of "<u>Beulah</u>" which impressed your aunt and friend,[1] with the idea, that Beulah's speculative doubts were not satisfactorily answered. The truth of the whole matter, lies in a nutshell—our religious states are determined by <u>Faith</u>, <u>not</u> <u>Reason</u>.[2] The preponderance of the Rationalistic element in "Beulah's" organization, necessitated her speculative career; she searched all creeds and systems,[3] rejected all, because in all she found inscrutable mysteries, which reason could not pierce and elucidate; consequently she trembled on the very confines of pyrrhonism,[4] (you must pardon the <u>seeming</u> pedantry, implied in the use of this term, for all sciences have their necessary, and peculiar phraseology). "Beulah" constituted her Reason, the sole criterion of trust, but found on all sides insolvable mysteries— found that unaided by that Revelation which her reason had ignored, that she was utterly incapable of ever arriving at any belief. She found that erudition and tireless research availed nothing; that without Divine aid, Man as Man was too finite to cope with the secrets of the universe, to solve the great questions of God! Eternity! Destiny! and discarding the belief that Reason alone could discover the truth, she rested her spent soul, in the Ark of <u>Faith</u>! whereby she was enabled to receive the sublime teachings of <u>Inspiration</u>. The object of the Book was to prove the fallacy of all human philosophical systems, the limited nature of human faculties, the total insufficiency of our reason, to grapple with the vital questions, which are propounded by every earnest mind, and the absolute necessity of <u>trusting</u> in the <u>revelations of Jeho-vah</u>! <u>the Great I Am</u>! (and pardon me dear Rachel,[5] I <u>must say what</u> I <u>believe to be true</u>,) of our blessed <u>Lord Jesus Christ</u>. Because "Beulah" trusted to Rationalism she was wretched and sceptical; but when she put <u>faith</u> in the word of the Living God, she <u>found</u> "<u>the ways of pleasantness and the paths of peace</u>." In the limits of a novel I could not introduce the vast systems of <u>historical evidences</u> of the truth of Revealed Religion; I could only glance at the proofs written by God's finger on the story pages of Geology, and dwell upon the necessity of trusting to that Revelation, which promises that, although "here we see through a glass darkly,"[6] "there we shall know and see <u>Him as he is</u>."[7] I am sorry that I have not time to enter more into detail on this subject; and if my brief analysis does not satisfy you I <u>will</u> <u>endeavor</u> to make my views more satisfactory in a future letter. Believe me my darling, nothing could give me more pleasure than the correspondence to which you allude. Rest assured if I can render you the slightest assistance in your reading, I will do so with the greatest delight. I am too inexperienced and full of defects to assume the post of <u>Mentor</u> my dear Rachel, but to what I can do, you are <u>more</u> <u>than</u> <u>welcome</u>! Oh! Rachel! Rachel! where have you hidden your conscience? My head will inevitably be turned, if you treat me to any more such <u>sweetly</u> <u>prepared</u> <u>allopathic</u>[8] potion of flattery! Don't spoil me darling! Don't spoil me! Mr Caldwell has <u>proved</u> himself one of my <u>best</u> <u>friends</u>! Pardon my haste, and stupidity: Au revoir

<u>Your</u> <u>sister</u>

1. According to William Perry Fidler, Rachel's friend is Henry Timrod, a South Carolina poet who would later become the poet laureate of the Confederacy. Timrod complained that Beulah's conversion from doubt to faith was not adequately explained in the novel. See Fidler, *Augusta Evans Wilson, 1835–1909: A Biography* (Tuscaloosa: University of Alabama Press, 1951), 64.

2. The advances of science in the nineteenth century precipitated a crisis of religious doubt and questioning for many people. In part, *Beulah* is autobiographical in that AEW herself experienced a brief and painful period of religious skepticism.

3. In the novel Beulah reads and analyzes the works of many nineteenth-century writers, including Poe, DeQuincey, Emerson, Carlyle, Coleridge, and the German transcendentalists. Her conclusion is that faith is more important than reason, that the heart can know truths that the mind cannot fathom.

4. Extreme skepticism. (Based on the teachings of Pyrrho, who founded a Skeptic school in ancient Greece.)

5. Rachel Lyons was Jewish.

6. "Now we see through a glass, darkly; but then [in Heaven] face to face" (1 Cor. 8:12).

7. AEW's paraphrase of the second part of this verse. See note 6 above.

8. Relating to the traditional system of medicine (as distinguished from chiropractic, homeopathy, etc.) in which a disease is treated by creating an antagonistic environment, such as administering antibiotics to treat infection.

❧ ❧ ❧

3 / MS Alabama   Mobile Dec 8 1859

My dear Rachel,

Do not imagine for one instant that because I have delayed answering your last kind letter, I have failed to remember you <u>daily</u>. Many very Many times I have come to my desk to write you, but something always called me off before I could even begin. You have no idea my dear friend how many claims I have on my time and attention. My correspondence is absolutely <u>for-midable</u> and you would pity me if you knew the number of unanswered letters staring me in the face as I write. Then the children's[1] winter clothes are all to make and you know I am <u>sewing</u> <u>machine</u> for the family: the girls have silk dresses on hand and I have to finish them by Christmas. Worse than all dear Rachel my brothers have both been sick for some time; my oldest Brother Howard is now confined to his bed with <u>typhoid</u> <u>fever</u>. Under these circumstances I hope you will excuse my long silence, which is to be attributed to every thing else than want of most affectionate remembrance. I thank you most sincerely darling for your <u>likeness</u>. It is excellent I think, and I prize it very highly I assure you—When I can spare the time to sit I will try to return you "evil for good." The weather here is intensely cold—Everything is <u>frozen</u>, and our <u>orange</u> <u>trees</u> are <u>all</u> <u>killed</u>, I am afraid. You must pardon this miserable scrawl my dear friend, for my fingers nearly freeze to the paper, though I have drawn my desk almost on the <u>hearth</u>—Such temperature is extremely uncommon in Mobile—I do not remember having known it so very <u>severe</u> before. I am very much hurried, but must tell you of some books I want you to get if possible—Rushkin's [*sic*][2] works, particularly his "<u>Modern</u> <u>Painters</u>,"[3] and if you can procure them his "Stones of <u>Venice</u>"[4] [*sic*]— Oh how I wish you were here with me seated near my desk where during these busy nights I pore over Rushkin's [*sic*] pages! Do read them and let me know whether you are much fascinated as your far-off friend—Also if you have not "Bayne's Biographical and Critical Essays"[5] you will find them extremely valuable—I presume ere this you have returned to Columbia and direct this wretched apology for a letter accordingly—Hear from Mr. Derby often—all well at Yonkers. Again my dear Rachel I thank you for your likeness—Please pardon my haste and believe me as ever—

Most sincerely yours
Augusta J Evans

PS—Can't you pay me a visit this winter? Oh I should be <u>so</u> <u>glad</u> to have you come. All my family say <u>come</u>.

1. AEW's younger brothers and sisters.
2. John Ruskin (1819–1900), English art and social critic and a major prose writer of the Victorian period.
3. *Modern Painters* (1843), a defense of the landscape artist J. M. W. Turner, dealt with such questions as truth in art and the importance of the imagination.
4. *Stones of Venice* (1851) argued against an industrialized society and in favor of a society that allowed individual expression in art and architecture.
5. Peter Bayne (1830–1896) wrote *Biographical, Critical, and Miscellaneous Essays* in 1859.

❧ ❧ ❧

My kind friend Col' Seaver[1]

A happy, sunny new year to you! unclouded by grief or care. Accept dear Sir my sincerest thanks for your cordial and welcome letter, and very flattering notice of "<u>Beulah</u>." For the several numbers of your paper, I am also much indebted, and regret extremely that a combination of unfortunate circumstances prevented my acknowledging your many kindnesses more promptly. I shall not weary you with apologies but simply state the truth and trust to your charity. Briefly then, several members of our family have been quite sick since my return,[2] and in addition, I have been so constantly engaged that I could not find a leisure half hour. Your name has become a sort of "household word" in my home and my Father wishes frequently that you could visit Mobile during the present winter. Amid the host of reminiscences connected with my stay in New York, I assure you none give me more pleasure than the memory of our reunions at the St. Nicholas,[3] and the friendly genial gathering at the tea table. Thank you for remembering me at your Delmonico[4] conclaves. I trust I shall yet be able to <u>merit</u> your good opinion of me. Ah Sir! if at Delmonico's there were only another "<u>ear of</u> <u>Dionysius</u>,"[5] into which I could steal <u>a la Gurney</u>[6] "the short haun [*sic*] writer" and jot down the bon mots; the good words, the crumbs that fall during your weekly "feasts of reason and flow of soul," what a benefit might I not render the world! What a budget of puns and witticisms might I not lay before the public until the name of Ambrose should be forgotten in the culmination of Delmonico! I do envy you (<u>not your dinners</u>, but) your circle of gifted, humorous friends where the icy fetters of formal etiquette are severed and congenial spirits meet, just as Christopher North, Tickler, and Ettrick Shepherd were wont to do in "Auld Reikie,"[7] in glorious days gone by. When do you go to Europe? You mentioned an earnest wish to visit in this year, and just now I am possessed by the same spirit to cross the water. From early childhood I have been singularly anxious to make myself acquainted with the wonders of the Old World, and as years roll their waves over my head, the desire increases. I am now studying French with the hope that I shall be able to go during the next summer. I wish to arrange matters so that I can spend the winter in Rome and Florence and give the summer months to Germany. If I go it will be to <u>study</u>. As yet it is only a bright dream with me, and only as the tangled web of 1860 unfolds itself, can I determine my future with any accuracy. Much of the enjoyment of such a tour depends on one's <u>Compagnon du voyage</u>, and I am extremely solicitous to find a pleasant party under whose care I can place myself. Doubtless I have written you into the conclusion of Sheridan's[8] servant who thought that <u>by far</u> the most eloquent portion of his Master's celebrated Hastings trial speech, was contained in the closing words, "<u>I have done my Lords, I have done</u>."[9] With renewed wishes for health and happiness, and a [obscured] New Year to your incomparable <u>Bohemian Fraternity</u>, I am dear

Truly your friend
Augusta J. Evans

PS If you should receive a Mobile paper during next week, containing a description of the 29th anniversary celebration of the <u>Cowbellion De Rakin</u>[10] Society, you may attribute <u>said article to my pen</u>.

1. William A. Seaver was famous in New York literary circles as a raconteur. As an editor of *Harper's New Monthly Magazine,* he was in charge of the "Editor's Drawer," a department so named for a desk drawer into which Fletcher Harper, one of the Harper Brothers who founded the magazine, would drop short humorous anecdotes and other writings. See Eugene Exman, *The House of Harper: One Hundred and Fifty Years of Publishing* (New York: Harper & Row, 1967), 71.

2. From New York City.

3. The St. Nicholas Hotel, at Broadway and Spring Street, was extremely luxurious, built at a cost of one million dollars. AEW and her uncle stayed there a few days before moving to the Derbys' home during their visit to New York. Ironically, almost five years after the date of this letter, on November 25, 1864, a band of Confederates from Morgan's Raiders, in an abortive attempt to ignite a firestorm in New York City, attacked the St. Nicholas and more than a dozen other hotels with Greek fire (a self-igniting chemical mixture). The St. Nicholas was moderately damaged. See Ernest A. McKay, *The Civil War and New York City* (Syracuse, N.Y.: Syracuse University Press, 1990), 287–90.

4. A famous restaurant on Fifth Avenue in New York City.

5. In Greek mythology, the god of wine and inspiration. From the revels and processions held in his honor evolved the forms of the theater: comedy, tragedy, and satiric drama.

6. Thomas Gurney (1705–1770), an Englishman who developed a system of shorthand that he called brachygraphy, or short writing.

7. AEW has confused two different pieces of literature here. North, Tickler, and Ettrick Shepherd were characters in a column called "Noctes Ambrosianae," which appeared in *Blackwood's Edinburgh Magazine* from 1822 to 1835. The characters met at a tavern and discussed topics of literary interest. "Auld Reikie" ("Old Edinburgh") is a poem written in Scottish dialect by Robert Fergusson (1750–1774). It portrays daily life in Edinburgh and includes a description of a social club to which AEW is apparently referring here.

8. Richard Brinsley Sheridan (1751–1816), known mainly as the British dramatist who authored *The Rivals* and *The School for Scandal.* However, he was also a statesman and member of Parliament.

9. Warren Hastings (1732–1818), English administrator in India who was accused of being dishonest and harsh in his dealings with his subjects. The House of Commons impeached Hastings in 1787, and the trial lasted until 1794, when he was acquitted. Sheridan brought the charges before the House on February 7, 1787, in a speech that lasted five hours and forty minutes. Later, in June 1788, Sheridan spoke, not for two days as the English historian Thomas Macaulay reported, but for several hours each day over a period of four days. He ended by collapsing exhausted into a friend's arms with the words, "My lords, I have done."

10. Michael Krafft, a cotton broker from Pennsylvania, founded the Cowbellion de Rakin Society in Mobile in 1830. Krafft and his friends marched through the streets at daybreak on New Year's Day carrying hoes, rakes, and cowbells, which they had acquired from a nearby store. Thus equipped, they called on the ladies of their acquaintance. (According to custom in Mobile, gentlemen called on their lady friends on New Year's Day and were served cake and wine.) As the years passed, the Cowbellion de Rakin Society became a prestigious and elite group. Members, wearing masks, staged a parade each New Year's Eve before hosting a ball for their guests (Harriet E. Amos, *Cotton City: Urban Development in Antebellum Mobile* [Tuscaloosa: University of Alabama Press, 1985], 65). If AEW did indeed publish an article on this subject, it has not been located. As Fidler points out, she published numerous articles anonymously in various Southern newspapers expressing her views on literature and the war (*A Biography,* 96).

❧ ❧ ❧

5 / MS Alabama   Mobile Jan 4 1860

My dear Rachel

A cloudless happy new year to you my darling! I regret extremely that a combination of most unfortunate circumstances, has prevented my answering your kind letter as promptly as I should like to have done. Indeed dear Rachel you must bear with me, and attribute my lack of punctuality to every other cause than want of most affectionate remembrance. You can have very little idea how constantly I am engaged, and how difficult it is for me to answer you. I have not had one leisure half hour at my command, for <u>2</u> months past, and I trust to your charity to excuse my epistolary short-comings, or rather in this instance, <u>long coming</u>. In addition to other things, I have had to write <u>two</u> newspaper articles recently,[1] and the claims on my time and attention are too imperative to be delayed. I am now studying French in the hope that I shall be able to go to Europe this spring or summer. From early childhood it has been a bright beautiful dream to me, that one day I should wander amid the ruins of the old world, and study art in the galleries of Rome and Florence. I am extremely anxious to arrange matters so that I can spend next winter in Rome. Much of the enjoyment of such a tour depends on one's companions, and I am now very solicitous to find a pleasant party under whose care I can place myself. Now my dear Rachel can't you arrange things so as to go with me? Do not some of your relatives contemplate a European trip this year? As yet it is only a bright, vague hope with me, and only as the tangled web of 1860 unfolds itself, can I determine my future with any accuracy. It would give me dear Rachel, very great pleasure to have you with me, if I should go, and if Beulah continues to sell well I think there is little doubt I shall go some time this year. I have just finished the "Fool of Quality" a quaint old English book of Brooke's,[2] recently republished by Derby & Jackson[3]—It is full of genuine pathos; and sublime morality—and it were well if the "Fool" were universally read—I am also studying Dante just now, and can only say, I consider his great work far superior to "Paradise Lost". I believe I wrote you of Ruskin.[4] Fully to appreciate "Modern Painters," one must possess an intimate knowledge of Dante. Since I wrote you, I have received a long sparkling letter from Col' Seaver.[5] A genuine Seaverish letter, wherein he "unbuttons himself" if I may employ one of his pet phrases. He is certainly the most incorrigible of all punsters—I also hear regularly from Mr Derby and am glad to be able to say, all are well at Glenwood[6]—Some time ago, I received a letter from Nina Moses. I wish if you please, you would thank her in my name and tell her I will try to write her just as soon as I can find ten spare minutes. And now dear Rachel I must beg you to excuse my haste, and brevity. I trust at some future time I shall have leisure to write you more at length—Meantime do not doubt that I love you very dearly and remain yours most affectionately

AJEvans

I shall try to send you my photograph next week if possible—Good bye my darling friend—Do tell Mr Caldwell how grieved I am at his wretched health.

1. This is probably a reference to a series of four articles published anonymously in the *Mobile Daily Advertiser* in October and November 1859. Fidler attributes these articles to AEW, and they are written in her style. The first two are titled "Northern Literature" and the last two "Southern Literature." By contrasting the literature of the two regions, AEW attacks Northern values. Northern writers, she claims, are cold and mercenary and use literature for political propaganda. Southerners, on the other hand, write to express beauty and truth. Fidler suggests that these articles are a reply to such Northern literature as *Uncle's Tom's Cabin* and the speeches of Abraham Lincoln and Daniel Webster (*A Biography*, 71–72).

2. *The Fool of Quality, or The History of Henry, Earl of Moreland,* by Henry Brooke, was originally published in 1766.

3. AEW's publishers.

4. See AEW to Rachel Lyons, December 8, 1859, notes 2 and 3.

5. See AEW to Seaver, December 31, 1859, note 1.

6. The Derbys' estate.

❧ ❧ ❧

6 / MS North Carolina   Mobile Jan' 21 1860
Alabama Archives (typed copy)[1]

My dear Rachel—

   Thank you darling for remembering me so kindly, and for promptly responding to my hasty letters—Do adhere to the determination of a European trip. I should enjoy it tenfold if you were only with me—Just fancy us both safely landed in Rome; once there we could place ourselves under the protection of Elizabeth Barrett Browning, and her scarcely less illustrious Lord, Robert. or if you did not particularly affect the "pets of Parnassus,"[2] we could doubtless prevail on Charlotte Cushman or Harriet Hosmer to <u>Chaperone us</u>. Apropos! of the two last, I see they have rented a house and are living together! Oh! what a privilege to reside in the City of the Ceasars[3]—albeit she is

> "Childless and crownless in her voiceless woe;
> An empty urn within her withered hands,
> Whose holy dust was scattered long ago."[4]

The Eternal City! the cradle, and Pantheon of the Arts! God grant I may see it! Ah! how the Titans of the century are falling away, sinking from the wave of Time, into the vast, echoless depths of Eternity. In one brief year[5] how many glory-crowned heads have been placed beneath monumental marble— Compte[6], Sir William Hamilton,[7] Prescott,[8] Irving,[9] Humboldt,[10] De Quincy,[11] Leigh Hunt[12] and Macaulay.[13] The brightest constellation of the 19th century blotted from our sky; one and only one of the magnificent group left—And he sitting in gloomy desolation at his lonely High-gate home—As the melancholy countenance of Carlyle[14] presented itself to me, I am constantly reminded of the mournful words of Lamb, which to Carlyle particularly must possess peculiar force and significance—

> "I have had playmates; I have had companions;
> In my days of childhood; in my joyful school days;
> All—all are gone; the old familiar faces—
>
> ———————
>
> Ghostlike I paced round the haunts of my childhood,
> Earth seemed a desert I was bound to traverse,
> Seeking to find the old familiar faces—."[15]

In the death of Humbolt [*sic*], Hugh Miller,[16] Hamilton and Macaulay the literary world is so planed. To whom shall we look as worthy to receive their mantles? When I read the announcement of Macaulay's death I could not forbear exclaiming with Southey—

> "Like clouds that rake the mountain summit,
> Or waves that own no curbing hands,
> How fast has brother followed brother,
> From sunshine to the sunless land![17]

Sic transit————[18] I am very much engaged; besides my French, and other necessary claims on my time and attention, I am reading <u>Grote's</u> Greece in <u>ten</u> volumes![19] It seems to me that like the fabled Danaides[20] I work hard and yet accomplish nothing of consequence. I received a letter from Mr Derby a few days since, acquainting me with the reorganization of the firm—Rest assured dear Rachel it always gives me very great pleasure to hear from you, especially when <u>as</u> <u>last</u> <u>night</u> you send me a <u>long</u> letter. Am also reading Bayard Taylor's "<u>Home</u> <u>and</u> <u>Abroad</u>."[21] It can with great truth be called the <u>refuse</u> bits of all his works—Kiss Nina for me—I went yesterday to have my picture taken for you, but <u>Pa</u> said it was so unlike me I should not send it— I will try a different artist as soon as possible. Good-bye dear friend—

Truly yours

Augusta Evans

Remember me to Mr Caldwell[22] and tell him I miss my consort very much! Am impatient for his recovery.

1. The Alabama Department of Archives and History has a typed copy of this letter. At the end of their copy is this note: "Copied by W.P.A. from original letter in possession of Mrs. Rosalie Heustis Clark, 2214 Tenth Court South, Birmingham. Letter written to Mrs. Rachel Heustis, Columbus, S. C."

2. A mountain in central Greece, considered by the ancients to be the home of Apollo and the Muses.

3. Rome.

4. Lord Byron, *Childe Harold's Pilgrimage,* canto 4, stanza 79.

5. AEW is referring to the previous year, 1859, which had just ended.

6. Auguste Comte, a French philosopher, died in 1857. AEW is apparently mistaken about the year of his death.

7. A Scottish philosopher who died in 1856. Again, AEW appears to have mistaken the date of his death.

8. William Hickling Prescott, an American historian, died in 1859.

9. Washington Irving (1783–1859), American writer and author of "Rip Van Winkle" and "The Legend of Sleepy Hollow."

10. Alexander von Humboldt (1769–1859), German naturalist and explorer.

11. Thomas De Quincey (1785–1859), English author known for his essays and criticism.

12. Leigh Hunt (1784–1859), English critic, poet, and political reformer.

13. Thomas Babington Macaulay (1800–1859), English man of letters, historian, and statesman. A major figure of the Victorian period, he advocated the importance of rationalism and science.

14. Thomas Carlyle, Scottish historian, philosopher, and social critic. He became a major influence during the early Victorian period when he wrote against the values of the Industrial Age.

15. Charles Lamb, "The Old Familiar Faces," stanzas 2 and 6.

16. Miller, an English man of letters and geologist, died in 1856.

17. These lines are not by Southey but by William Wordsworth in "Extempore Effusion upon the Death of James Hogg" (1835), lines 21–24.

18. Sic transit gloria mundi (Thus the glory of this world passeth away); from the coronation of Pope Sixtus V, May 1, 1585.

19. George Grote (1794–1871), British historian, wrote the *History of Greece* (1845–1856) in twelve volumes to the time of Alexander the Great.

20. In Greek mythology, the Danaides were the fifty daughters of King Danaus who, as punishment for murdering their husbands, were forced to spend eternity refilling leaky water jugs.

21. Bayard Taylor, an American author, wrote enthusiastically about his travels through Europe and the Middle and Far East. *At Home and Abroad* was published in 1860.

22. A friend of AEW and Rachel.

❧ ❧ ❧

7 / MS Alabama   Mobile Feb' 16th 1860
Historic Mobile Society (typed copy)

My dear Rachel—

Your kind and welcome letter reached me some two or three days since, and I snatch the earliest leisure to reply, and express my thanks. It is very sad to know that a gifted, genial noble soul like Mr Caldwell is passing away from earth forever. I wish I could see him—once more—wish I could sit down beside his bed, and talk to him of that "Other Land" to which we all are tending so rapidly. I enclose a note; will you be so kind as to take it to him; or at least know that he receives it—He has been verily a friend to me; and I should like to have him know I remember him in his suffering. Oh Rachel! how ephemeral is Man—! I find it so hard to realize all the time, the solemn fact, that <u>this</u> is not <u>my</u> <u>home</u>; that I am but a pilgrim journeying through Earth, toward that "Eternal City" whose walls are jasper and whose gates are pearl. Sometimes I smile when I find my heart bowing down before earthly idols; tightening the chain that binds it to dust—. It seems to me that this is the unsolved problem, vis [*sic*], to enjoy life; to be cheerful and happy; and yet to remember constantly, that this is but a probationary state; that Earth is thereby a vast vineyard in which the Father has laid out <u>work</u> for all of us—What matter if there are <u>dark</u> <u>corners</u>, where the sunshine rarely falls—He overlooks his laborers; and knows all the vast field before them—. Oh dear Rachel! may <u>you</u> and <u>I</u> hold up rich purple clusters, as the fruit of our toil, when the <u>Gathering</u> <u>Time</u> rolls round——. My European tour I am afraid I shall be obliged to give up, at least for this year——The party of Mobilians I once thought of going with, will not travel farther south than Germany, and as I am particularly anxious to spend some time in Rome and Florence, must defer my trip for the present——. Still I hope to go sometime——sometime Rachel I am going to Georgia, to Columbus,[1] in the course of the next ten days. Can't you meet me there? Do try darling——. I should be so glad——so glad to see you——and be with you——I only intend to make a short visit——say <u>two</u> or <u>three</u> <u>weeks</u>——So you hear from <u>Mr</u> <u>Fitch</u>——very often? <u>I</u> <u>never</u> <u>do</u>. Mr. Derby writes nearly every week, but <u>Mr</u> <u>Fitch</u>[2] has quite forgotten me——. I was so glad to hear through Mr Derby——of his admission into the firm. He was very kind to me during my stay in New York, and has my sincere <u>grati-</u> <u>tude</u> and <u>esteem</u>——. Our glorious spring time will soon be with us once more, pearly fragrant hyacinths, have "cheerfully glinted forth" like Burne's daisy[3]——pure and beautiful——I am very much engaged; and must beg you to pardon my hasty, and stupid letter——Direct your reply to Mobile——as it will probably arrive before I leave home——. Hoping to meet you in Columbus, my dear Rachel I am with warmest love——

AJE

PS——Please write me as soon as you see Mr Caldwell and tell me how he seemed——.

    1. The town where AEW was born and where many of her relatives still lived.
    2. An employee in Derby's publishing firm.
    3. "To a Mountain Daisy" by Robert Burns. (Burns's father spelled his last name "Burnes.") AEW is quoting from line 3 in stanza 3: "Yet cheerfully thou glinted forth / Amid the storm, . . ." The theme of the poem is similar to that of AEW's letter. Burns uses the death of the daisy to remind the reader of his or her own mortality.

8 / MS North Carolina   Mobile March 4th 1860
Historic Mobile Society (typed copy)

My dear Rachel

    I write in great haste, from the fact that I am momently expecting a housefull of company; but snatch a moment to introduce to your acquaintance Mr Gulio Hubbell who is a young friend I take great interest in. He is about to enter the college in your city,[1] and I will consider it quite a favor dear Rachel if you will receive him as a young friend of mine, and introduce him to your family——. He is a boy of noble principles, studious habits, and his family are among the first in Mobile. His Father's residence is just across the street from us, and consequently I know Gulio intimately——You will find him rather timid at first; but he is an <u>admirable</u> <u>musician</u> and I wish if possible you would prevail on him to play for you. I am very sorry my dear friend, that you cannot visit Columbus this spring; I had set my heart on seeing you; I shall leave home on Tuesday week March 13th; but if you write me your letters will be forwarded from Mobile. In great haste my darling so forgive me. I send <u>that</u> likeness, by <u>Gulio</u>, hope you will think it good. Good bye.

Your own
Augusta Evans

1. Probably the University of South Carolina, founded in Columbia in 1801.

❧ ❧ ❧

9 / MS Alabama   Mobile May 29 1860

My dear Rachel—

Your welcome letter arrived some days since, but I have been so unwell that I shrank from any exertion, and postponed writing till I felt stronger; but I am afraid I shall have to wait a long time for that; therefore I sit down to send you a few lines of most affectionate greeting. I have no disease, <u>no pain</u>, but am so feeble I can hardly creep about the house. Probably the warm weather has had a good deal to do with my feebleness; but I shall be well again soon I trust. You mentioned two letters; I never received but <u>one</u>, and that a day or two <u>after</u> I <u>wrote</u> <u>to</u> <u>you</u> by <u>Gulio</u> <u>Hubbell</u>. I am very much engaged my darling, for my two sisters Carrie & Sarah have left school and are under my charge. They are reading to me a course of History and Philosophy, which requires at least <u>half</u> <u>the</u> <u>day</u>. We are now deep in Grote's Greece[1] (<u>12</u> <u>volumes</u>!) and in connection with it, I am reading the Iliad to them. My evenings are almost always interrupted by company, and I find that after answering my numerous letters, I have very little time to spare. My reading is necessarily rather promiscuous for when volumes are sent me, I feel bound to examine them if possible. My generous and constantly considerate friend Mr Derby, kindly favored me with a copy of <u>"Rutledge,"</u>[2] which you mention in your last [letter]. The book is very well written; and I consider it a very remarkable one, if the <u>first</u> attempt of the author. I read it with pleasure and think you will find it very worthy of a perusal. I enclose you a brief notice, which I wrote last week; while suffering from indisposition; also a short <u>obituary</u> which I penned with scalding tears, pouring over my face. Armantine, was Gulio Hubbell's cousin and has always resided with his mother. She was a very beautiful, affectionate girl, whom I loved very warmly, and her strange untimely death, has thrown a gloom over me, which I can not dispel. I look across the street to her deserted home, and feel a bitter aching at my heart. "<u>Boast</u> <u>not</u> <u>thyself</u> <u>of</u> <u>tomorrow</u>"[3] saith the Preacher;

Ah! my dear Rachel I seem to see things so differently, during the past six months. Life and the stings of this world, appear so fleeting, so very trivial and uncertain—So we but do our duty faithfully what matter the clouds or shadows of these few vanishing years of pilgrimage—Many are called home, before the <u>morning-glory</u>, the dew sparkle fades; before the fierce struggles and withering heat of the <u>noon</u> come down upon them. May the Father help us dear friend to "work while it is called today" in the vast <u>world-vineyard</u> so that at Harvest, the ingathering time, we may hold up rich ripe purple clusters as the fruit of our labors. My dear Rachel I must say good-bye now, for company forces me to lay down my pen. When shall we meet again? <u>When</u>! In some surely-future day I trust; but if not on earth, at least there is an Eternal City of our God—where friends shall clasp hands forever. Remember me most affectionately to dear <u>Nina</u>. I saw Mr Moses and <u>Lee</u> in Columbus, and the latter dear noble boy, accompanied me to Montgomery, on my return. I am so glad you like my ambrotype[4]—You do not prise [*sic*] it as much as I do yours I am sure. Write to me my darling and next letter I will try to do better. I rejoice to hear your mother is better. Good bye for the present.

<u>Augusta</u>

1. See AEW to Rachel Lyons, January 21, 1860, note 19.

2. A popular romance by Miriam Cole Harris, published in 1860.

3. "Boast not thyself of tomorrow; for thou knowest not what a day may bring forth" (Prov. 27:1).

4. A picture printed on glass that was backed with black velvet, black paper, or opaque varnish to eliminate reflection. This process, developed in 1854, was used almost exclusively for portraits.

࿇ ࿇ ࿇

10 / MS Virginia   Mobile June 6th 1860

Mr Victor—[1]

Dear Sir—

Your kind letter reached me a few days since, and I beg leave to tender my grateful acknowledgments for your friendly remembrance—In the circulation and success of the Art Journal,[2] I am warmly interested and lose no opportunity of impressing upon my southern friends, my opinion of it's [*sic*] value. There is a lamentable want of aesthetic culture in our midst; an absolute dearth of Art associations or galleries. Even in New Orleans, except a few pictures in the Cathedral, there is no public collection of either paintings or statuary worth the seeing. That the "Cosmopolitan" would greatly aid in rousing our people from this inertia, I feel well assured and consequently whenever I can do so, I urge southerners to subscribe. Unfortunately political journals and the lighter class of magazines offer far greater attractions for the masses. As Teufelsdrockh[3] dolefully exclaimed in Sartor Resartus, "the <u>Monster</u> <u>Utilitaria</u>[4] holding the age in shackles goes forth to do her work, trampling down old Palaces and Temples under her broad hoof."[5] But I trust a brighter day is dawning upon us, and these shackles can be broken, by sowing seeds of <u>Beauty</u> among the youth of our country, and teaching them to seek and appreciate it in all it's [sic] Protean phases, whether of painting, sculpture, music or literature. That it is difficult, and sometimes very painful to tread the thorny path <u>journalism</u> I can readily understand and the constant proclamation of unwelcome truths, by a <u>conscientious</u> <u>Editor</u>, is frequently attended by just such a harvest as followed Jason's sowing of the Dragon's teeth.[6] But in matters of Art and literature, the people regard your fraternity much as a Pharos;[7] to warn from destructive errors. "A preaching friar, settles himself in every village, and builds a pulpit which he calls a newspaper;" consequently in handling his text, he is very apt to make personal applications or home-thrusts not very palatable to some of his hearers. Thank you for your kind invitation to contribute to the "Art Journal." It would afford me great pleasure to do so, and perhaps I may be able to furnish something in the course of the summer, though at present it will not be in my power. If I ever visit New York again, I hope I shall have the pleasure of meeting your Lady,[8] whose writings have long since rendered her name familiar as "household words" in our southern homes. Most particularly are my sisters interested in the fate of that much injured maiden, "<u>Elvira</u> <u>Slimmens</u>,"[9] and when the Magazine arrives there is always a scramble for the first reading. With best wishes for the prosperity of your several journals, I am believe me

Sincerely your friend
Augusta J Evans

1. Orville James Victor worked for a variety of New York publishing companies that produced popular books and magazines. In 1860 Victor made his mark in the literary world by inventing the American dime novel, published by Beadle and Company. He trained a corps of writers to produce these novels with their simple, fast-paced, and wholesome plots, often with a southwestern setting. The Beadle dime novels were extremely popular, especially among Northern soldiers. Later competitors discredited the dime novel by making it sensationalistic.

2. *The Cosmopolitan Art Journal,* one of several magazines which Victor edited, was published in New York City from 1856 to 1861. It was established to be "A record of art criticism, art literature and biography, and repository of belle lettres literature" (from the June 1857 issue).

3. The hero of *Sartor Resartus* by Thomas Carlyle who expresses Carlyle's theories about change and reality. Teufelsdrockh explains that institutions such as churches and

governments become worn out and must be replaced by new ones, just as an individual outgrows and must replace his old clothes.

4. Utilitarianism, a Victorian philosophy that Carlyle criticized, states that human beings should be motivated only by self-interest, specifically to achieve pleasure and avoid pain. On the societal level, decisions should be made according to which course of action would produce the greatest good for the greatest number, ignoring the needs of the others.

5. In this passage, from chapter 5 of *Sartor Resartus,* Carlyle states that even Utilitarianism has its purpose in that it tears down the old philosophies and institutions and prepares the way for new ones: "the monster Utilitaria . . . should go forth to do her work;—to tread down old ruinous Palaces and Temples, with her broad hoof . . . till the whole were trodden down, that new and better might be built!"

6. In Greek mythology, Jason, in order to obtain the Golden Fleece, was ordered to plow a field with a team of fire-breathing oxen and then to sow dragon's teeth in the furrows. The dragon's teeth yielded a harvest of armed men who attacked Jason and tried to kill him.

7. A famous lighthouse on the island of Pharos in the harbor of Alexandria, Egypt, it was regarded as one of the seven wonders of the ancient world. Its light was created by the use of fires and reflectors.

8. Metta Victoria Fuller Victor, Victor's wife, was a novelist.

9. A novel by Metta Victor.

❧ ❧ ❧

11 / MS Historic Mobile Society (typed copy)[1]   Mobile June 14th, 1860

My dear Rachel:

How can I sufficiently thank you for your affectionate and most welcome letter—. It helps me <u>marvellously</u> to know that you do remember and love me so kindly. If I had known of Mr. Hubbell's intended trip to Columbia even <u>two</u> days before he left, I believe I should have gone with him, <u>just for</u> a <u>sight</u> of <u>you</u> my <u>darling</u> Rachel. Thank you for thinking of the apricots. I am very sure 100 bushels would not have given me the pleasure your affectionate <u>wish</u> to send them has afforded me. Do not be troubled about me dear; I am better than when I wrote; and daresay I shall do very well. I do not overwork myself as you seem to think; I am just about as <u>lazy</u> as people ever get to be! I have been debilitated by the excessive heat of the weather; <u>that is all</u>; and the first autumn breeze will invigorate me wonderfully. <u>Sea</u> bathing is not good for me, else I would follow your suggestion. I have tried it often, and find it only relaxes my system. But Rachel, we have a beautiful little creek running through our lot; the water is clear as crystal and deliciously cool; and <u>such</u> baths as I take every evening. <u>How</u> I wish you were here, to enjoy it. Now could you not come, or is it asking too much at this season? Our country place is so healthy, I do not think you would be running any risk. Oh! I should be <u>so</u> glad! so preciously glad to have you with me. I hear frequently from my kind true friend Mr Derby—; All were well at Glenwood when he wrote last. Are you going North this summer? I have been strongly tempted to do so, but can not indulge myself; at least for the present. Oh! for an iceburg, or a glacier!!! It is most insufferably sultry this morning. Not a breath stirring; everything is still, as Coleridge's Ancient Mariner "As Idle as a painted ship— upon a painted ocean"—.[2] I have several letters to write today, so you must excuse my haste and brevity. Indeed dear Rachel I should like to sit and write to you by the hour—. Take care of yourself darling and keep a place for me in your heart,

Yours most affectionately
Augusta

1. This letter was transcribed from a typed copy held by the Historic Preservation Society of Mobile. Original unknown.

2. Samuel Taylor Coleridge, "The Rime of the Ancient Mariner," lines 117–18.

❧ ❧ ❧

12 / MS Virginia   Mobile June 27th 1860.

Mr. Victor[1]—
Dear Sir—

Allow me to introduce to your acquaintance my friend Mr H L Flash[2] of Mobile, whose poetical contributions to our periodical literature have doubtless familiarized you with his name—Mr Flash contemplates publishing a volume[3] soon, and during his visit to your city would be pleased to meet you.

Very respectfully
Your friend
Augusta J. Evans

1. See AEW to Victor, June 6, 1860.

2. Henry Lynden Flash was born in Cincinnati, Ohio, but settled as a young man in Mobile and became a successful merchant. His first volume of poetry was published in 1860, but the volume attracted little notice, possibly due to the advent of war. During the war, his poems received more attention and were published in several Southern newspapers, including the ones in Mobile. He published another volume of poems in 1906.

3. Flash's book, titled simply *Poems,* was published in 1860 by Rudd and Carleton of New York City.

જ્ર્ક જ્ર્ક જ્ર્ક

My darling Rachel

Your welcome letter saddened me, for I had not heard of the severe affliction that has fallen on my kind friend Mr Moses. How very sorry I am to
know that the circumstances were so melancholy. Yes dear, I did wonder why
you wrote me no letters this long while and thought that painted spectre
<u>Fame</u> has taken bodily possession of you; and set you to grinding at that ever-
lasting mill, yclept[1]—"<u>Novel-writing</u>." Rachel darling, I rather think you
should not "unbutton yourself" (as Seaver[2] says) to that same treacherous
worthy afore-said. <u>Fame</u> <u>don't</u> <u>pay</u>:—well—I take that back; but the <u>payments</u>
are in beautiful <u>looking</u> print, of an ancient variety,—first discovered on the
margin of the <u>Dead</u> <u>Sea</u>[3] and thence imported by all lands and people—; lus-
cious looking, glossy, rosy, fragrant <u>Apples</u> <u>of</u> <u>Sodom</u>.[4] Most folks swallow the
bitter dust, smiling all the time, and praising its <u>sweet</u> <u>juiciness</u>; N'importe![5]
But jesting aside my dear far-off, longed for friend; I knew you did not write
"<u>Rutledge</u>."[6] I believe you would have told me—Now Rachel—what are
you living for? What do you suppose your Creator gave you "good gifts" for?
I have often wondered why you <u>did</u> <u>not</u> <u>write</u>—Of course you know you
<u>could</u> if you would; and my darling you have <u>such</u> a glorious field stretching
out before you. Your—nationality—; your grand ancestral rights, all of the
sublime, that clusters around God's "<u>chosen</u> <u>people</u>."[7] Rachel write a Jewish
tale; and make it a substratum on which to embroider your views of life, men,
women, Art, Literature. You can do this: Give the world another Raphael
Aben Ezra![8] Your surroundings and education have familiarized you with all
the mystic points of your creed, and you might weave a tale of marvellous
power. Understand me though, darling; literary women have trials that the
world knows not of; are called on to make sacrifices whose incense floats not
before the public; but Rachel, beloved, though our Sisterhood work in dark
lonely corners, we have joys and encouragements peculiar to the vocation—
I speak not now of mere <u>gratified</u> <u>ambition</u>; I point you to the nobler arm of
doing <u>God's</u> <u>work</u>. There is a calm sweet reward, arising from the discharge
of duty like this, such as no one can take from us. I have thought much of all
this, and my deliberate conviction is, that while literary women as a class, are
<u>not</u> <u>as</u> happy, as women who have Husbands and Children to engage their
attention and monopolize their affections; yet in the faithful employment of
their talents, they experience a deep peace and satisfaction, and are crowned
with a glory such as marriage never gave. I have spoken of the two as antagonistic; I believe them to be so. No loving Wife and Mother can sit down and
serve two Masters; Fame and Love. It is almost impossible. If you were happily

married, I would say from the deeps [*sic*] of my heart—"Bless you dear Rachel: you are wise." But so long as you are not married, I wish you would write—Do. Now don't tell me you can't; Humbug! Try Rachel try. And now about my humble self. You "hear I am to marry soon"!!! You want to know about it; very natural you should. Rachel my darling; I may walk up the pyramids of Egypt, but I am not going to marry anybody. Do you believe me? Truly and solemnly my friend, I am not engaged; nor shall I ever be. What ever you may have heard, give it no credit. I am telling you the truth. You know I would not deceive you. I shall live and die, Augusta Evans. Write to me soon. Give me a long letter.

Your own
AJE

1. Old English for "named" or "called."

2. The editor of *Harper's New Monthly Magazine* and a friend of AEW. See AEW to Seaver, December 31, 1859.

3. A salt lake at the end of the Jordan River in Israel. With a salt content of twenty-five percent, the Dead Sea cannot support life.

4. The apple tree in the Garden of Eden was believed to have grown near Sodom, a city of wickedness, and was called "the apple of Sodom." Another Biblical reference was to the "vine of Sodom," which bore poisonous grapes. Moses compared Israel with this vine (Deut. 32:32). The fruit—pretty on the outside but with a dry, powdery interior—was used to represent the destruction of Sodom and Gomorrah (George Arthur Buttrick, et al., eds., *The Interpreters' Dictionary of the Bible,* 4 vols. [New York: Abingdon, 1962],1: 175-76, 4: 786).

5. French expression, "No matter!"

6. See AEW to Rachel Lyons, May 29, 1860, note 2.

7. The Jews. Rachel was Jewish.

8. Aben-Ezra (1119–1194), a Spanish Jew and an eminent authority and commentator on the Scriptures. He also excelled as an astronomer, mathematician, physician, linguist, and poet.

14 / MS Alabama Mobile August 28 1860

My dear Rachel—

I have just returned home after nearly three weeks absence at Bladon Springs,[1] whither I went for my health; and seize the very earliest leisure half hour to thank you for your last kind letter. It grieves me my dear Rachel to note the despondence in which you were plunged when you penned that letter; yet in all this broad sunny land there is no one who can more fully and perfectly sympathize with you than I. There come hours to all of us when hope folds her wings, and we sit listlessly holding our hands, despairing of success; well-nigh careless, indifferent to the future, asking nothing, hoping nothing, and immeasurably worse than all, <u>doing</u> <u>nothing</u>. I know what this disease is; am too familiar with each of its symptoms not to sympathize with the victim writhing in its grasp—In Hyperborean[2] regions, the weary traveller sits down by the way, pillows his head on murderous ice, and sinks to fatal sleep knowing that drowsiness is the avant-courier of Death; but a <u>faithful</u> guide, scourges him back to wakefulness, and hurries him forward exhorting to activity. My friend, my darling, be not offended if I call to you in your inertia; and say, <u>work</u>; <u>work</u> is the only medicine for a nature like yours. Oh Rachel! Rachel! God gave you talents; and will require them again at your hands. Where—where—have you <u>buried</u> your "napkin"?[3] Exhume it dear friend; and begin to increase it. Of the circumstances that surround you, of course I can know very little, but I feel assured you <u>could</u> accomplish <u>much</u> if you only <u>would</u>. I do not mean to flatter you; nothing is farther from my intention; but I believe you would write successfully—Perhaps I am mistaken; yet such is my conviction and at least you might make the attempt. I do not believe you will be happy until you faithfully begin God's work, in some of its varied departments—Some are called in the very dawn of life; some hear the summons later; all would hear them were not their ears obstinately closed. You admit that you are restless and dissatisfied with the weary round of fashion and gayety. Oh my friend; no <u>true</u> woman ever yet fed contentedly on these husks. Our hearts are shrines for holier idols than the world can erect; they must have either <u>Love</u>, or <u>Duty</u>. The fortunate and happiest women have <u>both</u>; but the <u>last</u> can give great comfort, pure joy, perfect serenity. I think you attach too much importance to the mere accumulation of information; for after all, it is an authors [*sic*] own deep, original thoughts, which are remembered, and prized; and not the rehashing of classical, or medieval sentiments. Some times I think that if you chose you might walk up and stand beside your national Sister Grace Aquilar.[4] Your religion is so full of grand immemorial themes, exhaustless, ever attractive. I often wish I might have been born a <u>Jewess</u>—You are a glorious old people; I would I belonged to you, sometimes—though of course <u>I</u> would combine the <u>Christian</u> <u>with</u> the Mosaic dispensation. Don't wait any longer; go to work at once; life is so short and fitful; you might be taken before middle age comes down upon you—Time is precious—who wastes it, wastes God's heritage. Do not be wounded by anything I have said—I <u>do</u> <u>love</u> you my darling, and long to know you are taking your own proper place as a writer. Make at last <u>one</u> <u>trial</u>. If in <u>any</u> <u>way</u> I can possibly aid you, call upon me—call upon me—how gladly will I do all in my power. Write to me speedily and tell me you are not hurt by my freedom of counsel. It is because I love you, that I am ambitious for you—Have you seen the "<u>Household of Bouverie</u>"?[5] Tell me what you think of it. How I want to see you! As yet I do not know exactly where I shall spend my winter—Will let you know soon—God bless you my dear friend—

With earnest love—
AJEvans

1. A resort near Mobile.

2. Relating to the extreme northern regions of the world, the Arctic.

3. In Jesus's parable of the talents, told in Luke 19:13–26, the servant who was given only one talent wrapped it in a napkin and buried it in the ground. When the master returned, this servant was punished. In contrast, the other servants, who had used and thereby increased their talents, were rewarded.

4. Grace Aguilar (1816–1847), Jewish author whose novels include *Home Influence: A Tale for Mothers and Daughters* (1855) and *The Women of Israel* (1857).

5. A novel by Mrs. Catherine A. Warfield, a Southern writer. See AEW to Victor, December 1, 1860, note 3.

❧ ❧ ❧

15 / MS Alabama   Mobile Nov 15 1860

My dear Rachel—

Do you wonder why I have suffered so long a time to elapse before answering your last kind and valued letter? Indeed my darling I have endeavored many, many times to send you a few lines of greetings, but the <u>Fates</u> have grimly conspired against me, and today, though I have but a mere <u>pittance</u> of leisure, I seize it in a fit of thorough desperation. We have just left our cottage home,[1] my dear quiet country sanctum—Sanctorum; my Mecca of rest; and removed to town, for the winter, perhaps for the year. <u>You</u> I am sure, can readily imagine, that in the confusion incident to moving, and the numberless calls on my attention, I have very little leisure at my command. The Hegira[2] is over now, and I trust I shall not be so beset in future, by engagements. I have been particularly anxious to write to you, that I might tell you how exceedingly glad I was to learn from your last letter, that you <u>really</u> contemplated <u>writing</u>. Do persevere dear Rachel; let nothing discourage you; at all events make the attempt! Elaborate your plot, trace clearly to the end, your grand leading aim, before you write <u>a line</u> and then you will find no trouble I think, in weaving the details, arranging your—chiaroscuro—in fine—polishing the whole. Let me beg of you not to waver in this project; set to work, and your labor will gather wonderful charms for you. I know you <u>can write</u>, and I believe you will, if you only <u>once</u> set about it. Once [*sic*] thing more, be sure to <u>select</u> the <u>very highest types</u> of character for the standard has sadly deteriorated of late in works of fiction. In a too close imitation of

Nature many of our novelists have fallen into the error of patronizing coarseness, vulgarity, and ignorance. I make this suggestion, because I think that it's [*sic*] truth is strikingly exemplified in "Adam Bede"[3] the most popular book of the age. The world needs elevating and it is the peculiar province of the Novelist to present the very highest noblest types of human nature. I know my dear Rachel you will not misunderstand my motive in making these affectionate suggestions, or think for one instant I presume to advise or dictate. I offer them as I would to one of my own sisters as the result of my own experience and observation. I presume that like myself, you are now all absorbed in considering the vital political question of the day.[4] It is an issue of such incalculable solemnity and importance that no true Southern man or woman can fail to be deeply interested and impressed. For this great political problem I can perceive but one solution—the unanimous cooperation of the Southern states in secession, prompt secession. South Carolina will inaugurate this movement I trust, indeed my hopes hang on her patriotism and fearlessness. The feeling here is intense; not noisy, but deep, and the faces of the people are stamped with stern, desperate resolve. Do not delay writing to me dear friend though I have suffered so long a time to elapse without thanking you for your last. Can't you come and make me a visit this winter? Do think of it—I should be so exceedingly glad to have you with me. Why can't you? Pardon my haste, dear Rachel and believe me as always yours ever

Augusta

1. Georgia Cottage, on the outskirts of Mobile. See AEW to Rachel, May 27, [1859], note 1.

2. A flight or journey to a more desirable location.

3. *Adam Bede,* by the English author George Eliot (Mary Ann Evans), was published in 1859. What AEW objected to in the novel was probably the character of Hetty Sorrel, a poor, orphaned young woman, who has a baby out of wedlock by the young squire Arthur Donnithorne. She abandons her baby in the woods after giving birth alone. After being sentenced to die for the murder of the child, she is reprieved at the last minute due to Donnithorne's efforts and is deported instead. The heroines in AEW's novels are also frequently orphaned young women, but they support themselves with honest work and usually get married—to wealthy, older men. As Nina Baym has pointed out, this is the basic plot of all the domestic novels (*Woman's Fiction: A Guide to Novels by and about Women in America, 1820–70* [Ithaca, N.Y.: Cornell University Press, 1978], 11).

4. In November 1860, what the South had most feared happened—Abraham Lincoln was elected president on an antislavery platform. Several Southern states began immediately to talk of secession.

❧ ❧ ❧

16 / MS Columbus   Mobile Nov 26th 1860

My dear Aunt—[1]

It is with a <u>very</u> <u>sad</u> <u>heart</u>, that I sit down to write to you and I hope that you will understand and appreciate the feeling which prompts me to tell you <u>one</u> cause of my sorrow. When I first accepted Mr S——,[2] though it was conditionally, I felt as if I wanted <u>you</u> to know it; but said to <u>Ma</u>: "I am not willing anybody but <u>Auntie</u> should know it; for it is so <u>uncertain</u>, and the others might speak of it." <u>Ma</u> answered, "your Aunt would be hurt if she thought you had not sufficient confidence in her family, to be willing to trust them; and besides, if you <u>request</u> <u>them</u> to <u>keep</u> your <u>secret</u>, of course they will do so." I confess I consented <u>very</u> <u>reluctantly</u>; and Auntie, you know I <u>begged</u> that the whole affair might be kept <u>secret</u>; I said it was only on condition the members of your family would promise not to mention it. Two nights ago, we received a letter from a young friend at <u>College</u>[3] in <u>Millegeville</u>[4] and in great astonishment he writes that "it is <u>now</u> <u>reported</u> <u>all</u> <u>over</u> <u>town</u> that Miss Augusta is <u>married</u> <u>to</u> <u>the</u> <u>Editor</u> <u>of</u> <u>the</u> <u>World</u>."[5] He said there were <u>Columbus</u>[6] <u>people</u> visiting there at the time. Auntie, do you not think I have a <u>right</u> to feel <u>hurt</u> when I <u>know</u> <u>Mr</u> <u>Benning</u>[7] <u>has</u> <u>said</u>, "<u>Augusta</u> <u>is</u> <u>going</u> <u>to</u> <u>marry</u> <u>a</u> <u>Mr</u> <u>Spalding</u> [*sic*] <u>a</u> <u>Black</u> <u>Republican</u>[8], <u>and</u> <u>the</u> <u>Editor</u> <u>of</u> <u>the</u> <u>World</u>"? <u>Even</u> <u>if</u> <u>he</u> had <u>believed</u> him to be an abolitionist, was it kind, was it the part of a <u>friend</u>, still less of a <u>relative</u> to publish his opinion to the world? To put such a report in circulation at such a crisis as this;[9] to tell that I was married or nearly so, to a Black Republican and that I was going to the <u>North</u> at <u>this</u> <u>juncture</u>! Oh Auntie! do you wonder that I feel this very keenly, when I tried <u>so</u> hard to shield the whole matter from the public; when I <u>begged</u> that nothing would be even hinted about it? This report is travelling <u>now</u> <u>in</u> <u>all</u> <u>directions</u>. Mother wrote to you that no time had been fixed, that all was uncertain, as events have proved, and I do not see how Mr Benning could speak so positively, as if the thing had already taken place. Think of having the whole matter in the mouths of gossips, at such a time as this. If he had merely mentioned the possibility of my marriage, and not branded <u>his</u> name as "<u>Black</u> <u>Republican</u>" I would not have been so grieved. To have <u>my</u> <u>name</u> so associated by the members of the Legislature in Millegeville!

We have removed to town, but though it is far better for <u>Pa</u> and the boys, I would infinitely prefer our quiet little country home. <u>Ma</u> wrote to you, a few days ago, I believe. How is <u>Uncle's</u> health now? I am so sorry he would not consult Dr Gescheidst last summer. Please <u>kiss</u> <u>him</u> for me, and give him my warmest best love. Tell him, too, that I intended writing to him, but have been <u>so</u> <u>troubled</u> <u>of</u> <u>late</u>, that I thought my letters would hardly afford him any pleasure.

I hope my dear Aunt you will not be wounded by anything I have written. I felt that if I wrote <u>at</u> <u>all</u>, I must tell you the reason why I was <u>so</u> <u>grieved</u>. All are well. I am about as usual. Believe me, my dearest Aunt <u>as</u> <u>always</u>

Your <u>grateful</u> & <u>affectionate</u>

Augusta Evans

1. This is probably Mary Howard Jones, the sister of AEW's mother and the wife of Seaborn Jones of Columbus, Georgia. A few years later, AEW used the Joneses' home in Columbus as the model for La Bocage, St. Elmo Murray's mansion in the novel *St. Elmo* (Barrett, family member of AEW; also see Fidler, *A Biography,* 14–15).

2. James Reed Spaulding, a young editor whom AEW met in October 1859 while visiting in the home of her publisher, J. C. Derby, in New York. Spaulding wrote a very favorable review of *Beulah,* which had just been published, and was so impressed with the novel that he came to the Derbys' home to meet the author. He and AEW were instantly attracted to each other and were tentatively engaged when she left New York to return home, with the understanding that he would visit her in Mobile.

3. Probably Oglethorpe University, founded in 1835.

4. Milledgeville, a town in central Georgia and state capital during the antebellum years.

5. Spaulding founded the newspaper *The New York World* in the spring of 1860 for the purpose of reporting the news from a Christian viewpoint.

6. A town in west central Georgia where AEW was born and where many members of her family still lived.

7. The Bennings were old friends and distant relatives of AEW.

8. The Republican Party was formed in 1854 on an antislavery platform and quickly gained support in the North. Opponents referred to its members as Black Republicans because of their stand against slavery.

9. Lincoln had just been elected president after campaigning against slavery, and several Southern states were already openly considering secession. Through his newspaper, Spaulding had espoused the Union cause, opposed slavery, and urged the Southern states not to secede. At some point during the autumn of 1860, he and AEW ended their engagement over irreconcilable political differences. No correspondence between the two has survived.

❧ ❧ ❧

17 / *MS Virginia*   Mobile Dec 1st 1860

Mr O J Victor[1]
Dear Sir—

The December No of the Cosmopolitan Journal[2] reached me last night, and I hasten to express to you my sincere thanks for the exceedingly flattering terms in which you speak of me and my literary efforts.[3] I assure you Sir it gives me very great pleasure to know that you think so kindly of me and the encouraging words contained in the <u>critique</u> will stimulate me to deserve in future the accolade so generously bestowed upon me. I regret very much that I have not been able to finish an article for the "Art Journal" and hope that I shall yet have the gratification of seeing my name in your list of contributors. That I am warmly interested in the prosperity of the Association and especially in the extended circulation of the Journal at [in] the South, it is not necessary to reiterate here. All that relates to Art has peculiar charm for me, and since I am debarred from the treasures contained in New York Galleries and Studios, I have learned to regard the "Cosmopolitan Journal" as my sole medium of communication. With renewed thanks for your kindness

Believe me very truly
Your friend
Augusta J Evans

PS
[Note obscured]

1. See AEW to Victor, June 6, 1860, note 1.
2. See AEW to Victor, June 6, 1860, note 2.
3. Victor's article, titled "Augusta J. Evans," appeared in the December 1860 issue of *The Cosmopolitan Art Journal* (154–66). The article included a biographical sketch of AEW and a very favorable review of *Beulah,* comparing it with *Jane Eyre.* Victor also claimed that *The Household of Bouverie* (see AEW to Rachel, August 28, 1860) and *Beulah* were "among the most *intellectually* original of any novels yet produced by American authors." Victor concluded his article by suggesting that book editors and reviewers were prejudiced against Southern authors and that AEW's novels would be held in higher esteem were she from another area.

❧ ❧ ❧

18 / MS Columbus   Mobile Dec 4th 1860

Dear Aunt—

Your letter has just arrived, and as Mother is writing to you I enclose my reply—if you will refer to my last letter you will see, that I did not say, I heard <u>Mr Benning</u>[1] <u>told</u> <u>it</u> <u>himself</u> in <u>Milledgeville</u>; but that it was reported I was <u>married</u> to the Editor of the World,[2] and that <u>Columbus</u> <u>people</u> were visiting <u>there</u> at the <u>time</u>. Now Aunt, <u>Cousin Mary Anne Williams</u> said, that "<u>Mr Benning</u> <u>told</u> <u>her</u> <u>Augusta Evans</u> <u>was</u> <u>going</u> <u>to</u> <u>marry</u> <u>a</u> <u>Black Republican Editor</u>."[3] He <u>told</u> <u>her</u> <u>so</u> <u>in</u> <u>Columbus</u>, when she went over to see you all immediately after you came from Virginia Springs; and knowing that <u>Charley Williams</u> was in <u>Milledgeville</u> I knew of course she told him what Mr. Benning told her; and thus the report was spread in Milledgeville. It makes no difference to me, whether he told it in Milledgeville <u>himself</u> or to people in Columbus who circulated it. Mr Benning might have known that when <u>he</u> <u>told</u> Cousin Mary Anne I was "<u>going</u> <u>to</u> <u>marry</u> <u>a</u> <u>Black</u> <u>Republican</u>" he might just as well have put it in the newspapers at once. It has <u>all</u> come from what he told her, and knowing that Charley Williams was in Milledgeville, I <u>knew</u> <u>of</u> <u>course</u> <u>he</u> or <u>some</u> <u>one</u> <u>else</u> <u>to</u> <u>whom</u> <u>she</u> told it, had set the report afloat. If Mr Benning had not been informed of the matter in <u>sacred</u> <u>confidence</u> I should have no right to complain. When I wrote to you I <u>knew</u> <u>he</u> had spoken of it to Cousin <u>Mary</u> <u>Anne</u>, but I had no desire to implicate her, and should not have mentioned <u>her</u> <u>name</u> if you had not asked about it. She only told others, what was <u>told</u> to her, and it was not strange that the tidings of my marriage with a "<u>Black</u> <u>Republican</u>" surprised her, <u>coming</u> from a member of your family; though one would have supposed that <u>common</u> <u>friendship</u> much less relationship would have kept <u>her</u> from <u>mentioning</u> the matter. Thus as I wrote you, it has come from Mr Benning, though he possibly did not speak of it <u>himself</u> in Millegeville. I repeat I have no desire to involve Cousin Mary Anne in the affair. As <u>I</u> never reposed <u>confidence</u> in <u>her</u>, I can not of course charge her with a betrayal of it.

Please give my love to Uncle and believe me

As ever
Affectionately
AJEvans

1. See AEW to Aunt, November 26, 1860, note 7.
2. See AEW to Aunt, November 26, 1860, note 5.
3. See AEW to Aunt, November 26, 1860, note 8.

❧ ❧ ❧

19 / Haverford   Mobile Dec 21st 1860

Mr C E Bennett

In compliance with the request contained in your very kind and flattering note of the 7th; I send you the desired autograph.

Very respectfully
Augusta J Evans

CHAPTER 2

"Thank God we are Southern women!"

20 / MS Columbus   Mobile Jan' 13th 1861

Hon' H. L. Benning—
My dear Cousin

I enclose a copy of a letter to Mrs L Virginia French,[1] <u>Editress</u> of the "<u>Crusader</u>" published in Atlanta Georgia, in reply to a communication from her praying me to append my name to a "<u>Memorial</u>" from the <u>representative women</u> of America,[2] to be presented to the Georgia State Convention.[3] Mrs French is a warm personal friend of Stephens,[4] and also of Ben' Hill,[5] and one of these two will be charged with the presentation of the "Memorial." I <u>suspect</u> the project was suggested to her by them, though she has not intimated it to me. I write to ask of you as a favor to me, <u>that</u> <u>if</u> the <u>Memorial</u> <u>is</u> <u>read before</u> <u>the</u> <u>Convention</u>, you will be kind enough to read my reply to her letter. I think it is an occasion when women should leave matters entirely to the wisdom of our statesmen, but if a number seek to exert their influence, at this time, in the form of a <u>memorial</u> I should like to have my native State, know that <u>I</u> for one do not belong to the band of latter day <u>Tories</u>. Of course, if the <u>memorial</u> is not mentioned, I have no desire to have my name alluded to at all. I believe you will appreciate my motives, and not suspect me of any wish to thrust my individual views on the public. Hoping that you will have <u>no occasion</u> to read my reply, I am in great haste

Your affectionate Cousin
Augusta J Evans

PS.
Please send me a line to let me know whether you received my letter. AJE

1. Lucy Virginia French, of Tennessee, was a poet, novelist, and editor of several magazines including *The Southern Homestead, The Southern Literary Messenger,* and the *Crusader.*

2. French wrote a "Memorial" urging support for the Union. To endorse this cause, she obtained the signatures of several hundred prominent women of both the

North and South ("Augusta J. Evans on Secession," 65). The Memorial does not appear to be extant. There is no record of it at the Tennessee State Archives, which houses French's other papers.

3. Alarmed by Lincoln's election on an antislavery platform, several Southern states began holding conventions in order to vote on secession. Hoping to sway the delegates' votes, French sent her Memorial to be read at these conventions. For the Georgia convention, she especially wanted the endorsement of AEW, who was already a well-known author and a native Georgian.

4. Alexander Hamilton Stephens, former governor of Georgia, was a moderate who fiercely opposed secession. However, when Georgia seceded, he bowed to the will of the majority and a few weeks later agreed to serve as vice president of the Confederacy.

5. Benjamin Harvey Hill, a Georgia state congressman, opposed secession at the Georgia state convention. However, he yielded when his state seceded and later served in the Confederate senate.

❧ ❧ ❧

21 / MS Columbus

<u>Copy</u>[1]

Mobile Jan 13th 1861

Mrs L V French—
Dear Madam—

Your very kind letter reached me yesterday, and I avail myself of the earliest leisure moment to send you a reply. As regards your request that I will append my name to a "<u>Memorial</u>" to be presented to the Georgia State Convention, you will I trust pardon me, when candor compels the avowal that with such a "<u>memorial</u>" I have no sympathy whatever. I regret most sincerely, that on this subject, our views are so widely at variance; you have warmly espoused the <u>Union</u> cause, while I am an earnest and most uncompromising Secessionist. Your predicate of "Southern rights <u>in</u> the <u>Union</u>," I now regard as more than paradoxical; and prompt and separate state action, I believe to be the <u>only</u> door of escape, from the worse than Egyptian bondage of Black Republicanism.[2] For fifteen years, we of the South, have endured insult and aggression; have ironed down our just indignation and suffered numberless encroachments because of our devotion to the <u>Union</u>; because we shuddered and shrank from laying sacrilegious hands on the magnificent Temple which our fore-fathers reared in proud triumph, and which has long blazed, the Pharos[3] of the civilized world. Presuming upon this devotion, northern fanaticism has <u>grown</u> <u>on</u> Southern endurance, and not all the diplomacy, the consummate statesmanship of patriotic men of both sections has weighed one iota against the waves of Abolitionism; which have rolled rapidly on, till

they threaten to pollute the sacred precincts of the "<u>White House</u>." <u>The
Union</u> has become a misnomer, and rather than witness the desecration of
our glorious Fane,[4] we of the South will Sampson-like lay hold upon its pil-
lars, and if need be, perish in its ruins. The present attitude of the Republican party, and the desperate and unscrupulous character of its leaders, pre-
clude the hope of a satisfactory redress of our grievances in the <u>Union</u>; and
since the <u>Aegis</u> of the <u>Constitution</u> has been contemptuously thrown aside,
I could place no confidence in the temporary concessions, which just so soon
as the storm of Secession swept by, would be cancelled as hitherto. The South
asks but her <u>sacred</u> <u>Constitutional</u> <u>rights</u>; these have been grossly and persistently violated; pleadings, expostulations and threats on our part, have been
answered with taunts, sneers, and defiance on theirs; and promises which
the present alarming crisis might <u>possibly</u> extort from them, would be kept
with their accustomed <u>Punic</u>[5] faith. I repeat it; the <u>Union</u> has been an Idol
with us all, too long, to admit of its being struck rudely from its lofty pedestal,
without sending a thrill of anguish to every true, patriotic heart, but my dear
Madam, the law of "<u>self-preservation</u>" is imperative and as the <u>thirteen</u> <u>States</u>
cut the chains of Great Britain to regain their birthright—Freedom; so we of
the South sever the links that bind us to a people, who guided by the Demon
of fanaticism, have insanely destroyed the noblest government, which the
accumulated wisdom of centuries has ever erected. The "Memorial" which
you propose to lay before the Convention of Georgia, from the "representa-
tive women of America," essays to accomplish what <u>our</u> ablest statesmen have
found impossible; and it is because I most earnestly deprecate as suicidal any
effort to delay the dissolution of the Union, that I must decline to add my
own signature. A few weeks hence, our rights would inevitably be maintained
at the point of the Sword; for the coercive policy of Lincoln is foreshadowed;
and since the South has resolved to defend her Constitutional rights at all
hazards, I regard it as an <u>economy</u> <u>of</u> <u>blood</u> for the fifteen States to secede as
promptly as possible. As a citizen of Alabama, I am proud to be able to tell
you, we have irrevocably linked our destiny with Carolina's and if necessary
will <u>drain</u> <u>our</u> <u>veins</u> rather than yield to the ignominious rule of Black
Republicanism. As a <u>native</u> of the <u>Empire</u> <u>State</u> of the South, my heart clings
to her soil, and I look forward to the meeting of her convention, with a triumphant assurance, that "knowing her rights, <u>she</u> <u>dare</u> maintain them"; and
that in the palmiest days of our <u>coming</u> Confederacy I shall look back to the
16th of Jan' 1861 and exclaim exultingly, "<u>I</u> <u>too</u> <u>am</u> <u>a</u> <u>Georgian</u>!" Perhaps my
dear Madam you will censure my warmth on this subject; but <u>my</u> <u>all</u> is at
Stake. My <u>Father</u> and my <u>Brothers</u> belong to the garrison of <u>Fort</u> <u>Morgan</u>;[6]
day after day, I ply <u>my</u> <u>needle</u>, making <u>Sand</u> <u>Bags</u> for the <u>ramparts</u> and <u>car-
tridges</u> <u>for</u> <u>its</u> <u>cannon</u>; and if, (which God in his mercy forbid!) the hour

arrives when Federal guns pour their fiery hail upon it; I feel that I would infinitely prefer to perish <u>there</u> with them, rather than endure the horrors which hundreds of John Browns would inevitably stir up in our midst, sheltered by the protecting mantle of Lincolns [*sic*] Administration. Were it my privilege to address my countrymen of Georgia on the 16th, I should point to the flag of Alabama; waving its magnificent folds in the balmy breezes of the Gulf, and with a serene trust in the God of Justice; say triumphantly, "let the Star of the Empire State blaze with ours along the way to <u>Freedom</u>; let us conquer or perish together; delay is ruinous, suicidal—; <u>the</u> <u>time</u> <u>has</u> <u>come</u>." Such are my views regarding the vital issues of the day, and having freely expressed them, you will not feel surprised that I do not comply with your request. With many and sincere thanks for your friendly feeling toward me, I am my dear Madam

Very respectfully yours
Augusta J Evans

1. This letter was appended to the previous one addressed to H. L. Benning (Jan. 13, 1861). The letter that AEW sent to Virginia French, identical to this one with a few minor variations in wording, was published in the *Alabama Historical Quarterly* 3, no. 1 (1941): 65–67. At that time, Mrs. Fred Frazier of Chattanooga, Tennessee, Virginia French's granddaughter, owned that letter.

2. See AEW to Aunt, November 26, 1860, note 8.

3. See AEW to Victor, June 6, 1860, note 7.

4. Temple or church

5. Referring to the three wars that Rome waged against Carthage (264–241 B.C.E., 218–201 B.C.E., and 149–146 B.C.E.). *Punic,* meaning treacherous or deceitful, was originally used by the Romans to describe the Carthaginians.

6. Located in the harbor of Mobile.

❧ ❧ ❧

22 / MS Alabama   Mobile Feb' 2nd 1861

My dear Rachel—

Your welcome letter arrived yesterday; and I snatch a few moments to send you thanks and a most affectionate greeting. Impute my silence to every other cause than want of remembrance. You have doubtless heard from the papers of our taking our <u>Forts</u> of <u>Arsenal</u>.[1] By far the most important of these is <u>Fort Morgan</u>,[2] situated <u>30</u> (thirty[)]miles below Mobile and commanding the entrance to our harbor. The fortifications are very strong, and with the addition of a few <u>Columbiads</u>[3] which are daily expected, will be almost impregnable. Immediately after its occupation by Alabama troops, the commander informed us that a number of Sand-Bags, for the ramparts were needed; and also flannel charges for the Cannon. We ladies went to work at once, and have finished over <u>9,000</u> Bags. This has kept me so busily engaged, that I have had no time for anything else; not even to write to you my dear friend. It is an anxious, terrible time——! My <u>Father</u> and <u>both</u> my <u>Brothers</u> <u>belong</u> to the garrison of <u>Fort Morgan</u> and you can readily imagine how restless their constant exposure to attack renders me. I do not now apprehend a collision at Fort <u>Morgan</u> but fear there will soon be trouble at Pensacola, over Fort Pickens[4] and if so, Mobile companies will go <u>over</u> at once. Several of my friends have <u>already</u> gone to Pensacola, and we are kept in continual apprehension on their account. I think Major <u>Chase</u> has been very culpable in allowing Skinner to take possession of Pickens.[5] He knew the importance of the position and after <u>Anderson's</u>[6] move at <u>Moultrie</u> should have been on the alert. We of Mobile feel almost as much interested in the affairs of <u>Sumter</u> as you Carolinians; it [is] a common cause, and the latest tidings from Charleston are most impatiently looked for. You ask of <u>Mr Derby</u> in your last. I hear from him frequently—had a letter <u>yesterday</u>. He is living in New York City this winter. Mr. Derby is of course a <u>Union Man</u>; and thinks <u>Secession</u> a grave sin. He is much distressed because <u>I</u> am so <u>very warm</u> a <u>Secessionist</u>, and believes southern rights might have been obtained <u>in</u> the <u>Union</u>; <u>which we</u> at the <u>South</u> know to be <u>impossible</u>. I am waiting most anxiously in hope that Virginia will secede at once. If so, the other border States will inevitably form our coming <u>glorious</u> <u>Southern</u> <u>Confederacy</u>. When I can find the <u>time</u>, I will write you of <u>some</u> <u>books</u> which I have read this <u>winter</u>; and consider extremely valuable. Write me what you are doing and thinking. I hope most sincerely that an amiable adjustment of National difficulties will soon enable me to dismiss all anxiety concerning my Father & Brothers, and attend as formerly to my correspondence. My health has not been good, for several months, but just now I am better, and I doubt not shall get quite well as soon as I return to my <u>country home</u>. <u>City-life</u> never <u>suited me</u>, in <u>any respect</u>. Good-bye my dear Rachel; do write to me soon, and believe that only pressing engagements prevented my writing to you <u>long ere this</u>. With <u>warm love</u> and <u>constant remembrance.</u>

Yours as ever

A J Evans

1. As soon as the Confederate states seceded from the Union, but before war had actually broken out between the North and South, the Confederates began seizing the Federal forts in their states. Obviously a "foreign power" could not be permitted to occupy territory in the new nation. See E. Merton Coulter, *Confederate States of America, 1861–1865,* vol. 7 of *A History of the South,* (Baton Rouge: Louisiana State University Press, 1950), 34.

2. Alabama seized Fort Morgan, located at the edge of Mobile Harbor (Coulter 34).

3. A type of heavy, cast-iron cannon used chiefly for coastal defense.

4. After Florida, with assistance from Alabama troops, seized Fort Barrancas near Pensacola, Federal troops relocated to Fort Pickens on Santa Rosa Island (Coulter 34).

5. Aware that the state of Florida, having already seceded, would want possession of the Federal forts on its soil, U. S. Lieutenant A. J. Slemmer (not Skinner, as AEW reports) quietly moved his forces to Fort Pickens. Colonel Chase, of the Confederate army, asked Slemmer to surrender, but he refused. Several Florida officials sent word to Chase that there should be no bloodshed, so the situation remained at an impasse until the attack on Fort Sumter in South Carolina. See Clement A. Evans, ed., *Confederate Military History* (New York: Yoseloff, 1962), 2: 21–22).

6. South Carolina had negotiated with the Federal government to obtain possession of the Federal forts on its soil and had been promised that the U.S. government would not take action at this time. However, on December 26, 1860, Major Robert Anderson, commander of the Federal army at Fort Moultrie on the edge of Charleston harbor, moved his troops to Fort Sumter, an island fortress which was easier to defend. South Carolinians, enraged over what they considered an act of bad faith, seized Fort Moultrie and began building up their fortifications around Charleston (Coulter, *Confederate States of America,* 34–35). Two months after AEW wrote this letter, the Confederates fired on Fort Sumter and the Civil War began.

❧ ❧ ❧

23 / MS North Carolina   Mobile March 13th 1861

My dear Rachel

Your kind and precious little note of invitation, reached me a few days since, when I was too ill to respond. Immediately after my return from Montgomery I was taken ill, and have been confined to my bed for some days. It was a low nervous fever, which had been hovering over me for weeks, and which suddenly swept down upon a feeble prey—The Dr thinks it the result of my visit to Montgomery, and the constant excitement I was subjected to,[1] but I don't believe one word of it; I should have had it if I had never seen Montgomery. Thank you my dear Rachel for the invitation to visit you in your home.[2] Ah! how I want to accept it! I told Mr Moses that if you did not come to see me this spring I should have to go to you! And he almost promised to take me from Columbus,[3] if I determined to go. It is a great temptation to me, my darling friend, for I do so long to see you but just now I can not leave home. I am far from well—; and Pa thinks a cold, mountain region is the place for me just as soon as warm weather sets in. I do not yet know what my plans are to be; my health only can determine them. Until I know most positively that there is to be no fighting[4] I am unwilling to get out of sight of Fort Morgan;[5] for in case of trouble my two Brothers would belong to it's [sic] garrison. Thus you see my dear Rachel, I can not say with any certainty what I shall do. I do want to be with you, but fear I can hardly come this spring. Things may change however and I hope for the best. I had the good fortune to meet Cousin John[6] and Mr Benning in Montgomery and it was a great joy to me. Cousin John looks remarkably well, and was in admirable spirits. You may be sure, we talked often of you, and regretted you were not with us. I met Mr Keith of your state, and several other gentlemen of the Carolina delegation. But dear friend I am not strong enough to write any more today—having already finished several other letters. When I am quite well again I will write at more length. Believe that I think constantly of you; and want to be with you—and write to your—

> Attached friend
> Augusta Evans

1. On February 9, 1861, delegates from the seven seceding states met in Montgomery, Alabama, elected Jefferson Davis president of the Confederacy, and adopted a provisional Constitution. AEW attended this convention as an onlooker.

2. Rachel lived in Columbia, South Carolina.

3. Columbus, Georgia.

4. The Confederate firing upon Fort Sumter, the event that precipitated war, did not occur until April 12, 1861.

5. Located at the mouth of Mobile Bay in Alabama.

6. AEW's cousin, John Jones of Columbus, Georgia, accompanied her to New York City in 1859 when she sold the manuscript of *Beulah* to publisher J. C. Derby (Fidler, *A Biography,* 68).

❧ ❧ ❧

24 / MS North Carolina　　　　　　　　　　　　　Norfolk June 26 1861
Alabama Archives (typed copy)[1]

My dear Rachel

I have intended writing to you ever since I reached this place; but a multiplicity of urgent engagements prevented my doing so as promptly as I could have wished. My brothers are both stationed near Norfolk[2] in the 3d Alabama Regiment, and we came to be with them, expecting an attack here very soon; but from all I can learn, I think there will be no trouble here, for a while at least. Our defences are very complete and formidable and I am disposed to believe the Phillistines [sic] will scarcely attempt to retake Gosport.[3] A few days since I went to Sewalls [sic] Point to visit some Georgia friends encamped there and during my stay went to an exposed point to take a look at Fortress Munroe[4] immediately opposite to us. While I stood looking at its savage port holes the immense Rifled Cannon at the Rip Raps, thundered angrily, and to our amazement, a heavy shell exploded a <u>few</u> <u>yards</u> from us. I turned my glass at once on the Rip-Raps, and distinctly saw the Muzzle of the villainous gun <u>pointed</u> at our party—saw the gunners at work reloading, and while I watched a second flask, sent it's [*sic*] missile of death right at us. When a <u>third</u> ball whizzed <u>over</u> our heads and exploded in a field just beyond us, the Officers insisted we should get out of sight, as they were very evidently firing at us, and our lives were in danger. Oh! I longed for a Secession flag to shake <u>defiantly</u> in their <u>teeth</u> at every fire! and my fingers fairly itched to touch off a <u>red-hot-ball</u> in answer to their <u>chivalric</u> <u>civilities</u>. <u>Ten</u> shells fell on land, but <u>Nobody</u> <u>was</u> <u>hurt</u> thank God. Not the slightest injury has been affected by all their firing at our batteries. Where do you suppose I spent yesterday? At <u>Fortress</u> <u>Munroe</u>! A number of persons in and about Norfolk, afflicted with Northern birth, and Northern proclivities, were very anxious to house themselves under old Abe's Mantle; and accordingly at Gen' Butler's request, Gen' Huger sent them down in a steam tug under a flag of truce. I went down with two or three friends and had a fine view of the Fortress, Rip-Raps, Hampton, Newport News and all other points of interest. We lay for three hours right under the <u>60</u> guns of the Flag Ship "Minnesota" and were very near the traitorous Cumberland, Monticello, Anacostia[5] and others. The day was one of the most eventful of my life and I think I shall never forget it. While we waited for Butler to receive his precious cargo of renegades, the Rip-Raps opened fire on our battery at Sewalls Point. We stopped on our return to the City and sent a boat ashore to know whether any injury was effected; but "<u>nobody</u> <u>hurt</u>" was shouted back amid bursts of <u>laughter</u> from the gunners. I wanted very much to pass through Columbia[6] on my way to Virginia in the hope of <u>seeing</u> <u>you</u> my darling; but the gentleman under whose care we travelled had decided to take the other route. I am very apprehensive we shall have a great deal of sickness among our troops here as warm weather advances. There are [obscured]. Of the future I know nothing. I want my Mother to remain here, and let me return home to take care of the children, and enable my Father to come on—But she is unwilling to have me leave her. I spent this morning at the Navy Yard, with an Officer of great intelligence; who had so much to show me in machine shops and laboratories, that I feel very very tired tonight and you must pardon my brevity. I went to the Charity Hospital today to offer my services to the sick—am not needed just now. God shield us all, from blood-shed and pestilence! Direct your letters to Mobile; I <u>may</u> leave any day; have been here <u>one</u> <u>month</u>. Do write to me, my dear Rachel and believe me as ever,

Yours most affectionately

AJ Evans

1. A typed transcript of this letter is held by the Alabama Department of Archives and History. A note at the end of their copy reads as follows: "Copied by W.P.A. from original letter in possession of Mrs. Rosalie Heustis Clark, 2214 Tenth Court South, Birmingham. Letter written by Augusta Evans to Mrs. Rachel Heustis, Columbia, S.C."

2. In April 1861, the Confederates had captured the navy yard at Norfolk, but Union forces held the nearby waterways and shipping channels of Hampton Roads (James M. McPherson, *Ordeal by Fire: The Civil War and Reconstruction* [New York: Knopf, 1982], 178).

3. A navy yard near Norfolk that the Confederates occupied after the Federals had evacuated it.

4. On the Virginia coast near Hampton.

5. Federal ships.

6. Columbia, South Carolina, where Rachel lived.

❧ ❧ ❧

25 / MS Alabama   Mobile August 20 1861

My dear Rachel—

Your truly welcome letter reached me some days since, but I have been busy, and could not find leisure even to write to <u>you</u> my darling. Attached to the Medical College of Atlanta Georgia as professor; is a Dr Powell, who has been writing to me for some months concerning a certain Utopian project of his; requiring my assistance. He proposed to publish a book called "<u>Voices from the South</u>"[1] composed of contributions from the <u>literary women</u> of the South, and the proceeds of the sale of said book to be devoted to the erection of a "<u>Female Charity Hospital</u>" at Atlanta. I advised him to defer the whole enterprise until the storm of war had passed; and the political atmosphere of our beloved country was tranquil once more. But it seems nothing daunted by existing obstacles, he has determined to make the attempt at this inauspicious juncture. Since I returned from Virginia, he wrote urging me to send him an article. So <u>bougre malgre</u>,[2] write I must; though my thoughts ran more on rifled cannon, Confederate cotton loan, and winter uniforms for our noble soldiery, than pen, and letters. Of course I could bring but a moiety of enthusiasm, or attention to the work, but by <u>sheer force</u> of <u>will</u> I contrived to throw together a few dim, thought <u>waifs</u>; and drilled them into line under the title of "<u>The Mutilation of the Hermae</u>."[3] If the volume ever struggles into existence, you will find at least a <u>bona-fide</u> "Mutilation" of a very classical and beautiful theme! If you love Greek history as dearly as I do, you will doubtless admit some interest in the subject. I received a letter from the Mr D[4] a few days ago, acknowledging the receipt of my precious <u>MS</u>;[5] and expressing himself as much pleased with it! Recently I have been much occupied; and yesterday finished a letter of <u>15</u> pages to <u>Motley</u> the <u>Historian</u> of <u>Dutch Republic</u> and <u>United Netherlands</u>;[6] whom our great Mogul, Abraham the 1st [7] has seen fit to appoint to the <u>Austrian Mission</u>. Have you read his histories? O tempora! O mores![8] The letter will be published <u>anonymously</u> tomorrow; and I will send you a copy of the paper.[9] My Brothers are still

stationed at Norfolk, and Cousin John is at Manassas. I Saw him in Richmond as I came home; and found him looking remarkably well. Poor Cousin
Mary! I sympathized so fully with her anxiety and suspense. What glorious
news we have from Missouri! how our holy cause brightens as the storm of
war thickens around us! Oh Rachel! I thank God that we are both <u>Southern
Women</u>! My heart swells with exultation, in view of the future of our Young
Confederacy! Who shall presume to limit its extent and magnificence! My
dear friend I wish I could write you a number of things which I find in my
heart, relative to our beloved country but I have a <u>number</u> of <u>letters</u> to write
today; and must debar myself from this privilege. Do write me whenever you
have leisure. Good bye my dear friend—God bless you—

Your <u>most</u> <u>affectionately</u>
Augusta

1. There is no evidence that this book was ever published. The article that AEW
wrote for it was published a year later in a newspaper. See note 3.

2. Literally, "in spite of the rascal" [her feelings].

3. This article was later published on November 9, 1862, in the *Gulf City Home
Journal* of Mobile. AEW begins the article by recounting the mutilation of the mar-
ble images of Hermes in Athens in 415 B.C.E., just as Athens was preparing to attack
Sicily. She compares this ancient sacrilege to the "mutilation" of the U.S. Constitu-
tion by the unscrupulous Northern politicians (see Fidler, *A Biography,* 96). Also see
AEW to Curry, November 10, 1862.

4. This is probably J. C. Derby.

5. This manuscript is probably an early draft of *Macaria,* which was published in 1864.

6. John Lothrop Motley (1814–1877), American historian and diplomat. He
wrote *The Rise of the Republic* (3 volumes, 1856) and *The History of the United Netherlands* (4 volumes, 1860–1867). He was also the U.S. minister to Austria (1861–1867).

7. Abraham Lincoln.

8. Oh the times! Oh the customs!

9. AEW's open letter to Mr. Motley was published in the *Mobile Advertiser and Register* of August 21, 1861, and was signed "A Southern Woman." In the article, AEW
criticized Motley for refusing to support the Confederacy after writing so eloquently
in his histories about other people's struggles for freedom.

❧ ❧ ❧

26 / MS Alabama   Mobile Oct' 3d 1861

My dear, dear Rachel—

Do not, I pray you, attribute to any <u>want</u> of affection or appreciation my long
delay in thanking you for your exceedingly kind and most welcome letter. I
assure you your cordial and friendly approbation of my Motley <u>tirade</u>[1] (?)
gave me great pleasure and I should have written immediately, but for

imperative engagements. I have been hard at work, for some <u>soldier</u> friends and relatives in Virginia, and this is the very earliest leisure day I could possibly command. Even now I find I have but little time for communion with <u>you</u> my dear—far off—friend. Besides to be candid, I have been in great degree <u>distrait</u> for some time past; for the national questions of the day have proved a vortex engulfing thought and feeling. Primarily and collaterally, our hopes, affections, and reflections all center in <u>one</u> magic word, potent as the spell of the Talmudish, "<u>Shemhamphorash</u>"[2] and <u>now</u>, infinitely dearer, <u>Country</u>! Of the <u>ultimate</u> achievement of our national Independence I have never entertained a doubt; and <u>three</u> months ago, I was sanguine in the belief of a speedy termination of this unholy and most unnatural war. Knowing that <u>unequalled</u> material crowded the ranks of our noble army, and trusting in the <u>skill</u> and sagacity of our Generals, I felt that Hercules–like <u>we</u> might strangle these infamous <u>Northern</u> <u>Serpents</u> at <u>our</u> <u>cradle</u>;[3] that we <u>could</u> and <u>would</u> crush out this iniquitous crusade in its' [sic] incipiency. In the thoroughly demoralized and panic-stricken condition of the Federal army subsequent to the battle of Manassas, <u>one</u> bold, vigorous, <u>Napoleonic</u> stroke <u>must</u> have decided the war; and the flames of <u>Washington</u> and Philadelphia would have furnished light to write the <u>terms</u> of Peace. The <u>inexplicable</u> policy of the Richmond Cabinet, the evident timidity of President Davis; the ruinous inaction of the Army of the Potomoc [sic], and the disgraceful conduct of affairs in Western Virginia;[4] all tend to impress me with the melancholy apprehension that the war will "drag to its' [sic] slow length along" possibly for years; expending the precious blood of our noblest and best and exhausting the resources of our Confederacy which I fondly hoped, had Pallas[5]—like sprung into existence, "<u>full-armed</u>, <u>invincible</u>." Rachel, I am <u>haunted</u> by the fear that <u>our</u> <u>leaders</u> <u>lack</u> <u>nerve</u>; that we have <u>no</u> Scipio[6] to carry the war into Africa. For months, the burden of the southern <u>press</u> has been <u>delenda</u> <u>est</u> <u>Carthago</u>![7] but today it seems as distant as ever; and the despotism of Washington grows stronger by every hours [sic] delay. I trust I am mistaken! Most earnestly do I hope that I am <u>short</u> <u>sighted</u> in this matter. I pray Almighty God, that future historians <u>may</u> <u>not</u> record of this our War of Independence, that <u>Manassas</u> <u>Junction</u> <u>was</u> <u>the</u> <u>Cannae</u>[8] of the <u>Confederate</u> Army. We are engaged in perfecting our coast defences, rifling cannon and preparing a rather <u>inhospitable</u> reception for the <u>latter-day</u> <u>Philistines</u>; the <u>plague</u> of <u>Puritanic</u> <u>locusts</u> that threaten our sunny borders. You will hear of famous performances of my beautiful little "<u>seven</u> <u>shooter</u>"[9] if any of these distinguished <u>peregrinating</u> gentry set foot near my home. My Brothers, my <u>two</u> darlings, are still in Virginia; both keep well thank God. Do write to me whenever you can spare the precious time, my dear Rachel. I am greatly hurried; so please pardon haste, <u>my</u> <u>darling</u> and <u>believe</u> <u>me</u> always yours most affectionately   A J Evans

You don't know how glad I am that you liked my article. Oh! I forgot the MSS! Well some day I hope I shall send you the book. After all, my contribution is very short.

Yours AJE

1. See AEW to Rachel, August 20, 1861, notes 6 and 9.

2. Shem Hameforash, another name for God, was used in the practice of magic. From the eleventh through the thirteenth centuries, some Jews practiced a "name magic," an invocation of names. The names of angels were invoked as well as the name of God Himself. God's "Ineffable Name" was sacred and could be uttered only once a year by the high priest. Therefore, many substitute names, such as Shem Hameforash, were developed for popular usage (Joshua Trachtenberg, *Jewish Magic and Superstition: A Study in Folk Religion* [New York: Atheneum, 1977], 88–90).

3. Hercules, the strongest man on earth, was the child of Zeus and a mortal woman. When Hercules was a baby, Hera, Zeus's wife, determined to kill him out of jealousy and sent two huge snakes to attack him in his crib. Hercules, however, awoke and killed both of the snakes.

4. The Battle of Manassas Junction, or the First Battle of Bull Run, which was fought on July 21, 1861, in northern Virginia, was a victory for the Confederacy.

Afterward, many Southerners were dismayed that the Confederates did not move on to attack Washington, D.C. Beauregard later claimed that Jefferson Davis had ordered the Confederates not to advance, but in fact Davis had urged his generals to take Washington. At any rate, it is not likely that the Confederates could have accomplished this feat. The Union army, reinforced by fresh troops, was firmly entrenched at Centreville and along the Potomac. Furthermore, a severe rainstorm had reduced the roads to mires of mud. Lastly, the Confederate army had exhausted its supplies of food and other resources and was not logistically capable of advancing (McPherson, *The Civil War and Reconstruction*, 206–10). AEW's criticisms, therefore, appear unwarranted.

5. Pallas Athena, or Athena, in Greek mythology was the goddess of war. Emerging from the head of Zeus, she was at her birth fully grown and armed.

6. Scipio Africanus Minor (185–129 B.C.E.) was the Roman general who defeated Carthage (in North Africa) in the Third Punic War (149–146 B.C.E.), sold the inhabitants into slavery, and sowed the land with salt.

7. Carthage must be destroyed!

8. The Battle of Cannae in 216 B.C.E. resulted in a decisive victory for the Carthaginians, led by Hannibal, who almost destroyed the entire Roman army.

9. A revolver with seven cartridges.

❦ ❦ ❦

27 / MS Alabama   Georgia Cottage[1] Jan' 22d 1862

My dear Rachel

What <u>has</u> become of you? Have the Yankees made an advance <u>at last</u>, and carried you off as an invaluable prize? I wrote you nearly three months ago, but of course was not waiting for a reply. For two months past I have been constantly engaged in nursing our poor sick soldiers, keeping vigil by day and night at their bedside; counting pulses, administering medicine, dressing blisters, and now I snatch a few moments to send you a few lines in token of constant and most affectionate remembrance. Oh! my darling if I could tell you of all I have witnessed, and endured since I became a hospital nurse! There has been an appalling amount of sickness among the Brigades stationed in, and around Mobile but at last it seems to be abating. Out of the 200 cases at our hospital[2] we have lost but two men. A number of them were alarmingly ill for weeks, with typhoid fever and pneumonia, and many might have rolled away as I sat with my fingers on their feeble fluttering pulse, stimulating them constantly with brandy, ammonia and quinine. God bless our noble army! and preserve it from the pestilence which has decimated its ranks during the past few months. Ah Rachel! I felt for and with you when the miserable hirelings of Puritandom desecrated the sacred soil of your state.[3] I felt every drop of blood boiling in my veins, as I read of their vandalic expeditions on the islands along your coast! Oh! that we had a government, capable of dealing with the wretches as they deserve. Not a soul, should ever be permitted to reembark, for their worse than Sodomic homes. I enclose a copy of a speech which I delivered some weeks since to the "Beulah Guards"[4] and you will see that I have inaugurated the black flag[5] on our coast. How I wish you could have been with me on the occasion! You would have enjoyed it I feel assured—Our Forts[6] you know are 30 miles from the city and the excursion required an entire day. My dear Rachel I have no time for more. Do write to me, and tell me what you are doing. When this miserable, unholy war ends, I hope to see you once more.

> Your own affectionate
>
> Augusta

1. See AEW to Rachel, May 27 [1859], note 1.

2. AEW established a hospital, named Camp Beulah in honor of her novel, near her home in Mobile. AEW, already known as a competent volunteer nurse, worked at the hospital and nursed sick soldiers from a nearby training camp (Fidler, *A Biography*, 90–91).

3. In November 1861, the Federal navy and marines captured Port Royal, which was halfway between Charleston and Savannah and the best natural harbor along the Southern coastline. In addition to Port Royal, the Federals also captured a string of islands along the coast from Savannah almost to Charleston (McPherson, *The Civil War and Reconstruction*, 177).

4. A "home guard," named for AEW's novel *Beulah*, stationed at Fort Morgan at the mouth of Mobile Bay (Fidler 90).

5. Since the black flag was a pirate flag, AEW is apparently suggesting that Federal ships should be captured as prizes of war (Fidler 90).

6. Forts Morgan, Powell, and Gaines were located around Mobile Bay.

☙ ☙ ☙

My dear Rachel—

For some weeks I have intended writing to you, but I have been so sad and anxious, so full of dread—forebodings, that I thought my letters could possibly give you no pleasure. Howard, my oldest Brother is at <u>Corinth</u>[1] as Lieut in a Mississippi Company; and <u>Vivian</u> my black-eyed broad-browed <u>young</u> Brother is at <u>Richmond</u>, with the 3d Ala' Regiment stationed at Dewey's Bluff. With immediate battles expected at both points you can I doubt not readily imagine my anxiety and suspense. My Father and Mother have been absent from home for <u>two</u> <u>weeks</u>, waiting in the vicinity of Corinth, so as to be near my Brother in case he were wounded, and I have been all alone at home with my young Sisters & little Brother, and my many, many fears. I struggle hard to be hopeful and contented, but it is a desperate and but partially successful effort. For several evenings past, I have had the pleasure of meeting your friend <u>Mr Timrod</u>;[2] he has spent the evenings here, with <u>J. R. Randall</u>[3] our noblest young southern Poet, whose magnificent appeals to poor Maryland have so stirred the heart of our people. I was glad to meet Mr Timrod, for his own sake, and have enjoyed his stay here very much, but I was doubly glad for your sake dear Rachel, because I could talk to him of <u>you</u>, my friend. He seems in delicate health, and shrinking and sensitive as a <u>mimosa</u>; but his <u>native</u> <u>reticence</u> wears away as I know him better. You would like Randall I feel assured, though the very antipodes of your quiet friend. Randall is a rich rare, tropical luxuriant soul, whose beautiful thoughts, and glowing images overflow continually, like a silver wine cup whose amber and purple foam ooze over the brim. A refugee from his home in New Orleans, he is of course rather sad just now, but I trust better brighter days are in store for us all. I have wished for <u>you</u>, very often during the past week, for I knew you would like Randall. I am afraid Mr Timrod will consider me very hopelessly <u>stupid</u> but indeed my dear Rachel, I have not been quite myself since my parents left home to wait for that battle; and many a time while talking to my gifted young guests, my heart and soul have been <u>far</u> <u>away</u>, on the bloody field of <u>Shiloh</u>[4] where I lost several friends, or hovering in dread over my brave young Brothers whose precious lives were in such startling danger. I am not fit for society, when I am so foreboding. When I meet Mr Timrod again I trust these sombre clouds will have all passed away, and white-winged Peace, and golden-eyed sunshine surround our homes and country. I feel sometimes as if I should like to sepulchre the last year of <u>trials</u> and suffering, and write <u>hic-jacet</u>[5] above. Rachel where are you? why don't you write to me? Do not I pray you, <u>count</u> letters with me, that is cold and unfriendly; I write—whenever I can; you must do likewise. I have much to engage me, much to occupy my time entirely. Pardon my brief, hurried letter, I am very unwell have a <u>wretched cough</u> which racks me mercilessly. Tell me what you are doing now, and believe me always my darling Rachel

Truly your affectionate friend
Augusta J. Evans

Do you ever hear from <u>Mr Fitch</u> or any of the <u>Derbys</u> now?

1. A town in northeast Mississippi.

2. Henry Timrod, a South Carolina poet, was called the "laureate of the Confederacy." His poor health prevented his serving in the army, but he wrote inspiring, patriotic poems about his beloved Confederacy. Also see AEW to Rachel, October 17, 1859, note 1.

3. James Ryder Randall wrote the song "Maryland, My Maryland," which became "the marching song of the Confederacy" (Fidler, *A Biography,* 99).

4. Following their defeat at Shiloh in Tennessee on April 6–7, 1862, the Confederates had retreated to Corinth, Mississippi.

5. here lies

❧ ❧ ❧

29 / MS Alabama Press [1]   Mobile, August 4th, 1862

General Beauregard[2]

With a heart throbbing with pleasure, and surely <u>pardonable</u> pride, I avail myself of the very earliest opportunity to attempt an expression of my earnest, cordial thanks, for the exceedingly flattering testimonial of remembrance, you so kindly conferred on me, through the courtesy of Co'l Roman.[3] I can imagine no compliment more delicate and valuable, than that, which you have so unexpectedly paid me; your consecrated Sword is the Nation's, and your Pen, around whose diamond point cluster such hallowed associations, has now become the property of one,[4] who, although undeserving of so distinguished a mark of favor, is at least fully capable of the most intense, and lasting appreciation of your kindness. Believe me, General Beauregard, <u>I am inexpressibly gratified by this priceless token of a friendship, I had not sufficient presumption to hope for, but will most earnestly endeavor to deserve</u>. I shall place your pen, and both your "Notelets" (as <u>par parenthese</u>[5] quaint Charles Lamb calls all such precious short letters,) in the Kaaba[6] of memory, whence, daily pilgrimages shall yield me reminiscences infinitely dearer, and more valued, than all those which flow from the possession of the celebrated treasure of Potsdam, the "blue velvet covered writing table" of Frederick the Great;[7] replete though it be, with indelible records of the "Seven Years War."[8] You tell me of your pen of victory, "it will still do its duty faithfully, if carefully handled!" Ah Sir! do you imagine, I would ever consent to desecrate it by <u>use</u> after it had left your hand? As soon, expect to find among curious archaeologic data, that the sacred Tripod of Delphi[9] become in the degenerated days of Greece, the "Dunce's stool," in the public schools of Athens. Your pen shall become an <u>heir-loom</u> in our family, to be touched only by the reverent fingers of the grateful people who have enshrined the image of their beloved deliverer in their inmost hearts; and around it, shall gather the <u>proudest</u> reminiscences of my life. Allow me to thank you in this connection, for the encouraging words you have kindly given, regarding my writings; I shall hang them on the walls of memory, "like apples of gold in Pictures of silver";[10] to furnish additional incentive to future exertion, and patient study. Since I have been so fortunate as to meet your approbation in any thing I have thrown out upon the stormy sea of public favor, I trust you will not consider me too presumptuous, or <u>entirely</u> <u>spoiled</u> by your kindness, if I enclose an article written during your Potomac campaign, and immediately after the acceptance of the Austrian Mission, by Mr. Motley.[11] It is not my privilege to enter the ranks, wielding a sword, in my country's cause, but all that my feeble, womanly pen could contribute to the consummation of our freedom, I have humbly, but at least, faithfully and untiringly <u>endeavored</u> to achieve.

> "Man for the field, and woman for the hearth;
> Man for the sword, and for the needle she:
> Man with the head, and woman with the heart:
> Man to command, and woman to obey!"[12]

And yet oh Sir! we of the Confederacy would fain cast our mite into the National-treasury of noble deeds, overflowing though it be, with acts of heroism, and grand self-abnegation, before which the storied-career of even Bayard[13] pales. Frequently during the past eventful year, I have felt disposed to lament the limited circle of action, the insignificant <u>role</u> assigned us,[14] in the mightiest drama that ever rivetted the gaze of the civilized world; and to envy the obsolete privileges of the young Hungarian Adjutant, the heroine of <u>Comorn</u>;[15] or even my dauntless immortal namesake of Saragossa;[16] but on such covetous occasions, I have consoled myself with the reflection that after all, woman's sphere of influence might be like Pascals,'[17] "one of which the centre is everywhere, the circumference nowhere;"[18] and though debarred from the "tented field," the cause of our beloved, struggling Confederacy may yet be advanced through the agency of its' [sic] daughters; for out of the dim, historic past, come words of cheer; when Sparta forsook the stern and sublime simplicity of the Lycurgus-Code,[19] "King Agis found himself unable to accomplish his scheme of redeeming his degenerate country from avarice and corruption, until the Ladies of Sparta gave their support to his plan of reform."[20]

Allow me to inquire, whether you received by mail, a short article styled "Memoria-in-Aeterna," on the subject of a gigantic Memorabilia at Vicksburg? I took the liberty of sending it to you about a fortnight since, because it was a suggestion, very near my heart, and one, in which I desired your approbation. Doubtless Sir, I have written you, into the conclusion of Sheridan's servant, who was once heard to remark, that he thought by far the most eloquent passage of his Master's celebrated three-days-speech in the Warren Hastings trial, was contained in the closing words, "I have done my Lords, I have done."[21] Pardon this trespass on your time and patience, which but for your great kindness, I should never have been guilty of, and permit me the expression of the earnest hope, that the improved state of your health, will very soon allow you to redeem the old cherished promise, of striking the manacles from the bleeding limbs of Maryland,[22] that—

"Patient Nemesis,[23] at sorrow's gate,"

and verify my own claim to prescience: for three days ago, I was sitting beside a sick soldier, who was entirely delirious with fever;—suddenly opening his eyes, he grasped my hand, and asked eagerly—"did you say, General Beauregard was on Arlington Heights?"[24] I answered, "be quiet, and go to sleep; he will be there, very soon." Accept my thanks for all your goodness, and also for the pleasure you afforded me, in the acquaintance of one of your Staff Officers, whom, without fear of contradiction I may venture to style, "the noblest Roman[25] of them all."

Gratefully and respectfully—
Your friend—
Augusta J. Evans

1. This letter is printed in Malcolm C. McMillan's *The Alabama Confederate Reader* (Tuscaloosa: University of Alabama Press, 1992). Used by permission. The original letter is owned by Mary Augusta Gaillard of Springhill, Alabama.

2. AEW met P. G. T. Beauregard, a prominent Confederate general, in Mobile in the summer of 1862, and the two began a long friendship and correspondence. Beauregard had become ill; left his troops without officially obtaining permission; and went to Bladon Springs, a resort near Mobile, to recuperate. While there, he was royally entertained by Mobile society. He greatly enjoyed the company of AEW, who was already known for her novels. Writing to a friend about her, Beauregard said that it "would not do for me to see [her] too often, for I might forget 'home and country' in their hour of need and distress" (quoted in T. Harry Williams, *P. G. T. Beauregard: Napoleon in Gray* [Baton Rouge: Louisiana State University Press, 1955], 160).

3. An officer and friend of Beauregard. See AEW to Beauregard, September 23, 1862, note 1.

4. According to Fidler, Beauregard sent AEW his writing pen in appreciation of her work nursing sick and wounded Confederate soldiers (*A Biography,* 94).

5. by the way

6. Relating to the Islamic shrine in Mecca to which Muslims turn while praying.

7. King of Prussia, 1740–1786.

8. The Seven Years' War (1756–1763) was a conflict between Prussia under Frederick the Great and Austria under Maria Theresa for dominance in Germany. The war also involved Britain as Prussia's ally, and France, Russia, and Sweden on the side of Austria. The war ended with Prussia as a major power in Europe. After the war, Frederick retired to Potsdam.

9. In ancient Greece, the Altar of Apollo at Delphi, composed of a caldron supported by a bronze three-legged stand.

10. "A word fitly spoken is like apples of gold in pictures of silver" (Prov. 25:11).

11. As an example of how she uses her writing to support the Confederacy, AEW is probably referring to an article she published on August 21, 1861, criticizing Motley's position on the war. See AEW to Rachel, August 20, 1861, notes 6 and 9.

12. Alfred Lord Tennyson, *The Princess,* part V, lines 437–40.

13. The Bayard family of Delaware, Maryland, and Pennsylvania produced several generations of prominent statesmen and diplomats.

14. the women of the Confederacy.

15. *Comorn* appears to be an error. AEW does not give enough information to identify this person.

16. Saragossa (also spelled Zaragoza) was part of the old kingdom of Aragon in northeastern Spain. When the area was attacked by the French in 1808–1809, one of the Spanish defenders was Maria Augustin, "the Maid of Saragossa," whose efforts were portrayed in Byron's *Childe Harold,* canto 1, stanzas 54–56.

17. Blaise Pascal (1623–1662), French mathematician and religious writer.

18. The statement, "The nature of God is a circle whose centre is everywhere and its circumference nowhere," is actually credited to St. Augustine and to Emerson in his essay, "Circles."

19. Lycurgus was a Spartan lawgiver who established the Spartan Constitution and the military system with its severe, communal lifestyle.

20. When Agis IV, King of Sparta from 244–241 B.C.E., tried to initiate reforms to benefit the poor—such as redistributing land and wealth—he was supported mainly by his wealthy mother and grandmother who voluntarily relinquished their property. However, his rivals deposed and executed Agis—along with his mother and grandmother.

21. See AEW to Seaver, December 31, 1859, notes 8 and 9.

22. The Confederates hoped fervently, but in vain, that Maryland would also secede from the Union and join them. The song "Maryland, My Maryland," which was written by AEW's friend James Ryder Randall and which became the marching song of the Confederacy, was a plea to Maryland to shake off the bonds of Federal tyranny and join the Confederacy. Maryland's proximity to Washington, D.C., would have, of course, made that state a valuable asset to the Confederacy.

23. In classical mythology, the goddess of retribution, whose purpose was to restore equilibrium by giving suffering and loss to those who had experienced too much good fortune.

24. In northeastern Virginia, near Washington, D.C., and the Maryland border.

25. A play on Colonel Roman's name.

ঞ ঞ ঞ

30 / MS Alabama   Mobile September 23^d 1862

General Beauregard—

For <u>palpable</u> <u>reasons</u> I write to request that no one except <u>Col</u> <u>Roman</u>[1] shall see the enclosed letter from Mr Yancy,[2] which I received several days since, and thought you might read with interest. As it is a matter of great delicacy, you Sir, will doubtless appreciate the motives that impel me, to obtrude these few lines upon you. Like Horace Walpole,[3] in the affair of the celebrated "Strawberry"[4] Edition of Hannah More's[5] "<u>Bas</u> <u>Bleu</u>,"[6] I feel that "I owe you an apology for this wretched <u>brown</u> <u>paper</u>,"[7] but rest in the consolatory reflection, that <u>my</u> <u>excuse</u> (the stringency of the blockade) if <u>not</u> <u>so</u> <u>graceful</u>, is at least, infinitely more cogent, than any my Lord Orford[8] of "Strawberry Hill" could possibly have offered. Hoping that your health continues good, and that my anxious heart will soon be gladdened, by tidings of your arrival in Tennessee,

> I am, very respectfully,
> Your friend—
> Augusta J. Evans

1. Colonel Alfred Roman was a friend and supporter of Beauregard. After the war was over, Beauregard began writing a book, *My Reminiscences of the War.* However, angered by what some former Confederates (particularly Jefferson Davis) wrote about him in their books, Beauregard decided to change tactics. He commissioned Roman to write his book for him with the title *Military Operations of General Beauregard* (New York: Harper's, 1883). Although Roman merely rewrote Beauregard's notes, he was listed as the book's author for obvious reasons. As the author, Roman could heap praises upon Beauregard and attack his enemies more effectively than Beauregard could do himself (Williams, *P. G. T. Beauregard,* 311–14).

2. William L. Yancey, a firebrand Alabama secessionist and member of the Confederate senate, was, like Beauregard and AEW, hostile to President Davis.

3. Horace Walpole (1717–1797), known mainly as an English letter writer.

4. Strawberry Hill was Walpole's country home, where he set up his own printing press and printed works by his friends and also some of his own writings.

5. A religious writer, poet, and friend of Walpole.

6. "The Bas Bleu, or Conversation," a poem by Hannah More.

7. According to Walpole's own records, the only poem by Hannah More printed at Strawberry Hill was "Bishop Bonner's Ghost" in 1789. Walpole did indeed print two copies on brown paper, one for Miss More and one for himself, with this explanation: "I know these two are not so good as the white: but, as rarities, a collector would give ten times more for them; and *uniquity* will make them valued more than the charming poetry" (Horace Walpole, *Journal of the Printing-Office at Strawberry Hill* [London: Cheswick, 1923], 75).

8. Lord Orford was Walpole's title.

CHAPTER 3

"These are dark hours . . ."

31 / MS Library of Congress (original)
Alabama (photocopy)
Duke (photocopy)   Mobile Nov. 10, 1862

Hon. J. L. M. Curry,[1]
My dear Sir,

Permit me to tender you my sincere thanks for the <u>speeches</u> you kindly sent me some weeks since, and which afforded me <u>much pleasure</u>. I should not have been so tardy, in my grateful acknowledgments, but for an unusual amount of sickness in our family and neighborhood, which has kept me constantly nursing for some weeks past. Allow me to enclose an article[2] published this week in a new paper established here, and yclept,[3] "<u>Gulf City Home Journal</u>."[4] Unfortunately the printers have <u>mutilated</u> my contribution almost as mercilessly as did the "Hermokopids"[5] my marble theme, but—

"A fellow feeling makes us wondrous kind,"[6] and doubtless your own typographical experience will enable you to sympathize with me. Like Horace Walpole, in the affair of the celebrated "Strawberry" edition of Hannah More's "<u>Bas Bleu</u>," I feel that I owe you an apology for this <u>wretched brown paper</u>,[7] but console myself with the reflection that my excuse (the stringency of the blockade) if not so polished and graceful, is at least more cogent than any Orford[8] offered, by my Lord Horace of Strawberry Hill."

With profound respect—

Gratefully your friend
Augusta J. Evans

1. Jabez Lamar Monroe Curry, of Alabama, was a Confederate congressman and educator. He and AEW met at the Convention of the Seceding States in Montgomery, Alabama, in February 1861 and began a lifelong friendship and correspondence.

2. This is "The Mutilation of the Hermae," described in the letter to Rachel of August 20, 1861.

3. Old English for "named" or "called."

4. Mobile newspaper (Fidler, *A Biography*, 96).

5. Those who deface herms, or monuments to Hermes. In Greek mythology, Hermes was the messenger of the gods and also the protector of travelers. Early monuments

(piles of stones) and later statues were erected at crossroads, along roadsides, and in markets in his honor.

6. David Garrick, "An Occasional Prologue on Quitting the Theatre," line 4 (June 1776), *Poetical Works of David Garrick,* vol. 2 (New York and London: Benjamin Blom, 1968), 325–27.

7. See AEW to Beauregard, September 23, 1862, notes 4–7.

8. A play on words (Orford—offered). Lord Orford was Walpole's title.

ↄ৯ ↄ৯ ↄ৯

32 / MS Library of Congress (original)
Alabama (photocopy)
Duke (photocopy)   Mobile Dec. 20, 1862

Hon. J. L. M. Curry
My honored friend

"What splendid weather?" "Ah yes: fine weather certainly, but Schiller is dead! Schiller[1] is dead." Such was the almost universal response in loving and appreciative Germany when one of her great masterminds passed from the "linden walks" to his everlasting home; and this sparkling winter day, as I look out from my desk, up at the blue depths brimmed with crystal light, my heart is bowed down with the sorrowful, haunting remembrance. Thomas Cobb[2] is dead. The ripe and elegant classical scholar, the astute, farsighted and comprehensive statesman, the Titan intellect holding all political problems in solution, the noble heart throbbing with generous impulses, the genial humorous sunshiny spirit exerting in social circles such marvellous magnetism, <u>the pure fervent consistent Christian</u>; the pride, the crowning glory of his state, one of the guardians of an infant nation. Agamemnon-like,[3] we have immolated our fairest and best. The long struggle of six thousand years[4] has not satiated Liberty with the precious blood of the brave and purest of our Cain-cursed[5] race. Since Bartow's[6] death, nothing has so grieved me, as the melancholy tidings of Gen'l Cobb's fate. Poor stricken Georgia, my mourning mother state; robbed of the two bright jewels that glittered in her diadem of dauntless sons—is she destined indeed, to become the <u>Niobe</u>[7] of the Confederacy "Childless and crownless, in her voiceless love?"[8] In pondering this irreparable loss, I have thought, frequently, of you, Sir, for I felt that to one who knew him as long and well as you have done, the blow must have fallen stunningly. God pity and comfort his bereaved family; For the slumbering warrior— <u>in calo quies</u>.[9] Thank you Mr Curry most cordially, for your kind and exceedingly welcome letter, which permits me to indulge the hope of seeing you in Mobile at no distant day. For more good reasons than I have time to enumerate, I trust it will be in your power to visit us before your return to Richmond. That portion of your letter relative to the rumors afloat concerning

General Forney,[10] I regret to say, did not at all surprise me, his waning popularity had ultimated in the harshest animadversions on the part of the public, and in painful and disgraceful reports, long before his removal to Gen'l Pemberton's army; which change was I believe, universally hailed with delight by our citizens. My knowledge of Gen'l F . . . . is limited to a mere casual introduction and bowing acquaintance; consequently I can give you no information on this subject; but from all I can learn from his intimate friends, I have not a doubt that his mind has become seriously impaired, through the partial paralysis which seems sadly enough, to have crept from his wounded arm to his brain.[11] It is I have <u>heard</u>, the opinion of his physicians that his physical condition is critical. Change of air, may and will, I trust, restore him to health. It was stated yesterday that Gen'l Buckner[12] would assume command of this Department, and if we are to be so fortunate, his presence coupled with that of our fearless, dauntless, veteran Buchanan,[13] insures the salvation of our City. Since writing the above, Col. Holtzclaw[14] has come in and assured us it is true that we are to have Gen'l Buckner—Thank Heaven. Concerning <u>our defences</u>, I have no apprehension, but I have entertained very <u>serious uneasiness</u> heretofore with regard to the <u>ability</u> of our commanding officers. Thanks to a merciful and righteous God, victory again nestled upon our banner at Fredericksburg; and I can not entirely divest myself of the belief, that it will have upon our enemies much the same effect as that produced upon Germany during the "Thirty Years War,"[15] by the battle of Leipsic.[16] Has it ever occurred to you, there is a parallelism between <u>McClellan</u>[17] and Wallenstein?[18] That Burnside[19] is playing the <u>role</u> of Tilly,[20] and that McClellan's speedy restoration to command, is Wallensteinlike, rendered more than probable by his late reverses? If parallelism there be, would <u>you</u> too, carp at my following it up, and finding in <u>Jackson,</u>[21] the latter day Gustavus Adolphus? I had hoped that the <u>speeches</u> which you sent me some days ago, and for which let me here return my earnest thanks, (though they merit <u>more</u> than parenthetic mention) would have contained your views and course with reference to the Exemption Bill,[22] which has caused such general dissatisfaction and which seems destined, I fear, to prove our political-social <u>Ate</u>.[23] In the unfortunate absence of that publicity of congressional debate for which Mr. Yancey[24] struggled so powerfully, the odium of an unpopular measure is unjustly and indiscriminately heaped on all who chance to constitute our Congress; and the appositives of Mr. Yanceys [sic] arguments in favor of <u>open session</u> could possibly find no more striking exemplification than at the present juncture. You have doubtless become to some extent acquainted with the spirit of insubordination and disaffection which is rife in our armies, and which has attained in this section of the Confederacy, melancholy and alarming proportions. Judiciously reticent upon this point at least, our papers have forborne any allusion to the disgraceful truth, but officers of grave experience and ripe judgment, do not hesitate to express their great uneasiness at the rapidly spreading spirit of defection in their commands. The number of desertions in Gen'l Pemberton's army, and even among the troops stationed in Ala,' is appalling; and fears are entertained of painful and disastrous consequences, unless the evil can be promptly remedied.[25] Courts Martial are everywhere in session, and it <u>chills</u> the blood in my veins to hear of the degrading and horrible punishments inflicted on <u>Southern</u> <u>Soldiers</u>, who plead in palliation of desertion, the cries of hungry wives and starving children. I have been told by officers of unquestioned veracity and prudence, that they almost daily see letters received by the privates in their commands, in which their families implore them to come home at <u>every</u> <u>hazard</u> and save them from the pinching penury that scowls at their thresholds. One wife asserted that she exhausted all other means of subsistence, and had just sold her <u>two</u> <u>last</u> <u>extra</u> dresses, to purchase at an exhorbitant [*sic*] price, meal enough to satisfy her children's hunger. Cursed as is our struggling country by the shameless tribe of speculators and extortioners who swarm in every nook and cranny of the Confederacy battening upon the pittances of families whose providers are toiling in snow, and sleet, and blood, on distant battlefields, or sleeping dreamlessly in nameless martyr-graves, it is not strange that murmurs are swelling ominously; and that disaffection stalks colossal, where cheerful endurance, noble self-abnegation, and sublime fervor of patriotism formerly challenged the admiration of the world, and earned the gratitude of coming generations. The burden of this deplorable state of affairs is laid upon the Exemption Bill, which it is alleged offers premiums for extortion, among all classes of artificers; instead of compelling them either to join the ranks of the army, or furnish such necessities as <u>shoes</u> and <u>meal</u> at reasonable rates. Moreover, one unfortunate clause, (though designed I know, to guard against servile insurrection) has resulted most unhappily in the creation of an antislavery element among our soldiers who openly complain that they are torn from their homes, and their families consigned to starvation solely in order that they may protect the property of slaveholders; who are allowed by the "<u>Bill</u>" to remain in quiet enjoyment of luxurious ease.[26] I was informed yesterday by a very intelligent officer, that his men were growing every day more discontented, in view of these facts; and that in one of our counties St. Clair, I believe, a band of 300 <u>furloughed</u> soldiers had organized and sworn never to return to their regiments, and to sternly <u>resist</u> all enrolling or arresting officers. However based upon an erroneous construction of the Statute in question, the growl of a discontented nation demands earnest consideration; and I look forward anxiously to the reassembling of Congress, hoping that such amendments will be offered, as shall speedily, and effectually, <u>crush</u> this insubordination which otherwise, may prove as potent in completely dividing our people, as the celebrated Talmudish gnome.[27] Thus much, your former generous indulgence, has emboldened me to believe, you would permit me to say, upon a matter very nearly touching the weal of our dear and common Cause; and now Sir, allow me to <u>thank</u> <u>you</u> once more, and <u>most</u> <u>cordially</u> for the kindness you have manifested toward my young Brother Vivian, and the friendly reception you gave him, on the occasion of that visit which he enjoyed so keenly. I have been hoping to have him at home during the next week and find myself growing strangely impatient to see him again in our dear home circle. Trusting that I may have the pleasure of greeting you in Mobile ere long, I wish you, a happy Christmas, in the bosom of your family—and remain

> With profound respect—
> Most sincerely your friend
> Augusta J. Evans

1. Friedrich von Schiller (1759–1805), German poet and dramatist and a major figure in German literature.

2. Thomas Cobb was "an emotional Georgia secessionist" and the brother of Howell Cobb (Coulter, *Confederate States of America,* 17). (Also see AEW to Curry, Jan. 1, 1902, regarding Howell Cobb.) Thomas Cobb was killed at Fredericksburg, Virginia, in December 1862. According to Coulter, the Confederacy mourned its fallen officers "with great emotional outpourings" (74).

3. In Greek legend, Agamemnon led the Greeks to victory over Troy in the Trojan War. After the war ended, Cassandra warned him not to return home to Mycenae, but he did. Upon his arrival his wife's lover murdered him.

4. In the early part of the nineteenth century, people reckoned the existence of humankind to cover approximately 6,000 years. This conclusion was based on the calculations of James Ussher, a seventeenth-century bishop, who used Biblical genealogy to arrive at this figure. By midcentury, however, new geological evidence about the age of the earth had undermined this theory. See Richard D. Altick, *Victorian People and Ideas* (New York: Norton, 1973), 98–99.

5. In Genesis 4 of the Bible, Cain, the first son of Adam and Eve, murdered his younger brother Abel.

6. Colonel Francis Bartow was killed in the Battle of First Manassas in 1861 (Coulter 492).

7. In Greek mythology, Niobe, the mother of seven sons and seven daughters, taunted Leto, who had only two children. To punish Niobe for her pride, Leto's children murdered all of her children.

8. Lord Byron, "Childe Harold," stanza 78. According to Byron, the Niobe of Nations is Rome—"Lone Mother of dead Empires."

9. rest in heaven

10. Major General John Horace Forney, after seeing action in Virginia, was stationed in Mobile for a year before being transferred to Vicksburg. He remained with General

Pemberton throughout Grant's siege of the city (Clement Evans, *Confederate Military History,* 405–6).

11. Forney was severely wounded in the arm during a battle at Dranesville, Virginia, in 1861 (Clement Evans 405). His countrymen no doubt held Forney, like Pemberton, culpable for the loss of Vicksburg. However, Clement Evans praises Forney as "a capable officer, cool and undaunted in danger, and skillful in the handling of his men" (406).

12. Brigadier General Simon Bolivar Buckner fought in the Kentucky and Tennessee campaigns and, years after the war, served as governor of Kentucky (1887–1891).

13. Franklin Buchanan was the senior admiral in the Confederate navy. See letter to Curry, January 27, 1864.

14. Colonel James T. Holtzclaw was stationed in Mobile in the fall of 1862 as a brigade commander. He had a noteworthy career in the Confederate army and was eventually promoted to brigadier general (Clement Evans, *Confederate Military History,* 417–19).

15. The Thirty Years' War, 1618–1648, began in Bohemia with a revolt by Protestant nobles against their new Catholic king, Ferdinand II. The conflict soon spread to include most of Europe, with Catholic countries aligned against Protestant ones.

16. The Swedish king, Gustavus Adolphus, entered the war to save Sweden and Protestantism. In a battle near Leipzig, he was killed, but his army was victorious. The result was that Protestantism was restored in Germany, and Sweden became a powerful country.

17. Major General George Brinton McClellan was a controversial Union officer who, like Wallenstein, was frequently in and out of favor with his superiors. In the spring of 1862, McClellan, planning to attack Richmond, moved his army to Fortress Monroe, Virginia, and incurred the displeasure of President Lincoln, who thought McClellan had disobeyed his orders to protect Washington. After Lee defeated Union Major General John Pope, McClellan, back in favor, was given command of Pope's disorganized men and quickly got them into order. At the Battle of Antietam (Sept. 17, 1862), McClellan had victory within his reach several times and lost it due to his faulty strategies and bad decisions. After this battle, Lincoln replaced McClellan with General Burnside and ended McClellan's military career.

18. During the Thirty Years' War, Wallenstein, a Bohemian nobleman, raised an army to assist Ferdinand II and won several important victories. Later Wallenstein fell into disfavor and was dismissed as commander of the army. However, when Sweden's Gustavus Adolphus attacked, Ferdinand had to reinstate Wallenstein. Eventually Ferdinand became convinced that Wallenstein was a traitor and had him murdered.

19. Ambrose E. Burnside, as commander of the Army of the Potomac, led the Union troops in the Battle of Fredericksburg on December 13, 1862. Burnside ordered his men to cross a long, open stretch of ground and attack the well-entrenched Confederate army at Marye's Heights. The result was slaughter: 12,600 Union casualties.

20. In the Thirty Years' War, Count von Tilly commanded the Catholic forces that were defeated by Gustavus Adolphus.

21. Thomas Jonathan Jackson, known as Stonewall Jackson, was a Confederate general and a brilliant military tactician. He defeated McClellan at Antietam on September 17, 1862, and Jackson and Lee won at Fredericksburg.

22. According to the Exemption Bill, men could avoid military service by paying a substitute to join the army on their behalf. This system was rife with abuse, with many substitutes joining the army, only to desert and be paid by someone new to join again. The system also created resentment among the troops who felt that they were engaged in "a rich man's war and a poor man's fight." The Confederate congress repealed the Exemption Bill on December 28, 1863 (Coulter, *Confederate States of America*, 318–19).

23. In Greek mythology, the goddess of discord and mischief, Ate influenced men to take actions that brought about their own downfall.

24. William L. Yancey, an Alabama congressman and a friend of AEW.

25. Actually both armies had a high desertion rate. Although exact figures cannot be known because of incomplete records, the desertion rate for the Union army is estimated at 9.6 percent and for the Confederate army at 13 percent (McPherson, *The Civil War and Reconstruction,* 468).

26. Under the Exemption Bill, a man who owned at least twenty slaves was exempt from military service. This exemption was based on the belief that overseers were necessary on the farms and plantations to ensure adequate crop production (Coulter 319–20).

27. During the Jewish Diaspora in Egypt, the Jews were not allowed to be governed by their own laws. Instead, Egypt had overlapping systems of jurisprudence, courts, and laws to cover various groups of people and various offenses. If the laws did not apply adequately to a specific case, then the judges were to follow "the most equitable view" or the gnome dikaiotate. This principle, of course, was subject to interpretation and to arbitrary application (Hecht, *History and Sources of Jewish Law,* 81–83).

꙳ꙮ ꙳ꙮ ꙳ꙮ

33 / MS Virginia   Mobile Feb 22nd 1863

Messrs West & Johnston[1]
Gentlemen,

Your very kind letter of the 14th inst[2] has been received, and I write to acquaint you with my acceptance of the terms specified; namely $1000 cash and ten percent on every copy published;[3] with the understanding that as soon as you deem it advisable you will republish "Beulah," allowing me the same percentage—I recapitulate, that no possible misapprehension may exist on either side—Having a very decided preference for your [publishing] house, above all others in the Confederacy, you must permit me to add, that I feel much gratified, that we have been able to enter into satisfactory arrangements concerning the publication of my books. Owing to unavoidable and unexpected interruptions, my new work[4] is not as near completion as I had hoped it would be by the middle of this month. The <u>story</u> is finished, and I am now engaged in revising and <u>copying</u> it for the press. This is necessarily a tedious process, necessitating great particularity, but I shall devote my entire time to it until it is accomplished. I fully appreciate the <u>expediency</u> of bringing it out as early as practicable, and shall therefore work as rapidly as possible. When will you be ready for the MS? I know of course that it will require some weeks to make the requisite arrangements, as you have other publications on hand. Do you purpose bringing it out in pamphlet form, and what are your facilities for stereotyping?[5] Hoping that our relations may prove in every respect as satisfactory, and agreeable as I am prepared to expect, and that I shall hear from you at your earliest leisure, I am gentlemen—

Very respectfully
Your friend
Augusta J. Evans

1. A publishing company in Richmond, Virginia, which published AEW's third novel, *Macaria.*

2. instant—here meaning occurring in the present month.

3. The terms of this contract are more generous than those AEW received from Harper and Brothers for the publication of *Inez,* her first novel. The original, handwritten contract for *Inez* is held by Columbia University. See Appendix.

4. *Macaria,* which AEW had been working on since June 1862.

5. AEW is asking if the publisher can print artwork (perhaps an illustration for a frontispiece or cover). By 1860 stereo photography had become common, and stereo images were often produced and then cut apart for single images. Thus "stereotyping" is used here as a generic term meaning "artwork" (Michael L. Carlebach, *The Origins of Photojournalism in America* [New York: Smithsonian Institute, 1992], 51–53).

꒰ঌ ꒰ঌ ꒰ঌ

34 / MS Duke[1]   Mobile March 17th 1863

General Beauregard—

Fearful as I am, of intruding upon your valuable time, especially at this juncture when you must be so constantly occupied; and hoping that the reasons I shall assign will plead my pardon; you must permit me to express my earnest gratitude for your exceedingly kind and gratifying letter, and also for the confidence you repose in me, as manifested by the gift of a copy of your "<u>Review</u>," which it seems you deem inexpedient to publish at this crisis. As I read the analysis, and complete refutation of the illnatured, venomous, ungenerous and jealous remarks, elicited by the presentation of that petition; (which embodied the hopes and wishes of the entire Confederacy,) and reflected upon the systematic injustice that had been heaped upon you, by the President;[2] the blood tingled in my veins, and I could not forbear recalling the words of Tennyson

> "Ah God! for a man with heart, head, hand,
> Like some of the simple great ones gone
> Forever, and ever by!
> One still strong man in a blatant land,
> Whatever they call him, what care I?
> Aristocrat, democrat, autocrat,—one
> Who can rule, and dare not lie."[3]

The day is not distant I trust, when all the facts connected with the infamous persecution of yourself and General Price[4] may be laid before an indignant and outraged people. Apropos! of the Western Scipio,[5] I recently had the pleasure of becoming acquainted with him, as he passed through Mobile en route for Vicksburg, and as I looked into his noble gentle face, beaming with generosity and enthusiasm while he spoke of you Sir, in terms of unmeasured admiration and exalted esteem; I felt the lines of the great Ode to Wellington, creeping across my lips:

> "Oh good gray head which all men knew!
> Oh face from which their omens all men drew
> Oh iron nerve, to true occasion true!"[6]

In alluding to your removal from Department No 2,[7] which he said he should never cease to deplore, and regarded as the most flagrant Administrative faux pas of the war, he added with his genial smile, and humorous twinkle of the eye; "in fine, General Beauregard has certainly been treated with more rank injustice than any other man in the Confederacy, except one, far less important individual."[8] Some weeks since, I had the good fortune to meet Gen'l Joseph E Johnston[9] at Admiral Buchanan's,[10] where I was spending the evening. As the Admiral presented me to him, he said; "General, here is an extremely fortunate lady; she knows General Beauregard and tells me, that she occasionally has the honor of hearing from him." The General's face flashed instantly, he put out both hands, and immediately spoke of you in glowing language, that brought tears to my eyes. He has surely a noble magnanimous Soul; is a stranger to the miserable weakness of envy, and I found that my acquaintance with you, was an "open Sesame"! to his friendship and sympathy. Again has our country been called on to witness the immolation of another illustrious victim on the altar of Presidential Jealousy, and everywhere the people are deploring and muttering angrily about the forced resignation of Gen'l G. W. Smith.[11] Ohe! jam satis.[12] Mr Davis seems to have learned but one rule of government; that laid down by Machiavelli[13] in the celebrated sophistical dictum; "the dissensions of great men, contribute to the welfare of the state." Allow me if you please, to detail my reasons for inflicting a letter upon you at this time, when any interruption must be annoying. You may perhaps remember that I mentioned to you, that I had a MS Novel,[14] containing a chapter relative to the Battle of Manassa [sic], where one of my characters was killed.[15] I was very anxious to read it to you, but could find no appropriate opportunity. At the time that I spoke of it to you, I intended not to publish it until the close of the war, but recently circumstances have determined me to bring it out, as soon as I can finish copying the MS upon which I am now employed. The chapter to which I allude, is the XXXth and before I copy it, I am extremely desirous to know that I am entirely accurate in all my statements relative to the Battle; I am afraid to trust to my memory of the conversation I had with you concerning it, and to avoid the possibility of error, I beg permission most respectfully to propound the following inquiries. Am I correct in saying—1, That you and Gen'l Johnston were not acquainted with the fact that McDowell had left Washington with the main Fed army to attack you at Manassa's [sic] Junction until a young Lady of Washington (I give no name), disguised as a market woman, and engaged in selling milk to the Fed soldiers, succeeded in making her way through their lines to Fairfax Court House and telegraphed you of the contemplated attack?[16] 2nd, That you immediately telegraphed to Gen'l Johnston, then at Winchester, and in consequence of this information he hastened to Manassas?[17] 3d At what hour did you learn that your order for an advance on Centreville by your right wing, had failed to reach its destination?[18] 4th Did you not lead in person the second great charge which recovered the plateau and took the Batteries that crowned it?[19] Could I satisfy myself of the correctness of my views or impressions regarding these points, elsewhere than by applying to you, believe me Sir, I would not annoy you, for I shrink from the thought of becoming troublesome to you, or imposing upon your generosity. I regret exceedingly that I could not have submitted this chapter of my new Novel to you, before sending it to press. It is dedicated to the Army of the Confederacy. In view of the impending attack upon Charleston, your name is constantly on our lips, in our hearts, and believe me, in our prayers. Yet apprehension does not mingle with my interest in all the tidings that come from your Department; I rest in perfect assurance that with the blessing of our God, victory will, as everywhere else, nestle upon your banner. Have you heard recently from Mrs. Beauregard? Earnestly, most earnestly do I hope, that ere this, her health has been perfectly restored;[20] and that the day is not very distant, when in peace and prosperity, you may return laden with the love, and followed by the prayers of a redeemed and grateful people, to your rescued home, and the bosom of your beloved family. That God will shield you, from all the dangers that threaten, and preserve you to the country which so demands your services, and rests it's [sic] hopes upon you, is the heartfelt wish of

Yours most respectfully and gratefully
Augusta J. Evans

P.S. My Sisters desire me to tender you, their love and gratitude for your kind remembrance.

A.J.E

1. The manuscript of this letter is housed in the Special Collections Department of the William R. Perkins Library at Duke University. The letter was also published, with an introduction by Ben W. Griffith, in *Mississippi Quarterly*. See "The Lady Novelist and the General: An Unpublished Letter from Augusta Evans to P. G. T. Beauregard," *Mississippi Quarterly* 10 (summer 1957): 97–106.

2. Confederate General P. G. T. Beauregard was constantly at odds with President Davis, a relationship that Griffith compares with that of President Truman and General Douglas MacArthur. After Beauregard lost at Shiloh and a few weeks later left his troops without officially obtaining permission when he was sick, Davis relieved him of his command of the Western forces (Tennessee, Mississippi, and Alabama) and reassigned him to a less important post in Charleston. Forty-nine Confederate congressmen signed a petition asking President Davis to reinstate Beauregard in the West. Davis angrily replied that he would not return Beauregard to the West even if the entire world should ask him to do so (Griffith, "The Lady Novelist and the General," 100–101).

3. Alfred, Lord Tennyson. "Maud," section 10, stanza 5.

4. Sterling Price was a hero in the Mexican War and later governor of Missouri. When war broke out he was appointed major general in the Confederate army. However, he always felt that President Davis undervalued him and constantly placed him under officers who were his inferiors (Griffith, "The Lady Novelist and the General," 99).

5. "The Western Scipio" is AEW's title for Major General Price. Scipio was the Roman general who defeated Carthage in the Third Punic War (149–146 B.C.E.).

6. Alfred, Lord Tennyson. "Ode on the Death of the Duke of Wellington," stanza 4, lines 17–19.

7. Beauregard was removed as commander of the Western forces.

8. Price is referring to himself here.

9. Johnston, a general at Manassas with Beauregard, later infuriated Beauregard by hinting that *he,* not Beauregard, deserved the credit for the victory at Manassas (Griffith, "The Lady Novelist and the General," 99).

10. Franklin Buchanan, the only admiral in the Confederate navy, led the *Merrimac* against the *Monitor* and later commanded the ironclad *Tennessee* in the Battle of Mobile Bay (Griffith 99).

11. General Gustavus Woodson Smith also had his differences with President Davis. Davis relieved Smith of the command of the Army of the Potomac and gave that position to Lee. After six officers were promoted over him, Smith resigned in 1863, but he later fought against Sherman as the commander of the First Division of the Georgia Militia (Griffith, "The Lady Novelist and the General," 99).

12. "Hold! That is enough." Horace *Satires* 1.5.12.

13. Machiavelli (1469–1527), an Italian statesman and political philosopher, known for his cunning and duplicity.

14. *Macaria* (1864).

15. Russell Aubrey, the young man who wanted to marry the novel's heroine, is killed in this battle.

16. Beauregard, in his reply to AEW dated March 24, 1863, verifies the assistance of this spy, a Miss Duval (quoted in Griffith, "The Lady Novelist and the General," 102). In *Macaria* Electra Gray, an art student studying in Europe when war breaks out, plays the role of Miss Duval. When asked to smuggle some important dispatches to Richmond, she glues the papers on the back of one of her sketches, sails to Havana, and then takes a blockade-runner to Mobile.

17. According to Griffith, Beauregard delayed sending this message and AEW politely omits any reference to this issue in the novel ("The Lady Novelist and the General," 102).

18. Beauregard hedged in this answer (Griffith, "The Lady Novelist and the General," 102), and in the novel AEW states merely that ". . . the General learned with unutterable chagrin that his order for an advance on Centreville had miscarried, that a brilliant plan had been frustrated . . ." (Augusta Jane Evans, *Macaria; or Altars of Sacrifice,* 1864; reprint, intro. by Drew Gilpin Faust, *Library of Southern Civilization* [Baton Rouge: Louisiana University Press, 1992], 334).

19. Beauregard could answer this question in the affirmative (Griffith, "The Lady Novelist and the General," 102), and in *Macaria,* AEW grandly states: "Not a moment was to be lost; General Beauregard ordered forward his reserves for a second effort, and with magnificent effect led the charge in person" (Evans, *Macaria* [1992], 334).

20. After a two-year illness, Beauregard's wife died in March 1864 (Williams, *P. G. T. Beauregard,* 203–4), almost a year to the day after this letter.

❧ ❧ ❧

35 / MS Alabama   Mobile March 20 1863

My dear, dear Rachel—

Peccavi! peccavi![1] I throw myself on your known mercy and generosity, and believe that the reasons which I shall assign, will plead my pardon. You ought to know me too well to imagine, that because I have been silent, I therefore ceased to remember, to think of, or to love you. What has made you so suspicious of me? The truth simply is, that for one year past, I have been wretchedly anxious about one of my Brothers,[2] in Bragg's[3] Army, who in

addition to the dangers of the battle field, has been in <u>miserable</u> health. I have
been so sad, that I thought my letters would give pleasure to no one, except
the members of my family who entered into my feelings. Thank God! he is
stronger and better now, and though I am very uneasy in view of a probable
battle near Tullahoma,[4] still I am less unhappy than I was; and try to commit
both my Brothers to the care of a merciful God. In addition to this cause of
silence, I have been literally <u>over-run</u> with <u>company</u>. We have a Brigade of
Soldiers encamped <u>in sight</u> of my home, and the officers are constantly here,
claiming my time. But the <u>reason</u> of <u>reasons</u>, dear Rachel remains to be told;
I am now constantly occupied (when <u>not</u> in the parlor) in copying the <u>MS</u>
of a new Novel[5] which I intend to publish just as soon as I can complete said
<u>MS</u>. This is tedious work; you can have no idea how tedious and wearing
upon heart and brain. Sometimes I sit at my desk from <u>eight</u> in the morning
till after midnight. Under these circumstances you readily imagine, I have no
leisure for anything else. Occasionally I snatch a few minutes to write to my
Aunt Jones, and to General Beauregard and my <u>two</u> precious <u>Brothers</u>. When
Billie Brooks came out and brought me your welcome letter, I was grieved,
pained to see that you were disposed to doubt my affection for you. Ah
Rachel! had you so little faith in me? Hereafter if long intervals occur
between my letters, feel assured that I am too much engaged, or am sick, or
that anything <u>else</u> has happened, than diminution of my love, and friendship
for you. I hope before very long that this, my bondage to midnight lamps will
be ended; until that time, bear with me my darling. I hope you will like my
new book; I believe that you will. In some respect, I think it is superior to
"<u>Beulah</u>." I can't tell exactly when I shall finish <u>copying</u> it; in the course of a
very few weeks I hope. Meantime write to me, as in the olden days, before
these dark days of blood and horror; and when my work is ended, you shall
have no cause to complain of my silence. Are you uneasy concerning
Charleston. [sic] I have no apprehension of the result of an attack upon it; we
have there the ablest General, and I believe one of the <u>noblest purist</u>, most
devoted patriots of the Land.[6] If human skill can avail, he will save Charleston
& Savannah. Knowing both Beauregard & Price,[7] I have for them a <u>reverence</u>
and <u>admiration</u>, such as <u>none other</u> of our Generals, whom I have met, have
excited. Dear Rachel do believe my assurance of love and write soon to

Your most truly AJ Evans

PS. What has become of our friend Mr. Timrod?[8]

1. "I have sinned." AEW is alluding to a famous statement by Sir Charles Napier
who in February 1843 defeated the Ameers of Scinde (or Sind, in Pakistan) and
acquired their territories. In notifying his superiors of his success, Napier sent one
word: "Peccavi" ("I have sinned"), a play on words to signify, "I have Scinde."
2. Captain Howard Evans, AEW's brother, was in Bragg's army.

3. General Braxton Bragg.

4. A town in central Tennessee. On June 30, General Bragg, outmaneuvered by the Union General Rosecrans, was forced to retreat from Tullahoma (Charles P. Roland, *An American Iliad: The Story of the Civil War* [Lexington: University Press of Kentucky, 1991], 151).

5. *Macaria,* published in 1864.

6. General Beauregard.

7. In 1862 General Sterling Price was driven out of Missouri and defeated at the Battle of Pea Ridge. After this, Price and his army were reassigned east of the Mississippi, a serious error on the part of the Confederate high command. With Missouri unprotected, the Union army was able to invade Kentucky and push down through Tennessee and all the way into northern Mississippi (Coulter, *Confederate States of America,* 49). AEW seemed to feel that the bungling of their superiors had undermined the ability of both Beauregard and Price. See AEW to Beauregard, March 17, 1863.

8. Henry Timrod, the poet laureate of the Confederacy, had at one point courted Rachel Lyons. He wrote a poem to her, "La Belle Juive," and many love letters. At the time of this letter, however, Rachel was engaged to Dr. Heustis, whom she later married, and Timrod was in love with Katie Goodwin (Fidler, *A Biography,* 73), for whom he wrote the poem "Katie." Timrod and Katie married in 1864 (Introduction, *The Poems of Henry Timrod,* xix–xx).

❧ ❧ ❧

36 / MS Alabama
Historic Society of Mobile (typed copy)   Mobile March 28th [1863]

My dear Rachel

Your letter arrived two days ago, and I should have answered it immediately, but for a <u>rush of company</u> which left me no leisure whatever. After all that you said to me about Dr. Heustis[1] and especially <u>your laughing</u> at the idea that he could interest you and his saying that your tastes were congenial, I confess I was very much surprised at your declaration that you <u>loved him</u>. I knew that he was interested in <u>you</u> but from <u>what you told</u> me concerning <u>your estimate of him</u>, and your repeated assurances that he was your inferior intellectually, and you could never marry a man like Dr Heustis—you ought not to wonder that I was not prepared for your avowal of affection. You are well aware of my friendly appreciation of his <u>rare worth</u>; I have known him long and well, and understand his character better than any one else beside his own family. His nature is remarkably generous and magnanimous; he has one of the <u>noblest truest hearts</u> I have ever known, and I have always entertained a warm and sincere friendship for him. If <u>you do indeed love him</u> as <u>you say</u>, then he will make you happy, and you could not make a better selection, could not possibly give yourself to a nobler man. His affectionate nature can not fail to make a happy home for the woman who really loves him, and I have no friend whom I should be so glad to see happily married, as Dr Heustis, for he deserves a good and devoted wife. To be candid with you, my dear Rachel I must tell you, that I was very much astonished to find from your letter, that you had not informed your Parents of <u>your</u> <u>engagement</u>. Oh Rachel! You owe it to them to acquaint them immediately with the solemn step you have taken; and the holy relationship which you occupy to Dr Heustis. They are your <u>best</u> <u>friends</u>, dear Rachel, and do you suppose they would oppose you in a matter which you say involved your happiness? Since your conscience does not forbid your marriage, do you think that the difference of faith will present an insurmountable obstacle to their consent?[2] That they would of course prefer otherwise I have no doubt, but they must feel that it is a matter which <u>you</u> <u>only</u> can decide. Beside [*sic*] you said while in Mobile, that under such circumstances you would follow the dictates of your own heart. If you love Dr Heustis, no one has the right to forbid your marriage, and I believe that your Father and Mother <u>will</u> <u>give</u> <u>their</u> <u>consent</u>, if they are assured <u>your</u> <u>happiness</u> is at stake. Were I circumstanced as you are, I would <u>go</u> <u>at</u> <u>once</u> to my home, and <u>inform</u> <u>my</u> <u>parents</u> of <u>all</u> that had transpired. They must know it some day, and the sooner the better; perfect frankness on your part, will prove a powerful advocate before your loving Mother's heart, whose happiness centres in that of her child. Moreover, so long as your family remain in ignorance of your engagement, you keep both the Doctor and yourself in painful suspense. Do you not <u>owe</u> it to Dr Heustis to be candid and ask your Parents [*sic*] blessing on your engagement? You say dear Rachel, that you "<u>do</u> <u>not</u> <u>see</u> <u>your</u> <u>way</u> <u>clearly</u>." There is but <u>one</u> <u>path</u>, and duty points you to your Father & Mother. It is utterly impossible that you can be happy, until perfect confidence is established between <u>your</u> <u>heart</u> <u>and</u> <u>theirs</u>; and <u>procrastination</u> brings endless evils. Pardon me dear Rachel if I say aught that displeases or wounds you, but you asked me to write to you freely, to advise you on this point, and I have done so, as conscientiously, as honestly as though I were writing to <u>one</u> <u>of</u> <u>my</u> <u>own</u> <u>sisters</u>, who was situated as you are. From <u>my</u> Parents, I keep <u>nothing</u>; they know all my thoughts and feelings, my hopes and sorrows, and they should be the <u>first</u> to know of my relationship to the unfortunate man (<u>if</u> <u>he</u> <u>is</u> <u>upon</u> <u>the</u> <u>face</u> <u>of</u> <u>the</u> <u>earth</u>) who had the promise of my hand. You know very well how <u>solemn</u> a thing I hold engagements, and therefore I am so surprised at your reluctance to have your family acquainted with yours. I should think you would want to hurry home, and have a family <u>talk</u> as soon as possible. Dr Heustis loves you sincerely, and I shall not forgive you if you do not make him the happiest man in the Confederacy. Write me what your plans are, and <u>how</u> <u>soon</u> <u>you</u> <u>are</u> <u>coming</u> <u>to</u>

Mobile <u>to</u> <u>live</u>. That chronic nuisance yclept[3] "Macaria"[4] will probably make
its bow to the "dear people" next week. Did you know Mr Evans had a lit-
tle son, born last month? He is very proud and happy, as this is the first boy.
<u>Gen'l</u> <u>Shoup</u> is ordered away from Mobile and was out to see me two days
since, before he knew he was to leave the City. He goes to Johnston's Army,
and will have command of all the artillery. I see Gen'l Quarles <u>very frequently</u>
and we have become[5] most <u>excellent</u> friends, we have ceased skirmishing and
signed a treaty of <u>Peace</u>! He has sent for one of his children, now in Tennessee, and is expecting him by every flag of truce. Alice Vivian has had the
measles, and I <u>hear</u> the mumps!! I can almost as soon fancy Aphrodite rising
out of the Agean [sic] Sea, convulsed with a spell of whooping cough!!!!! She
is however quite well again, and will I expect come down this spring, before
the weather becomes too warm. Do give my love to your family when you
write, and tell them I say Dr Heustis is the noblest hearted friend I have and
they must not object to him as a <u>son</u> <u>in</u> <u>law</u>. By the way, he gave me a photograph of himself, but as he said you were not satisfied with the <u>one</u> <u>you</u> <u>had</u>,
I advised him to send you the one he gave me, and I hope you will like it
better. It is a fine likeness [obscured]. AJE

 1. When Rachel visited AEW in Mobile in the summer of 1860, AEW introduced her to Dr. James Fontaine Heustis, a widower with a young daughter (Catherine L. Druhan, "Louise Lyons Heustis: Southern Artist," *The Vulcan Historical Review* 4
[2000]; http://www.sbs.uab.edu/history/varticles/Louisely.htm [accessed 10 December 2001]).
 2. Rachel was Jewish and Dr. Heustis was Christian. Apparently Rachel's parents
gave the young couple their blessing, for Rachel and Dr. Heustis were married on
February 4, 1865 (Fidler, *A Biography,* 78).
 3. Old English for "named" or "called."
 4. AEW's third novel, published in 1864.
 5. This final section from this point to the end of the letter was written in crosshatch across the text of page 1.

❧ ❧ ❧

37 / MS Historical Society of Pennsylvania   Mobile April 29th 1863

General Beauregard—
 Knowing your warm interest in all that appertains to the Kentucky Campaign which resulted so disastrously through the rejection of your plan of
operations,[1] permit me most respectfully to submit to you, a paper of more
than ordinary interest and value. A few days since, the author, a gentleman
of very fine intellect, extraordinary culture, and great promise as a lawyer
and politician of Lexington Kentucky sent the <u>MS</u> to me, having heard that
I was compiling a history of the war, and desiring to furnish me <u>correct data</u>

concerning the campaigns in Kentucky and Middle Tennessee. He was misinformed; I have not presumed to become the historian of our great Revolution; the mantle of Xenophon,[2] Thucydides[3] or Tacitus,[4] would ill become my shoulders, but I read the MS with absorbing interest, and was so impressed by the melancholy truths he uttered, (for I have heard from various officers of corroboration of the statements therein contained) that I asked him why he had not published his admirable critique? The answer he gave was ominous, sadly indexing the slow approach of the very despotism, which Confederate Soldiers are hourly yielding up their lives to avert. He said that Gen'l Bragg had issued an order prohibiting officers in Dept No 2, from publishing any article, which reflected in any respect upon the conduct of the Commander of the Army.[5] He thought that the people should be made acquainted with the truth which had been studiously suppressed, but added that publication was not his privilege. I asked his permission to make two copies, one for you Sir, and one for my noble friend Mr Yancey.[6] He gladly assured me that the MS was entirely at my disposal, but observed that it required much pruning as regards polish and elegance of style; that it was penned in a tent, by the flickering light of camp fires, rendered inconstant by rain and snow, and debarred from books and sources of embellishment. He claims for it only accuracy of narration, unimpeachable veracity. I have had the enclosed copy made for you; it is not as neatly executed as I could desire, owing to the indifferent character of the paper. The author of the "Apology" is Captain R. W. Woolly, a nephew of Gen'l Preston[7] of Kentucky, whom he accompanied as Charge d'Affaires, when the latter was our Minister of Spain. He left his home in Lexington at the beginning of hostilities, went through both campaigns, and is now Judge Advocate on Gen'l Buckner's[8] Staff. He is a man of great earnestness of purpose and rare talent. I will only add that Captain Woolley [sic] submitted his "Apology" to "Gen'l Hardee"[9] who pronounced the statements accurate and incorporated a portion of the "Apology" in his Official Report of the Battle of Murfreesboro.[10] Hoping that it will interest you in some degree, I am General, with profound respect

Sincerely your friend

A.J.Evans

1. Beauregard advocated abandoning Bowling Green, Kentucky, which was a weak position for the Confederates, and concentrating their forces at Fort Donelson, from which they could mount an attack on Grant's army. According to Williams, Beauregard's strategy was sound. On February 12, 1862, Grant attacked Fort Donelson with an army of 15,000. If Beauregard's plan had been adopted, the Confederate General Johnston could have met Grant at Donelson with an army of 30,000 and defeated him before Union reinforcements could arrive. Johnston's refusal to adopt Beauregard's plan seemed utterly irrational. Instead he insisted on personally leading the retreating

troops from Bowling Green to safety. He appeared to be in a "fog of mental paralysis" precipitated by this military crisis (Williams, *P. G. T. Beauregard,* 118–19).

2. Xenophon, a Greek historian, essayist, and soldier (431–352 B.C.E.), wrote several volumes of Greek history. Also, after fighting in the army of Cyrus the Younger, Xenophon wrote seven books describing Cyrus's military campaign and ultimate defeat.

3. Thucydides, a Greek historian (c. 460–c. 426 B.C.E.), wrote a history of the Peloponnesian War based on his own experiences as a general in the war.

4. Tacitus (c. 56–c. 120 C.E.), remembered as one of the great Roman historians, is especially well known for his histories of the emperors of the first century C.E.

5. General Bragg had several reasons to be sensitive to criticism. Many Confederates resented him for replacing Beauregard, a very popular general, as the Confederate commander of the Western theater (Kentucky, Tennessee, and Mississippi). Also, Charles Torrey, museum researcher at the City of Mobile Museum, explains that the people of Mobile, especially the women, blamed Bragg for the deaths of so many of Mobile's young men who were soldiers in his army (letter to the author, July 26, 1994).

6. William L. Yancey, a firebrand, Alabama secessionist, and member of the Confederate senate, had become hostile to President Davis over a series of slights—some imagined and some real (Coulter, *Confederate States of America,* 385). AEW probably assumes that Yancey will share her feelings toward Bragg, who was a Davis supporter.

7. William Preston, former United States Minister to Spain, was later commissioned to go to Mexico on behalf of the Confederacy. Preston attempted to win Napoleon's support for the Confederacy through the intermediary of Maximilian, Napoleon's puppet emperor over Mexico. Preston's mission failed (Frank Lawrence Owsley, *King Cotton Diplomacy: Foreign Relations of the Confederate States of America,* 2nd ed. [Chicago: University of Chicago Press, 1959], 508).

8. Simon Bolivar Buckner was a former United States army officer and veteran of the Mexican War who joined the Confederate army in 1861 as a brigadier general. After the war, he served as governor of Kentucky from 1887 to 1891.

9. Major General Hardee served under Johnston in the ill-fated Kentucky campaign (Roland, *An American Iliad,* 56) and under Bragg when Bragg was forced to retreat from Tullahoma, Tennessee. Hardee, like many other Confederates, was very critical of Bragg. At Tullahoma, Bragg's will to fight was "eroded by the distrust and recrimination of his corps commanders Polk and Hardee" (151).

10. Shortly after assuming command of the Western army, Bragg saw an opportunity to make a great advance against the Federals. He planned to march through middle Tennessee and central Kentucky, all the way to the Ohio River. However, due to his inept leadership, he was stopped at Perryville, Kentucky (Oct. 8, 1862) by Federal General Buell and prevented from taking Louisville. After losing an opportunity to make huge gains in territory for the Confederacy, Bragg returned to Tennessee and fought an "indecisive" Battle at Murfreesboro (Jan. 2, 1863) against the Federal General Rosecrans (Coulter, *Confederate States of America,* 357).

In early 1862, Beauregard's plan to defeat Grant in Kentucky had been rejected. At the time of this letter, a few months later, Bragg bungled a second opportunity for Confederate victory.

❧ ❧ ❧

38 / MS Library of Congress (original)
Alabama (photocopy)
Duke (photocopy)   Mobile July 15 1863

Mr. J. L. M. Curry—
My honored friend—
    For three weeks past I have been absent at Bladon,[1] visiting my cousin Alice Vivian; and on my return yesterday I found your exceedingly kind and welcome letter, for which I hasten to express my cordial thanks. To your friendly interest and perseverance, I am I assure you, greatly indebted for the passage of the Act securing Copyrights;[2] which is (as far as I am capable of judging,) sufficiently protective, and perfectly satisfactory. Accept my grateful acknowledgments for its successful accomplishment. Touching your prospective <u>Lecture</u>,[3] permit me to say <u>par parentheses</u>,[4] that I fully appreciate the compliment implied in your flattering consultation with reference to a theme; and believe me, were I capable, I should be both <u>proud</u> and <u>happy</u> to render you all possible assistance. Waiving for a moment, the absurdity of supposing that I could suggest an idea which had not been already weighed and canvassed by you, labelled for use, or rejected as vapid and irrelevant,—let us discuss your contemplated theme, in some of its most ordinary aspects. 1st "<u>Is the character of Southern women prejudicially affected by Slavery</u>? <u>Entre nous</u>[5] I believe that it is, though the evils are not necessarily inherent, nor are they an inevitable sequence of the institution. Ignoring for a time, the consideration of climatic influences, look at the physical and mental <u>status</u> of Southern women. Are they not enervated, lethargic, incapable of enduring fatigue, and as a class, afflicted with chronic lassitude? Why? Simply because they never <u>systematically exercise</u>. Why not? From the fact that having a number of servants always at hand, whom she scarcely knows how to employ, the Southern matron accustoms herself to having every office in the household performed by others; while she sits passive and inert, over a basket of stockings, or the last new novel. The less she exercises, the less she feels inclined to do so; gradually her constitution succumbs,—she finds herself listless, querulous, fretful; an incubus to her Husband, and utterly incapable of properly educating and attending to her children. To perfect health, <u>regular exercise</u> is absolutely indispensable; occasional spasmodic exertion will not avail, and where a woman feels that the comfort of her family is involved in <u>her performance</u> of certain domestic duties, systematic exercise will not be

neglected. The consciousness of conducing to the happiness of those she loves, is the most powerful stimulant which could be administered to a careless indolent wife or mother. In communities where white labor is employed, fewer domestics are engaged, and infinitely more of the household work necessarily devolves on the mistress. She who kneads her own bread, is very rarely troubled with dyspepsia; and one who habitually churns her butter, or industriously handles her broom, is a stranger to the horrors of asthma, and nervous headaches. You might here point in refutation to the fact that many Northern and English women entirely abjure household work. But remember that they have methods of habitual daily out-door exercise, from which we are debarred by climate. A southern woman who emulated the peripatetic performances of her English Sister, would unquestionably find herself the victim of Sun stroke, or brain fever. Our work must be indoors. Such are the practical results of the system of labor now existing; though I believe these evils might be counterbalanced by the advantages which are concomitant. Southern women have more leisure for the cultivation of their intellects, and the perfection of womanly accomplishments; but do they properly employ it? Thoroughly educated women are deplorably rare among us; we have thousands who are graceful, pretty, witty, and pleasant companions for a promenade or pic-nic, but their information is painfully scanty; their judgment defective, their reasoning faculties dwarfed, their aspirations weak and frivolous. We can boast no Herschel[6] or Willard,[7] or Sommerville,[8] or Mitchell[9] in Southern circles. Were we stronger in body, from systematic household work, we should be characterized by more intellectual vigor and originality. I believe that women should daily perform a certain amount of physical labor, and such is not the habit of Southern families. Brooms, rolling pins, dashers and hoes have grown obsolete. I repeat, I do not regard this inertia as inseparably bound up with the system, but as far as my observation extends, I find it the practical and melancholy result. Southern women might be exalted by the institution, but such is not the fact. In tropical climes (where slavery flourishes) women are generally more richly endowed than in colder latitudes; their imagination more vivid and glowing, their susceptibility to emotions or impressions of beauty, or sublimity, infinitely keener; and nature seems to stamp them devotees at the shrine of Aesthetics; noble, perfect instruments for the advancement of Art. But the sacred mission is not fulfilled; they fold their listless fingers, and failing in requisite energy, become the victims of chronic inertia. 2. "Does history throw any light on the subject?" After a hasty survey of the hoary evidence of dead centuries, I am afraid it would cause a verdict against us. Except Penelope[10] and Lucretia,[11] I can recall no examples worth adducing in favor of slavery; and the most brilliant women of the past, barring Hypatia[12] & Damo,[13] were certainly from northern climates where

slavery had no existence. In the <u>East</u> where the institution has been maintained from time immemorial, women are sunk in semi-barbarism, and rank
lowest in the social scale. Perhaps you will urge that her degradation is to be
attributed less to the institution, than to the absence of the refining and elevating influence of our Religion. Sir, do you find the <u>status</u> of the mass of
women in Christian Russia, any more encouraging? <u>Under</u> <u>the</u> <u>old</u> <u>regime</u>
will they ever lift themselves to a purer, loftier sphere of usefulness? I am
afraid a <u>rigid</u> <u>analysis</u> might prove unfavorable to us; but lest you should mis-
interpret my views, I beg to add, that <u>I</u> <u>do</u> <u>not</u> consider it an inexorable necessity. Mr. Curry, will you forgive my presumption, if I <u>humbly</u> and most
respectfully suggest that there is <u>another</u> <u>theme</u> which you might handle with
magnificent effect, and incalculable usefulness? <u>Political</u> <u>and</u> <u>social</u> <u>quicksands</u>
<u>of</u> <u>the</u> <u>Future</u>. My friend, in casting our national horoscope, my heart is
weighed down with ceaseless apprehension; and I feel that here on the
threshold, warning tones should be heard, and warning hands lifted toward
the mouldering mournful ruins, which blacken the <u>past</u> <u>of</u> <u>Republics</u>. Corruption stalks through the land, grim and merciless as Carlyle's monster "Utilitaria"[14] and if not speedily vanquished, we might as well relinquish all hope
of a <u>permanent</u> <u>republic</u>. With the downfall of this form of government, we
surrender all that makes American soil dear; and today, I would rather lay my
head in my grave, than survive such a wreck. All the evils which History
proves inherent in Democratic Republics, now threaten us in an aggravated
form; and to point the people to them, pleading for reform, seems the <u>impera-</u>
<u>tive</u> duty of our Statesmen. <u>Our</u> <u>national</u> <u>salvation</u> <u>depends</u> <u>on</u> <u>certain</u> <u>modi-</u>
<u>fications</u> <u>of</u> <u>our</u> <u>Constitution</u>, to effect which, the masses must be trained and
elevated to a <u>higher</u> <u>stand-point</u>. For instance the restriction of our suffrage
is a delicate matter for politicians to handle; but the people must be brought
to a realization of its importance, or we shall ere long, (even after attaining
our Independence), be plunged in hopeless anarchy, or crushed under the
iron heel of despotism.[15] The dangers to which I allude, are too numerous in
their ramifications to admit of recapitulation here, but doubtless they are as
palpable and deplorable to you, as to myself. In a Lecture you might <u>popu-</u>
<u>larize</u> <u>the</u> <u>remedies</u>, and certainly no nobler theme could be found, in the
whole range of literature. You have the vast experience of bygone ages,
heaped with melancholy wrecks, to furnish illustration and syllable a solemn
warning, which uttered by your lips, could never prove Cassandran;[16] and oh
Sir! great, great good might be accomplished. I have a very valuable little
book which would render you assistance in such a subject; if you have not
already studied it: "Reflections on the Rise and Fall of Ancient Republics;"
by Montague.[17] It is a rare volume, and I have sometimes thought I would write
an analytical sketch of our old Republic, and with this addition republish the

work. But my courage fails me, I am not competent to the noble task; the mantle of Tacitus[18] or Xenophon[19] would ill-become my shoulders. If you desire it, I will with great pleasure, prepare and send you a compend of the causes of the decline of each of the Ancient Republics, as furnished by Montague; and you will I think, find many startling points of analogy between the Bygone and the Present. You could I feel assured, make a splendid and valuable Lecture, upon this comprehensive and vital subject. Need I add, that if I can serve you in so noble a project, I shall be inexpressibly happy to be allowed such a proud privilege? Thank you Mr. Curry, for your kind remarks relative to "Beulah." You have probably seen from the papers that I have a new work now in the hands of the publishers, West & Johnston; "Macaria" or "Altars of Sacrifice." It will be ready within a month, if Mobile and Charleston do not fall, and I hope to have the pleasure of sending you an early copy. What think you of my resurrecting "Macaria?" The title impresses me as singularly appropriate,[20] and the book is on the whole superior to "Beulah;" though it contains less philosophic lore, and no metaphysical disputation. In this book I discuss some of the dangers threatening our government,[21] which I am so anxious to have treated by your masterly hands; for my feeble touches are very inadequate to the demands of the crisis. I regret that I can not furnish your enthusiastic Virginia friend, with the real Guy Hartwell,[22] she has done me the honor to admire. Tell her she has only to look into the ranks of our matchless armies, to find hundreds who are nobler than my carping, self-indulgent, cynical, sceptical Guy. The hero of "Macaria" is not happily married at the close of the book, but dies—gloriously at Malvern Hills.[23] Vicksburg has fallen, through official imbecility.[24] I feel as did Queen Mary over the loss of Calais: "when I am dead it will be found engraven on my heart."[25] Unless Johnston can defeat Grant at Jackson, he will be forced to retreat,[26] and thus leave Mobile at the mercy of an invading army,[27] flushed with victory. In such emergency, which may Almighty God forbid! we, like thousands of others shall be homeless refugees; for I will never remain an hour under Yankee rule. Ten thousand times rather would I see the city destroyed, than polluted by their presence, but a different policy has been adopted by our Government. Grave fears are entertained by many of our citizens, but under any and all circumstances which may arise, I have implicit confidence in Gen'l Johnston, whom I regard as the ablest General in the Confederacy. Some, who were totally ignorant of the facts, have been weak and unjust enough to censure him for not relieving Vicksburg, when the treachery or stupidity (in times like these a blunder is almost a crime) of Pemberton had rendered matters desperate in Mississippi. Johnston has toiled ceaselessly to repair Pemberton's errors, he has done all that human skill and tireless energy could possibly accomplish, and a just and grateful people will not quietly submit to the gross injustice, which the Administration is striving to heap upon him. These are dark hours, but: "Onward in faith! and leave the rest to Heaven."[28] I shall not apologize for this <u>raid</u> on your valuable time, because in the first place Sir, I have not said the half I intended to bore you with, and secondly, excuses like homeopathic remedies, would only increase the affliction. Pardon me if I have presumed upon your kindness, and believe me, dear Sir

Very sincerely your friend—
A.J. Evans

1. Bladon Springs, near Mobile.

2. The Confederates at first viewed the war as an opportunity, among other things, for the South to develop its own literature, free from Northern and European influences. To this end, the Confederate congress established copyright laws to protect literary works for twenty-eight years, with the possibility of renewal for an additional fourteen years. Also, to stop literary piracy, which the United States laws had not done, the Confederacy planned to establish international copyright agreements with European countries. However, these treaties were never negotiated (Coulter, *Confederate States of America,* 507–8).

3. Curry had originally planned to lecture on "The Influence of African Slavery on our Southern Women" (Jessie Pearl Rice, *J. L. M. Curry: Southerner, Statesman and Educator* [New York: King's Crown Press, 1949], 191n. 10). In this letter AEW convinces him to change topics. Following her advice, Curry wrote the speech "Two Wants of the Confederacy," which he later delivered both in Richmond and in Petersburg. In this speech Curry denounced the tyranny of the majority and claimed that the two "wants" of the Confederacy were for an enlightened populace and for an "enlarged liberal Christian statesmanship" to control government (39).

4. in parentheses, by the way

5. between us

6. Caroline Lucretia Herschel (1750–1848), an Englishwoman, assisted her brother William in his work in astronomy, but also established her own reputation in the field and is known as the first notable woman astronomer.

7. Frances Elizabeth Caroline Willard (1839–1898), a prominent educator and reformer. Most of her fame (as president of a women's college, dean of women at Northwestern University, and national president of the Woman's Christian Temperance Union) came after the time of this letter.

8. Mary Somerville was a Scottish mathematician and scientific writer, prominent in the early nineteenth century. She taught herself advanced math and astronomy. See Kirstin Olsen, *Chronology of Women's History* (Westport, Conn.: Greenwood, 1994), 115.

9. Maria Mitchell (1818–1889), the first woman astronomer in the United States.

10. In Greek mythology, Penelope was the wife of Odysseus. She is known for her faithfulness to Odysseus during his twenty-year absence due to the Trojan War.

11. Lucretia, according to legend, was raped by the son of the king of Rome, who threatened to kill her and make it appear that she had committed adultery. She

submitted but later told the truth to her family, who overthrew the monarchy. Lucretia committed suicide as self-punishment for her sin.

12. Hypatia was a philosopher of the fifth century C.E. and was affiliated with the Neoplatonic school in Alexandria.

13. Damo (late sixth century) was the daughter of Pythagoras. She worked to promote education for women and was affiliated with the Pythagorean school of Greek philosophy (Olsen, *Chronology of Women's History,* 10).

14. See letter to Victor, June 6, 1860, notes 4 and 5.

15. AEW seemed to fear a tyranny of the masses. As Fidler points out, she thought this "demagogism" (power held by uneducated, uninformed voters) is what elected Lincoln to the presidency and what defeated her friend Curry in his re-election bid to the Confederate congress. Fidler points to chapters 20 and 21 of *Macaria* for a statement of AEW's views on suffrage: through one of the main characters, Russell Aubrey, AEW argues that voting rights should be limited for the foreign born, that ownership of property should be a prerequisite for voting, that members of the judiciary should be appointed for life, and that the president should have a longer term of office (Fidler, *A Biography,* 111–12).

16. In Greek mythology, Cassandra had the gift of prophecy but the curse that no one would believe her.

17. Edward Wortley Montague (1713–1776), *Reflections on the Rise and Fall of the Ancient Republic adapted to the present state of Great Britain* (1759).

18. See AEW to General Beauregard, April 29, 1863, note 4.

19. See AEW to General Beauregard, April 29, 1863, note 2.

20. In Greek mythology, Macaria saved her beloved Athens by offering herself as a human sacrifice, an act that appeased the gods and guaranteed victory for Athens against her enemy, Eurystheus. The full title of AEW's novel, *Macaria: Altars of Sacrifice,* reveals the author's theme: the sacrifices required of the (Confederate) *women* during the Civil War. In addition to doing all that they can to aid the war effort, the women also must sacrifice their fathers, husbands, and brothers to the war.

21. See previous note 15 on restriction of suffrage.

22. The man Beulah marries at the end of AEW's novel *Beulah.*

23. Malvern Hill was the last of the Seven Days' Battles, June 25–July 1, 1862, in Virginia. At the Battle of Malvern Hill, the Confederates suffered enormous losses from Union artillery, to the point that Confederate General Daniel Hill declared that this was murder—not war (McPherson, *The Civil War and Reconstruction,* 247–48). In *Macaria,* AEW has one of her main characters, Russell Aubrey, die in the Battle of Malvern Hill.

24. In 1863, after many unsuccessful attacks on Vicksburg, General Grant surrounded the city and cut off all supplies to the Confederates for six weeks. Finally, his army starving, Confederate General Pemberton surrendered on July 4. Many Southerners reviled Pemberton for failing to anticipate and thwart Grant's moves. General Joseph Johnston had amassed an army of 30,000 troops within twenty miles of Vicksburg, and the Confederates at first hoped that Johnston could save the city. However,

Johnston's army lacked adequate supplies, weapons, and transportation. Johnston himself reported to his superiors that he considered it hopeless to try to save Vicksburg (McPherson 332–33).

25. Mary Tudor (1516–1558), daughter of Henry VIII and Catherine of Aragon, was convinced by her husband, Prince Philip of Spain, to join Spain in its war against France. As a result of this decision, England lost Calais, which was all that had remained of the once vast English holdings in France (Norah Lofts, *Queens of England* [Garden City, N.Y.: Doubleday, 1977], 115).

26. Johnston retreated to Jackson, Mississippi, which was heavily fortified, and hoped to engage the Union army in battle there. Instead, General Sherman began surrounding Jackson, apparently planning to starve the Confederates out, as the Union forces had done at Vicksburg. To prevent this, Johnston retreated and left central Mississippi to the enemy (McPherson, *The Civil War and Reconstruction,* 332).

27. Mobile Bay fell in 1864, but the city itself was not conquered until after Lee's surrender at Appomatox.

28. Robert Southey, "The Retrospect," line 176.

Top and bottom: Georgia Cottage, where Augusta Evans lived with her parents and siblings, has been restored and is now the home of a family in Mobile. (Photographed by George Wright)

Jabez Lamar Monroe Curry (courtesy of the Alabama Department of Archives and History, Montgomery, Alabama)

Sketch of General P. G. T. Beauregard by an unknown artist, supposedly for publication in *Harper's Weekly*

Augusta Evans Wilson (courtesy of the Historic Mobile Preservation Society
Archives, Mobile, Alabama)

Mobile Nov.' 14.th 1863,

General Beauregard —

I am frequently reminded of the words of Horace Walpole to Gen'l Conway: " My friend, when the press teems with tributes of praise, and your name is fondly throned on the lips of a grateful and admiring nation, have you the time or the patience to listen to my feeble but heartfelt congratulations; — a can you peruse with any interest, my dull, and merely friendly letters? " When your welcome and valued letters arrive, I often think that perhaps

Example of Evans's handwriting in letter to Gen. Beauregard, Nov. 14, 1863 (courtesy Mobile Museum)

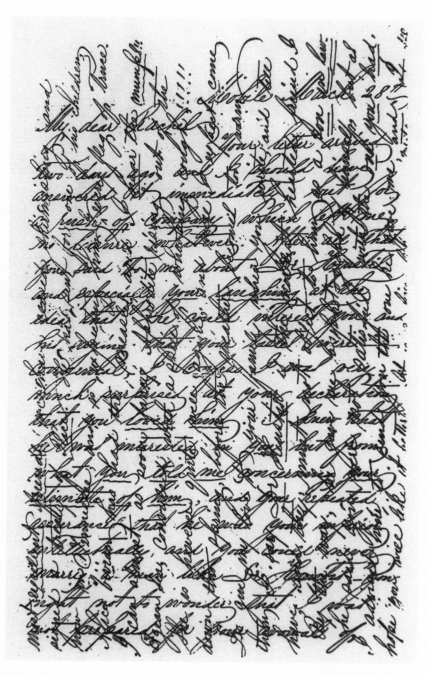

Example of Evans's crosshatch handwriting in letter to Rachel, March 28, [1863] (courtesy University of Alabama Library)

CHAPTER 4

"Amid the Sombre Shadows . . ."

General Beauregard—

Lamb has remarked in one of his admirable essays: "The greatest pleasure I know, is to do a good action by stealth, and to have it found out by accident."[1] This keen enjoyment was certainly mine, when I received your kind, valued letter, enclosing my own article, "<u>Ohe!</u> <u>jam</u> <u>satis</u>";[2] and containing your unexpected and <u>most</u> flattering commendation. I had intended sending you a copy and acquainting you with the <u>authorship</u>, but you anticipated me; my style, (as frequently happens) betrayed my <u>nom</u> <u>de</u> <u>plume</u>; and I see that you <u>suspect</u> <u>me</u>. The eulogy which you pronounced upon the article, has thrilled my heart with <u>inexpressible</u> pleasure. Praise from your lips is <u>very</u> <u>precious</u> to me,—and as I reread your words of approval, I recall a celebrated criticism on the delicacy and value of Pope's inimitable compliments: "<u>Each compliment</u> <u>is</u> <u>worth</u> <u>an</u> <u>estate</u> <u>for</u> <u>life</u>."[3] My desire to remain incognito arose from no reluctance to assume the responsibility of my article, but is attributable solely to my aversion to that species of notoriety, which newspaper contributors so often acquire. To institute reforms in any department of State, is regarded as unsuitable work for womanly hands; and though I have sometimes been impelled to this painful task, by a stern sense of duty to our country,—I can not avoid deploring the necessity, and shrinking from the publicity incident to such contributions. Although reluctant to transcend the proper sphere of womanhood, and always fearful of encroaching upon the prerogatives of your sex, I am not to be deterred from fulfilling what I occasionally feel to be a sacred duty,—by fear of the ridicule or wrath of those who contend that women have no interest in matters appertaining to Government errors. Consequently while I am neither ashamed of my opinions, nor <u>afraid</u> to <u>avow</u> them, I still endeavor to escape all unnecessary notoriety. That some good has already resulted from the publication of the said article, I have good reason to believe, and this, in conjunction with your flattering encomium, is matter of <u>proud</u> gratification. Ah! General Beauregard! what friendly discriminating "<u>familiar</u>" whispered in your ear, my earnest desire to peruse that plan of campaign, which you mentioned in a former letter, you had submitted to Gen'l

Johnston?[4] Thank you Sir, most cordially for this token of your kind confidence, which I had no right to expect; and which despite my curiosity, I should never have <u>presumed</u> to ask for. I read you plan, with mingled emotions of pleasure and pain; admiration for its happy conception, and the brilliant fruitage it could not fail to have gathered,—and profound chagrin, not free from bitterness, when I reflected how different our national <u>status</u> would have been, had your noble campaign been honored with the respect which it merited. The rejection of your Kentucky plan, twelvemonths since, finds a parallel for stupidity, or <u>willful</u> <u>error</u>, only in the ignoring of the one recently submitted; and induces the melancholy conviction that you are casting your pearls of strategy before swine, who seem disposed to trample them, and rend you. As we ponder the singular spectacle presented by the incorrigible obtuseness, or deliberate obstinacy of the Administration at Richmond, we are painfully reminded of the old classical ejaculation: "Whom the Gods would destroy, they first make mad!"[5] Unexampled gloom settled upon that section of the Confederacy, after the reverses in Mississippi, and though I hoped for brighter hours, and was sanguine of our ultimate triumph, I mourned the loss of our gallant Vicksburg,[6] as inconsolably as did Queen Mary the fall of Calais: "when I die, Calais will be found engraved upon my heart."[7] But thank God! Gen'l Johnston[8] remains to us! A sheltering palladium,[9] a conquering aegis! In him, our people repose the most implicit confidence, which the future will only justify and strengthen. To Charleston, the Mecca of our hopes, all eyes are now turned; for its preservation in the iron storm hurtling round it, all hearts are lifted in fervent supplication to the God of Battles. In Him and in you, General Beauregard, we put our trust,[10] feeling assured that like Richelieu, <u>in</u> <u>your</u> <u>lexicon,</u> <u>there</u> <u>is</u> <u>no</u> <u>such</u> <u>word</u> <u>as</u> '<u>fail</u>.'[11] We can bear to know that in a fiery translation the noble old city passed into immortality; we can proudly look upon the smouldering ruins that may attest the spot where once stood the nations grand pyre; and in the midst of our sorrow for its destruction, we can smile triumphantly and show the world that no footprint of the enemy ever marred its sacred ashes;—but we <u>could</u> <u>not</u> <u>bear</u> that Federal banners should flout the skies that once bent above hallowed Sumter[12] and Moultrie.[13] That a just and merciful God will spare you and Charleston to us, is the supplication which rises hourly, from the great throbbing heart of the nation; and to that passionate petition, stained with the tears, and broken by the sobs of countless widows and orphans, will <u>He</u> not lend his ear? Oh! that like the women of Harlem and Seyden and Maestrich, we of the Confederacy might render you some assistance during the siege, and by laboring day and night upon your fortifications, prove our devotion to the noblest Cause, for which warrior ever yet drew sword or historian assayed to panegyrize [*sic*] or epic bard to immortalize. The privilege enjoyed by our sisters in dead centuries, is not accorded to us; in my great anxiety, I can only pray for you, and for Charleston, and exclaim with Southey: "Onward in faith! and leave the rest to Heaven!"[14] Some time since, you did me the honor to send me a copy of your "Principles and Maxims of the Art of War."[15] I did not acknowledge its receipt, or answer your last most welcome and valued letter, because I feared to intrude upon your time, and was haunted by the dread of becoming troublesome to you. I have studied your compilation, and here beg to express my warm thanks for the great pleasure and profit which I have derived from its perusal. You must not smile at my vanity in presuming that I can understand it; for such incredulity on your part, would reflect as unfavorably upon the perspicuity of my Teacher, as upon the aptness of the pupil. Just now, my heart is weighed down with grief for my noble peerless friend, William Yancey.[16] His death at this crisis, is an irreparable loss to the country he loved so devotedly, and a bitter, bitter blow to me. None can fill his place in the Councils of this nation or the sad hearts of his sorrowing friends. Pardon I pray you, this long trespass on your precious time. As Pascal once observed on a similar occasion: "I have not time to make it shorter."[17] Thanking you most earnestly for your great kindness in remembering me at this crisis, when so much of anxiety must necessarily be yours, I am, with daily, heartfelt prayers for your happiness, safety, and success, in your fiery ordeal,—

Respectfully and gratefully

Augusta Evans

1. "Table Talk by the late Elia," *The Athenaeum,* Jan. 4, 1834.

2. "Ohe Jam satis est." "Hold, that is enough!" From Horace's *Satires* 1.5.12. This article has not been located. As Fidler points out, AEW published numerous articles anonymously in a variety of Southern newspapers (*A Biography,* 96).

3. According to his biographer, Lamb made this comment in 1817 during a conversation with friends about the merits of Pope's writing. AEW apparently did not realize that Lamb was speaking facetiously when he claimed to especially enjoy reading Pope's "compliments"—which were really jibes. Lamb said that Pope's compliments were "The finest that were ever paid by the wit of man. Each of them is worth an estate for life—nay, is an immortality" (quoted in E. V. Lucas, *The Life of Charles Lamb,* 4th ed. [London: Methuen, 1907], 384).

4. In the spring of 1863, Grant had laid siege to Vicksburg, Mississippi, a key to the Mississippi River, which the Confederates wanted to hold at all costs. Beauregard's battle plan called for Johnston to amass 30,000 troops in Tennessee and defeat the Federals first at Nashville and then at Vicksburg. Williams describes this plan as "impractical and impossible" and "a military fantasy" because Beauregard ignored the capabilities and resources of the Confederate army (*P. G. T. Beauregard,* 181–82). Needless to say, Beauregard's plan was not adopted.

5. "Whom Jupiter would destroy he first makes mad." Sophocles, *Antigone* c. 450 B.C.E. This quotation is paraphrased in English as the proverb, "whom the gods would destroy, they first make mad" (H. L. Mencken, *A New Dictionary of Quotations on Historical Principles from Ancient and Modern Sources,* [New York: A. A. Knopf, 1942], 732).

6. Vicksburg fell on July 4, 1863.

7. See AEW to Curry, July 15, 1863, note 25.

8. General Joseph Johnston (1807–1891) frequently quarreled with Davis over his ranking among the other generals and his and Davis's differences in military strategy. Undermined by his own peevishness and feuding with Davis, Johnston could not stop Grant from winning Vicksburg. He seems to have remained popular with the masses, however. Because of pressure from public opinion, Davis assigned Johnston to the Army of Tennessee in late 1863, after that army had suffered several losses.

9. A statue of Pallas Athena, the preservation of which was supposed to ensure the safety of Troy.

10. Beauregard had already repulsed a naval attack on Charleston on April 7, 1863. The Federals sent a fleet of ironclad ships to retake Fort Sumter, but they had to turn back under heavy Confederate fire: "The accuracy of the Confederate firing was amazing and a tribute to Beauregard's training" (Williams, *P. G. T. Beauregard,* 177).

11. "In the lexicon of youth, which fate reserves / For a bright manhood, there is no such word / As 'fail'" (Bulwer, *Richelieu,* act II, scene 2).

12. An island fortress in Charleston harbor.

13. Fort Moultrie is at the mouth of Charleston harbor.

14. Robert Southey, *The Retrospect,* line 176.

15. Beauregard's book was published in 1863 in Charleston by the firm of Evans and Cogswell. The full title: *Principles and Maxims of the Art of War, outpost services, general instructions for battle, reviews.* The book was written for "the use of general officers in the Department of South Carolina, Georgia, and Florida."

16. Alabama secessionist and member of the Confederate senate.

17. Blaise Pascal (1623–1662), French mathematician and physicist. "I have made this [letter] longer than usual, only because I have not had the time to make it shorter." *Lettres Provinciales* (1657), no. 16.

❧ ❧ ❧

40 / MS Alabama   Sept. 12th 1863

My dear Rachel—[1]

Since my return from Tennessee (whither I went to see my Brother who belongs to Bragg's army) I have been <u>constantly engaged</u>, or I should have replied more promptly to your two last letters. As regards the rumors you mentioned with reference to the corruption existing in official circles at Charleston, and <u>especially</u> the charge of negligence as a disciplinarian, which you preferred against Gen'l Beauregard,[2] I confess I was pained and astounded, but <u>did not for one instant</u> place credence in them. That you <u>heard</u>

them, I knew, but I felt equally well assured that the <u>on</u> <u>dit</u>[3] contained no truth. I have for Gen'l Beauregard, the <u>profoundest</u> <u>admiration</u>, <u>veneration</u> and respect; I regard him and Gen'l Johnston as the <u>ablest</u> <u>strategists</u> and Gen'ls in the Confederacy; and as men whose purity, whose nobility of soul, would frown down every species of corruption which dared show its shameless face in their departments. I was on the eve of writing to Gen'l Beauregard and acquainting him with the injurious reports which you said were in circulation concerning himself and Staff, for I felt it <u>my</u> <u>duty</u> to <u>do</u> <u>so</u>, though of course <u>your</u> <u>name</u> would never have been mentioned, in the matter. But just before I would have written, your second letter arrived, requesting me to <u>keep</u> <u>silent</u> which I accordingly did. I have not alluded to the matter at all. Do you know Genl Jordan, and how came he to write a refutation of the rumors? Tell me dear Rachel the cause of Gilmer's promotion from Lt Gl, to Major Genl, in order to rank Genl Ripley. Is not Ripley a <u>popular</u> and <u>efficient</u> <u>officer</u>; or does he happen to be no <u>pet</u> of <u>Davis</u>? God grant that Beauregard may hold Charleston successfully. If any human being <u>can</u>, <u>he</u> <u>will</u>. My book is being printed in Charleston, <u>now</u>, though published by <u>West</u> & <u>Johnston</u>.[4] I hope it will soon be ready. I am much hurried. Write soon, dear Rachel to

your affectionate AJE

PS. I have been and <u>still</u> <u>am</u> in <u>great</u> <u>sorrow</u> over the death of my <u>beloved</u> Cousin, John Jones.[5] Oh! it is a bitter blow to all of us, who loved him so dearly.

1. The following words were written on the envelope containing this letter: "Augusta Evans [*sic*] letters to Mama Miss Augusta's letters to Mamma—Rachel Lyons Heustis" Printed on the flap of the envelope was the following: Mrs. George Huntington Clark [Rosalie Heustis Clark, Rachel's daughter].

2. On April 7, 1863, Beauregard repulsed a Federal naval attack on Charleston. The city was saved and he was a hero. However, his repeated requests for additional men and supplies were denied, and in June the Federals attacked again, this time by land and sea. Expecting the Federals to attack James Island in order to gain an approach to Fort Sumter, Beauregard had concentrated most of his forces there. Instead, the Federals, led by General Quincy Gillmore, attacked and captured most of Morris Island, a victory that brought criticism for Beauregard. For the next two and a half months the Federals bombarded Battery Wagner and Fort Sumter and, for a brief time, even the city of Charleston. Daily bombardments created a morale problem for some troops, especially those at Battery Wagner, who were in desperate straits. Finally on September 7, the Confederates were forced to abandon Battery Wagner and the rest of Morris Island. Fort Sumter had been badly damaged. Still, the Federals, held at bay by the guns on James and Sullivan's Islands, could not penetrate Charleston harbor (Williams, *P. G. T. Beauregard*, 185–96). The situation was at a stalemate at the time of this letter.

3. Literally, "they say," or in other words, the rumor.

4. West and Johnston of Richmond, Virginia, published *Macaria,* but the firm of Walker, Evans, and Cogswell of Charleston, South Carolina, did the actual printing.

5. AEW's cousin Colonel John Jones accompanied her to New York City in 1859 when she sold her manuscript for *Beulah* to J. C. Derby. Jones, "a fiery young Southerner," had planned to throw a book at Derby's head if he had declined the manuscript (Fidler, *A Biography,* 68–69).

※ ※ ※

41 / MS Library of Congress (original)
Alabama (photocopy)
Duke (photocopy)   Mobile Oct 16th 1863

Hon. J. L. M. Curry
My dear friend—

Peccavi! peccavi![1] is the cry of my heart, as I revert to the date of your last kind and exceedingly welcome letter;—and reflect that the charge of neglect, or want of appreciation of its valued contents, may seem sanctioned by my long silence. Fain would I make the silvery accents of "<u>Lucille</u>"[2] plead my pardon: "Excuses are clothes which, when asked unawares, Good Breeding to scanty Necessity spares. <u>You</u> must have a whole wardrobe, no doubt!"[3] Believe me my dear Sir, I prize your friendship and your letters far too highly to be guilty of ingratitude, or of any delay, which is other than <u>unavoidable,</u> in expressing my thanks for both. I was in Chattanooga, visiting my Brother Howard (who belongs to Bragg's Army,)[4] when your last most acceptable letter arrived; and on my return, an accumulation of work at the Orphan Asylum, of which I am one of the Managers,—and a multiplicity of imperative engagements, absolutely debarred me from the pleasure of writing to you. Today I sweep everything else from my desk,—turn my back upon all other claims, and indulge myself in the luxury of a high communion with my distant, but ever-remembered and honored friend. Ah! that I could only talk to you, face to face, of many things in connection with our struggling country, which press heavily, <u>mournfully</u> upon my heart. <u>A la</u> North and Ettrick Shepherd in the immortal "Noctes -Ambrosianae,"[5] or the "Snuggery" in Auld Reikie[6]—permit me to nestle down into an armchair in your study, and to tell you in the first place;—how <u>grieved</u> and <u>astounded</u> I was, to hear of your defeat. That the fatuity of your quondam constituency could reach the extreme of sending Cruikshank to Congress,[7] I was utterly sceptical; and the disgraceful fact painfully attests how imperatively the great national ulcer,—Demagogism—demands prompt cauterization. Universal Suffrage is an effete theory of Utopian origin,[8] which might find acceptation in the shadowy realm of "Bensalem,"[9] but certainly not in this sternly real, rushing, <u>explosive</u>

19th century. The correction of the multitudinous evils which may be justly denominated as ramifications of its <u>practical</u> <u>abuse,</u> is one of the gravest problems which can engage the attention of our legislators; and anxiously do I wait for the hour, when the Peneus of political reform shall be turned through the Augean department of our system of Elective Franchise.[10] Though deeply pained at the result of the Congressional elections, I consoled myself with the hope of your obtaining a seat in the Senate; but the appointment of Mr. Jemison,[11] and the published letter of Mr. Clay,[12] announcing that he "would serve again if reelected," leads me and all your friends here, to fear very much that we are to be again disappointed. That Mr. Jemison should now occupy the position so nobly and gracefully filled by my lamented friend, Mr. Yancey, chagrins and annoys me beyond expression; for I happen to be personally acquainted with the former, and his political antecedents I confess I find it impossible to tolerate.[13] Moreover I know him sufficiently well to dread the <u>incorrigible</u> <u>obstinacy</u> which forms the substratum of his character, and <u>crops</u> <u>out</u> bold and flint-faced on every occasion. His honesty and sincerity of purpose I do not for an instant question, nor his orthodoxy in all that appertains to State-fiscal schemes, but his qualifications for the important and responsible post of Senator, I most certainly doubt. At this juncture we particularly require men of enlarged capacity of astuteness, <u>pre-science</u>, and enlightened Statesmanship, and Mr. Jemison's political bigotry excludes him peremptorily [*sic*] from such a category. Dismiss the thought that I am prompted by mere idle curiosity, and tell me, what are the probabilities of your superseding Mr. Clay?[14] Will you contest the election with him before the next session of the Legislature? I know that when you consented to become a candidate, you shared the general belief that the feebleness of his health, precluded the possibility of his again filling the position. Feeling the most earnest interest in your welfare, success, and usefulness I am especially anxious that you should share in the deliberations of our next Congress upon whose <u>nerve</u>, ability, energy, so much of the gravest import depends,—I can not forbear an expression of my anxiety; and as an Alabamian jealous of the Congressional <u>status</u> of our noble state, I trust you will at least <u>pardon</u> <u>me</u> if I have presumed upon your kindness in the inquiry propounded. How shall I sufficiently express my gratification at the undeservedly flattering reception, which you so kindly extended to my crude, waif-like suggestions, concerning, "Political & Social Quicksands," <u>versus</u> your selected theme of "Influence of African Slavery?"[15] Verily Mr. Curry! The delicacy of your unexpected compliment reminds me vividly of Lamb's <u>critique</u> on the value and elegance of Pope's encominous [*sic*]: "<u>Each</u> <u>of</u> <u>his</u> <u>compliments</u> <u>is</u> <u>worth</u> <u>an</u> <u>estate</u> <u>for</u> <u>life.</u>"[16] At what time do you contemplate delivering the Lecture in Richmond? And may I not anticipate the pleasure of receiving a copy? Would it be practicable for you to redeliver it in Mobile during the course of the winter? I shall not attempt to tell you, how rejoiced I should be to entertain the hope of hearing it. The Federal reverses in Georgia, and more recently in Louisiana have, I doubt not, <u>indefinitely postponed</u> the attack upon our little city; which we now regard as quite safe,[17]—at least for the present. I have cause to congratulate myself upon the acquisition of an extremely agreeable acquaintance, who is I believe a personal friend of yours; Hon. C. I. Villere of Louisiana; brother in law of Gen'l Beauregard. Temporarily a refugee from his home, he is now in Mobile; and told me during his last visit, that he was very apprehensive that the occupation of his state by the enemy, would prevent the Congressional elections, and consequently deprive Louisiana of all representation;—in which event, he would be thrown adrift. He allowed me the privilege of perusing a late letter from Gen'l Beauregard, which breathed the nobly defiant, hopeful, cheering, invincible spirit, which characterizes Beauregard, and stamps him one of the <u>World's Heroes</u>. All the fiery, magnetic ardor and stern unconquerable bravery of Aytoun's[18] grand old Cavaliers, throb in his great, great heart. Thank God! for the precious gift of such men as Beauregard and Johnston. Mr. Curry, I should like to know your estimate of Mill's celebrated work on "Political Economy."[19] I have recently finished that feast of "Labor," and flow of "Rents,"[20] and must confess I closed the second volume with a mingled sensation of great relief and bitter disappointment. Perhaps I am not sufficiently <u>au fait</u>[21] in the occult lore of Catallactics,[22] to fully appreciate its worth; but I can not avoid regarding Say's[23] great book as vastly superior. Mills is tediously, tiresomely, tormentingly prolix, and tautological; and his style is involved, confused, and unsatisfactory, in comparison with the perspicuous, sparkling, delightful diction of the greatest of French Political Economists. If my favoritism in the matter, is that of a tyro, tell me so roundly and unequivocally; for on all topics, I desire my criteria to be correct; and with reference to this one [obscured] I am afraid to trust my own judgment. There are several matters which I designed mentioning to you, but unfortunately for <u>me</u>, and most luckily for <u>your long-abused patience</u>, company comes, to your relief, and I am summoned from my letter. Accept many and most cordial thanks for your exceedingly kind invitation to your house. Should it ever be my good fortune to visit Talladega, rest assured I shall be most happy to accept the hospitality of your pleasant home, and make the acquaintance of your wife & children. Hoping that you will send me at least a few lines, <u>as early</u> as possible, I am my dear Sir,

Most sincerely your friend
Augusta Evans

1. "I have sinned." See AEW to Rachel Lyons, March 20, 1863.
2. A book-length verse drama by Edward Robert Bulwer-Lytton (1831–1891), a Victorian poet and a British diplomat. He wrote *Lucille* in 1860 under the pseudonym of Owen Meredith.

3. In the opening pages, Alfred asks his cousin John to help him think of an excuse to avoid visiting Lucille and returning her letters, as she had requested (Bulwer-Lytton, *Lucille,* 16). AEW misquoted the second line: "Good Breeding to Naked Necessity Spares. . . ."

4. AEW and her mother traveled to Tennessee to visit Howard Evans before the impending Battle of Chickamauga. In the middle of the night, a crowd of soldiers who had heard of AEW's arrival and wanted to hear her sing awakened them. Over her mother's objections, AEW "went out into the moonlight with her mass of hair streaming in the wind like a flying cloud" and sang "Maryland, My Maryland." Her song was followed by cheers and sobs from the soldiers and finally the "high, shrill, quavering, penetrating note of the rebel yell" (LaSalle Corbell Pickett, *Literary Hearth-stones of Dixie* [Philadelphia: J. B. Lippincott, 1912], 289–90).

The song "Maryland, My Maryland" was the "marching song" of the Confederacy and was written by James Randall, a friend of AEW, who once courted her sister Caroline (Fidler, *A Biography,* 99–100).

5. "Noctes Ambrosianae" literally means "nights of ambrosia." In Greek and Roman mythology, ambrosia was the food of the gods. Here the title refers to intellectual "food" or evenings of intellectual discussion. The "Noctes Ambrosianae" was a series of imaginary conversations that were published in *Blackwood's Edinburgh Magazine* from 1822 to 1835. The conversations, which sometimes took place in a tavern, were playful and witty and usually centered on a discussion of literary criticism. They sometimes involved a character named Christopher North and the Ettrick Shepherd, who spoke in Scottish dialect and presented an instinctive, nonintellectual response to literature. See J. H. Alexander, "Literary Criticism in the Later 'Noctes Ambrosianae,'" *The Yearbook of English Studies* 16 (1986), 17, 25.

6. "Auld Reikie" ("Old Edinburg") is a poem written in Scottish dialect by Robert Fergusson (1750–1773). The poem portrays daily life in Edinburg and includes a description of a social club, to which AEW is apparently referring (Fergusson, *The Poems of Robert Fergusson,* 2: 109–20; 276–80nn. 19, 33).

7. In 1863 Curry was defeated in his reelection bid to the Confederate congress. In Alabama, dissatisfaction with the progress of the war and with Davis's administration was a key issue in the election. According to the *Montgomery Advertiser,* whenever the Confederacy suffered a setback, the Whigs put up an obscure candidate for Congress with no record that those loyal to the Confederacy could attack. Marcus H. Cruikshank, an "obscure editor and a suspect reconstructionist," defeated Curry because of Curry's "identification with the Government" (quoted in Wilfred Buck Yearns, *The Confederate Congress* [Athens: University of Georgia Press, 1960], 55–56). Curry's biographer attributed his defeat to the Confederate losses at Vicksburg and Gettysburg; opposition in his district to secession; and the toll taken by inflation, high taxes, and the blockades (Rice, *J. L. M. Curry,* 44–45).

8. AEW feared the power of the masses. See AEW to Curry, July 15, 1863, note 15.

9. An imaginary utopian community that Francis Bacon describes in "The New Atlantis" (1623).

10. In Greek mythology, Augeas, the king of Elis, had a stable that had not been cleaned for many years. Hercules cleaned it in a day by diverting through it the rivers Alpheus and Peneus. Augean as an adjective means filthy or corrupt.

11. The Alabama legislature appointed Robert Jemison to replace AEW's friend William Yancey, who had recently died (Yearns, *The Confederate Congress,* 56).

12. Clement Claiborne Clay, an Alabama senator (Yearns 282).

13. Jemison actually continued Yancey's policies, although in a less flamboyant style. AEW's dislike of Jemison is perhaps due to the fact that he had opposed Alabama's immediate secession following Lincoln's election (Yearns 56, 236).

14. Clay fell into disfavor and was replaced in November 1863 not by Curry but by Richard W. Walker. Clay claimed he was defeated because he had voted against a pay raise for the Confederate soldiers, but historians blame his defeat on his support of President Davis (Yearns 56).

15. See AEW to Curry, July 15, 1863.

16. See AEW to Beauregard, August 19, 1863, note 3.

17. Mobile Bay fell to the Federals in 1864, but the city itself was not conquered until the end of the war, a few days after Lee's surrender.

18. William Edmondstoune Aytoun (1813–1865), a Scottish writer known for his ballads and other works. His *Lays of the Scottish Cavaliers* (1848) celebrates the gallantry and courage of the Scottish soldiers who fought against the British from the sixteenth to the eighteenth centuries.

19. John Stuart Mill (1806–1873), an English economist, philosopher, and reformer, wrote *The Principles of Political Economy* (6 volumes) in 1848. His basic theories were that the value of goods is based on the amount of labor and time needed to produce them, that a country's production is limited by how much land it has, and that the standard of living can improve only when population growth is controlled.

20. "Of Labour as an Agent of Production" and "Of Unproductive Labor" are chapters 2 and 3 of volume 1, and "Of Rent" is chapter 16 of volume 2, of Mill's book.

21. in the know, informed

22. That part of political economics that deals with commercial exchanges or the exchange of equity.

23. Jean-Baptiste Say (1767–1832), a French economist who supported the theories of Adam Smith. Say is best known for his Law of Markets, which states "A supply of goods generates a demand for the goods." Understanding this principle, Say thought, would eliminate economic depressions and unemployment.

❧ ❧ ❧

42 / MS Mobile Museum   Mobile Nov' 14th 1863

General Beauregard—

I am frequently reminded of the words of Horace Walpole to Gen'l Conway: "My friend, when the press teems with tributes of praise, and your name is proudly throned on the lips of a grateful and admiring nation, have you the time or the patience to listen to my feeble but heartfelt congratulations;—or can you peruse with any interest, my dull, and merely friendly letters?"[1] When your welcome and valued letters arrive, I often think that perhaps the best, and most acceptable proof of my appreciation of your kindness, would be my silence; or failure to annoy you with an answer. But alas! cacoethes scribendi![2] my anxiety to express my thanks, triumphs over my judicious and self-sacrificing resolutions,—and I find myself nolens volens[3] inflicting a letter of acknowledgment upon you. The celebrated English jeu d'espirit,[4]— "Rejected Addresses,"—is destined to pale in future ages, before the mournful monument of Administrative obtuseness, which the "Rejected Campaigns" of the Revolution will furnish for your historic archives. As I read the plan of concentration,[5] which you forwarded to Gen'l Bragg, and a copy of which, you did me the honor to enclose in your last highly-prized letter, I felt more than ever perplexed for a solution of the great mystery of Davisonian stupidity, or obstinacy, or je ne sais quoi.[6] Surely the President must desire the triumph of our arms; and yet his course with reference to the conduct of military affairs, has been fatuitously [sic] suicidal. Movement whose expediency can be realized and appreciated by the veriest tyro, (vide your humble correspondent) and which you have faithfully and persistently impressed upon him,—he seems utterly incapable of comprehending; or is vindictive enough to be willing to sacrifice irremediably the interests of the Confederacy,—rather than accord you the glory of saving our holy cause, by your prescience and strategy. I confess, this is a Sphinx, of which I can not prove the Oedipus.[7] It seems verily, that the ancient jealousy of Hanno towards the Barcan family,[8] has revived at Richmond, in all its dire bitterness;—that the days of Demosthenes[9]—(Heaven save the mark!) and Phocion[10] had dawned again. I indulge the hope however, that during his recent visit to Charleston, you succeeded in convincing the President of the absolute necessity of executing your oft-rejected plan, for the defence of Georgia, and the redemption of Tennessee & Kentucky.[11] Should this hope be doomed to disappointment, God only knows how we are to maintain ourselves, and subsist our armies. Cut off from Texas and Tennessee, the great granaries of the Confederacy, with a constantly narrowing circle of territory whence to draw our supplies,— the feasibility of properly provisioning our troops, becomes a question of grave importance. A spirit of reckless speculation broods cormorant-like over every department of civil and military affairs; and the disaffection induced in the army, by these gigantic evils, threatens consequences the most serious. In view of the existing difficulties, and impending campaigns in Virginia and Northern Georgia, does it not impress you as expedient that the next session of Congress should repeal the Substitute statute,[12] as promptly as possible? Also, that stern measures should immediately be taken, to enforce the order, whereby Regiments & indeed <u>Brigades</u> of <u>young</u> <u>athletic</u> bread & butter Captains & Majors will be driven from the ignominious shelter of Commissary and Quartermaster Dep'ts, into the thin ranks of our noble army? To meet the new levies of the enemy, which will be ready to take the field early next spring, what other method of strengthening our needy armies, suggests itself to you? This critical juncture is not the time for despondency on the part of the masses at home, nor for the chronic <u>vis</u> <u>inertiae</u>,[13] the wonted <u>laissez</u> <u>nous</u> <u>faire</u> of our Government; but calls for the most vigorous exertions, the most herculean [*sic*] energy, which a brave people ever manifested. From the mouldering and dusty crypts of Rome, comes a sepulchral voice, to stir our pulses and our stagnant powers. Doubtless you remember that during the first Punic War,[14] when the Carthagenian [*sic*] armaments darkened the blue bosom of the Mediterranean, and hovered devouringly around every Levantine[15] port, threatening the Roman Empire with destruction; a wrecked African galley drifted upon the coast of Italy. Duilius the Consul,[16] seized it as a model; the decree went forth, that Rome would have a navy, and cope with Carthage on the seas. No governmental sluggards,—no paralyzing Mallory[17] (Malheureux?)[18] barred the work; every harbor of Italy rang with the hammers of mechanics, and <u>in three months</u> a Romish armament bore its eagles proudly across the Mediterranean,—crushed the maritime power of its ancient rival, and verified the famous boast of latter-day Martin Harpertzoon Tromp.[19] With similar <u>determination</u> on the part of government and people, what might <u>we</u> not accomplish for our armies, during the ensuing winter? Upon two measures depends in great degree the salvation of our beloved country. First, the reinforcement of the troops now in the field; and secondly, the vigorous and immediate correction of our vitiated currency, which has fallen almost to the old Continental standard of worthlessness.[20] From this paper plethora ramify countless evils and abuses, which demand the wisest legislation, and most rigid reform in our financial system. But unfortunately that department of political economy, denominated "<u>catallactics</u>,[21] seems to have been completely ignored by those to whom it should have specially commended itself, for earnest consideration. Oh! for one hour of <u>Sully</u>![22] or <u>Colbert</u>![23] or Necker.[24] Ere this, you have doubtless learned the discontent among the subordinate officers of Gen'l Bragg's army;[25] and of the withdrawal of Cheatham,[26] which I very much fear, will operate disastrously upon the Tennessee troops in Bragg's command. He wields a powerful influence over them, and his absence, in conjunction with their proximity to their invaded homes, will almost offer a premium for desertion. At all times deplorable, these dissensions in the western army are peculiarly unfortunate at this crisis, when entire harmony can alone insure our success. A Revolutionary witticism here suggests itself; "We must be unanimous," said Hancock on the occasion of signing the Declaration of Independence; "There must be no pulling different ways." "Yes, we must all hang together, or most assuredly we shall hang separately," answered Franklin. Since the subordinate commanders are so extremely averse to serving under Gen'l Bragg,—the good of the cause which is paramount to all personal considerations, demands that Gen'l Bragg should be removed to some other field of operations, where his usefulness will not be marred by the disaffection and want of confidence manifested by his Lieutenants. Do not, I beg of you, General Beauregard, suppose me the advocate of individual ostracism, because of popular clamor. But whatever Gen'l Bragg's abilities as a military leader may be, he has certainly been singularly unsuccessful from the moment he assumed command of Tupelo; and since after nearly 16 months trial, he fails to inspire confidence in his army, his officers, and his country, it seems to me that he should be sent to some other department; and his present command, (the most important in the Confederacy) entrusted either to your Sir, or to Gen'l Johnston. Personally, I have no prejudice against Gen'l Bragg; I believe that he is a pure patriot, exerting himself to the utmost, to accomplish the triumph of his noble army; but I confess, a study of his career since he first entered Tennessee, leads me to the conviction that the success of our cause would be promoted by his removal. Oh! if you, or Gen'l Johnston could only take command at Chattanooga! what a shout would go up to heaven! what a fervent thank God! would leap from every anxious heart. Yesterday in a conversation with Gen'l Polk,[27] he informed me that twice since the failure of the Kentucky campaign[28] he had earnestly urged upon Mr Davis, a plan exceedingly similar (as he described it) to that which you long ago proposed. When I remarked the priority of your suggestion, he expressed very great gratification at hearing that his views corresponded with yours, and were sanctioned by your "superior strategic wisdom." He spoke sadly, rather than bitterly, of his separation from his old Corps, to which he seems warmly attached. Permit me to thank you most sincerely for your kind letter, and also for the copy of your withering stricture upon the Munchausen[29] circulars of Seward[30] and Gilmore.[31] Northern mendacity often recalls the pithy dictum of Dean Swift: "Satan is generally regarded as the Father of Lies, but like other great inventors, he seems to have lost much of his reputation by the continual improvements that have been made upon him."[32] Ah Gen'l Beauregard! I almost envy you the proud exultation with which you must look day after day, upon grand and unconquerable Sumter,—battle-scarred and glory-crowned! With an immortal halo circling its crumbling parapets, and stern deathless defiance graven on its sacred ruins. Not the world-renowned Mound of Marathon[33] bears a record more sublime, than that which future ages will peruse in the falling debris of Sumter; whence an invincible people flung their hallowed Banner of the Cross to the Atlantic breeze,—signaling via victis.[34] Among the officers of your engineer corps, I have a heroic young cousin, Cap't John H. Howard[35] of Georgia, whom you may possibly have noticed; though he is too modest to thrust himself upon your attention. He is now at Fort Johnston, and writes to his family: "I would rather belong to the garrison here, than be a Brigadier General anywhere else, than in Charleston." Such is the trust your officers repose in you. Would to heaven! that the Army of Tennessee[36] furnished a parallel. Ever since you left Mobile for Charleston, I have been searching for suitable materials to make a "comforter" or "neck-tie" for you, which would protect your throat from the humid atmosphere of the seabord. After many unavailing efforts, I am convinced there is <u>nothing</u> <u>really</u> <u>pretty</u> to be found in the Confederacy; but as I hear you are still suffering with <u>your</u> <u>throat</u>, I have knitted the accompanying scarf, of the best worsted I could possibly obtain. It <u>is</u> <u>not</u> <u>as</u> <u>handsome</u> as I could wish it, nor of the colors which I should have preferred and selected, had it been practicable to procure them; but I hope Sir, that you will accept and wear it during <u>inclement</u> weather, as a very slight and inadequate token of my profound esteem, and <u>earnest</u> <u>gratitude</u> for the friendly remembrance with which you have honored me. I made it shorter than usual, so as to be worn inside your coat; (for it is not pretty enough to venture among your stars) and I <u>trust</u> that the stringency of the blockade, will plead in extenuation of its <u>want</u> of <u>beauty</u>. I am well aware that <u>many</u> <u>physicians</u> entertain a sublime contempt for all such feminine suggestions and inventions, but ask <u>Dr</u> <u>Brodie</u>, for my sake, <u>please</u> <u>not to give verdict</u> against my little protectionist, or advise you not to wear it. Present my respects to him, and to <u>Captain</u> Beauregard,[37] whose recent visit, I recall with pleasure, and believe me, General Beauregard—

> Most respectfully
> Your sincere friend
> A.J.Evans

1. Horace Walpole (1717–1797), English letter writer, historian, and amateur architect, is now remembered mainly for his letters. General Henry Seymour Conway was one of his correspondents and closest friend. Also see AEW to General Beauregard, September 23, 1862.

2. an incurable itch to write!

3. not wanting / wanting [to inflict]

4. game of wit

5. Beauregard's plan of concentration, based on the strategies of masters such as Napoleon and Jomini, consisted merely in engaging the enemy with a larger number of troops than he had. This principle—the key to all of Beauregard's strategies—caused frequent disagreements between him and President Davis. Beauregard, unlike Davis, would willingly sacrifice cities and states to amass concentrated armies. Beauregard's overall strategies were generally sound, but the government usually rejected

his battle plans. Beauregard's weakness was in the specifics: he frequently devised unrealistic plans that looked good in theory but that were beyond the capability of the Confederate army to execute (Williams, *P. G. T. Beauregard,* 93–94). In planning the Battle of Manassas, for example, Beauregard planned for Johnston to reinforce him with 20,000 men, conveniently ignoring the fact that Johnston had only 11,000 troops (74). AEW, however, consistently supported her friend Beauregard and sided with him in all his disagreements with other officers and his superiors.

6. I don't know what.

7. According to ancient Greek legend, the Sphinx, with the body of a lion and the head of a woman, killed anyone who could not solve her riddle: "What walks on four feet in the morning, on two at noon, and on three in the evening?" Only Oedipus could defeat the Sphinx by giving the correct answer: Man—crawling as an infant, walking erect as an adult, and walking with a cane as an elder.

8. Hanno the Great of Carthage was a bitter enemy of the Barcid family of Hamilcar and Hannibal in the third century B.C.E.

9. Demosthenes (384–322 B.C.E.), a great Athenian orator who argued that Athens must oppose the growing power of King Philip II of Macedon.

10. Phocion (c.402–318 B.C.E.), Athenian general and politician who argued against Demosthenes on the Macedon issue and urged Athens to cooperate with Philip II.

11. AEW is probably referring to a plan that Beauregard presented first to General Bragg and then to Davis in October 1863. Bragg had bottled up the Federal army at Chattanooga but had, nevertheless, not been able to defeat them. Beauregard proposed that Bragg be reinforced with 35,000 troops from Lee's army in Virginia and other sources. Bragg could then drive the Federals out of Tennessee, after which he could go to Lee's aid in Virginia. Davis liked Beauregard's plan but refused to weaken Lee's army by removing 35,000 troops for Bragg. Davis said he would try to find the reinforcements from another source but never did. Thus, the Confederates lost their last chance to regain the Tennessee line (Williams, *P. G. T. Beauregard,* 197–98).

12. The substitute statute allowed a man to avoid military service by paying a substitute to go in his place. (The substitute had to be someone not subject to conscription.) Many of the substitutes were ne'er-do-wells who made terrible soldiers and frequently deserted only to be paid to reenlist for someone new. The substitute statute also undermined morale in the Confederate army by encouraging the belief that this was "a rich man's war and a poor man's fight." On December 28, 1863, the Confederate congress abolished the substitute statute (Coulter, *Confederate States of America,* 318–19).

13. inability to act

14. The First Punic War (264–242 B.C.E.) was the first of three wars between ancient Rome and Carthage for the control of the Mediterranean Sea.

15. Relating to the countries bordering the east Mediterranean.

16. Gaius Duilius was the commander of a fleet of Roman ships that defeated a Carthaginian force off Mylae (in Sicily) to win Rome's first naval victory.

17. Stephen Russell Mallory (c. 1813–1873), the Confederate secretary of the navy. Since the Confederate navy suffered a serious shortage of ships and supplies, Mallory

encouraged the government to look toward other areas, such as experiments with naval torpedoes and submarines, as ways to gain an advantage.

18. The French word for unlucky or unsuccessful. Here, of course, a play on Mallory's name.

19. Maarten Harpertszoon Tromp (1598–1653), the Dutch admiral who defeated first the Spanish and then the English fleet and obtained control of the English Channel in 1652.

20. Since most of the capital of the Confederacy was invested in slaves and land, the government did not have an adequate financial structure to support the war. It hesitated to impose new taxes for fear of losing public support for the war. Loans (bonds) raised some money but not nearly enough. The only remaining alternative was to print paper money, a decision which created a "dizzying spiral of inflation that could not be stopped" (McPherson, *The Civil War and Reconstruction,* 198–99). For example, in Richmond in October 1863, a barrel of flour cost $70.00, an exorbitant price. Four months later, flour was $250.00 a barrel (377).

21. A branch of the political economy dealing with commercial exchanges.

22. Maximilien de Bethune, the duke of Sully (1560–1641). As finance minister under France's Henry IV, Sully stabilized the country financially.

23. Jean-Baptiste Colbert (1619–1683), the finance minister under Louis XIV and the first controller general of France. He did much to improve France economically.

24. Jacques Necker (1732–1804), director general of finances under King Louis XVI. He introduced efficient management and fair taxation in the French government.

25. Although Bragg had defeated the Federals at Chickamauga in Tennessee, he and his officers blamed each other for not obtaining more decisive results. Some of Bragg's officers wrote President Davis that Bragg was unfit for command and should be removed. Davis's response was to visit Bragg's headquarters and ask the generals— in Bragg's presence—to state their opinion of their commander. Several of them spoke up and called for Bragg's removal. Davis, however, never acted on their demands (Williams, *P. G. T. Beauregard,* 198). Roland lists Davis's decision to leave Bragg in command at Chattanooga (Tennessee) as one of the five or six most serious mistakes that either side committed during the course of the war (*An American Iliad,* 189).

26. Major General Benjamin F. Cheatham was sent to Georgia to help fortify Atlanta. He took part in the Battle of Atlanta a few months later (Roland 189).

27. General Polk served under Bragg in Tennessee and, like General Hardee, was very critical of Bragg's performance as commander (Roland 151).

28. See AEW to Beauregard, April 29, 1863.

29. Baron Munchausen was a character in the novel *The Adventures of Baron Munchausen* by Rudolf Erich Raspe. Munchausen told far-fetched, fabricated stories about his travels.

30. William Henry Seward (1801–1872), secretary of state under both Lincoln and Johnson.

31. This could possibly be James R. Gilmore, a freelance journalist who wrote for Northern newspapers.

32. Jonathan Swift, *The Examiner,* number 14.

33. The Battle of Marathon occurred in 490 B.C.E. and resulted in a victory by the outnumbered Athenians over the Persians. When the Athenians buried their dead, they marked the graves with a high mound.

34. woe unto the conquered

35. AEW was related to the Howards through her mother's side of the family.

36. General Bragg's army.

37. Captain Rene T. Beauregard was General Beauregard's older son.

꙳ꙫ ꙳ꙫ ꙳ꙫ

43 / MS Alabama   Mobile Nov' 21st 1863

My dear Rachel—

Long, long ago, I supposed my new book would have been issued, but the removal of Evans & Cogswell from Charleston to Columbia, has necessarily delayed it.[1] Unforseen [*sic*] difficulties have also arisen, with reference to punctuation, and to the proof-reading. I find that in order to have the <u>MS correctly printed</u> I shall have to revise the proof sheets myself, and it will not be practicable for me to do so, without being in Columbia. As I am very fastidious concerning the typography of my books, I am afraid to trust the proof to any one else. Consequently, I write to ask if you will please try to obtain board for me in some private family for <u>three</u> <u>weeks</u> or a <u>month</u>.[2] I should dislike to be at the hotel, because being alone, such a position would not be pleasant, but I should like a private house, or a private <u>boarding</u> <u>house</u>. Will you inquire for me, and let me know, the result. I can not tell exactly when Evans & Cogswell will be ready to furnish my proof, but I <u>hope</u>, early in December, or it may be, not until January.[3] The delay is very provoking, for the <u>MS</u> has been in the hands of the publishers, ever since the <u>first</u> <u>of June</u>. I assure you dear Rachel, the prospect of seeing you, is now a delightful anticipation. Please make inquiries for me, and let me hear from you. Pardon my haste dear friend, I am <u>expecting</u> <u>company</u>, and have <u>no</u> <u>time</u> for <u>more</u>.

Most affectionately yours
A.J.Evans

1. With Charleston under constant threat of attack, the firm of Walker, Evans, and Cogswell relocated to Columbia, South Carolina, for safety. The move delayed the publication of *Macaria.*

2. Rachel lived in Columbia.

3. Scholars dispute *Macaria's* publication date. Fidler (*A Biography,* 1951) and Hubbell (*The South in American Literature,* 1954) claim it was published in 1863. However, more recent scholars (such as Drew Gilpin Faust in her introduction to the 1992 edition of *Macaria* [Baton Rouge: Louisiana State University Press]) seem to agree that *Macaria* was first published in 1864.

❧ ❧ ❧

44 / MS Mobile Museum   Columbia South Carolina
Dec' 14th 1863

General Beauregard

Availing myself of the courtesy of Captain Mordecai[1] who leaves immediately for Charleston, I hasten to express my great gratification at the receipt
of your last most valued letter; containing papers, and photographs of Fort
Sumter,—for all of which, please accept my earnest gratitude. Among many
precious souvenirs of these dark days of blood and horror, none are more
highly prized, and carefully preserved, than the pen,[2] the reports, the letters,
and the photographs which you have done me the honor to send me. Having read with great interest the report relative to the defects of our Confederate gun-boats, I was powerfully tempted to submit it to Admiral Buchanan's
perusal; hoping that your valuable suggestions might materially aid him in
improving the formidable vessels now in course of construction at Mobile;[3]
but conscious of my ignorance of the minutiae of military etiquette in such
matters, I felt unauthorized to do so, without first obtaining your sanction.
Before I could ask your permission to lay the papers before him, I was called
to this city, upon business concerning my new book,[4] which has been in the
hands of the publishers, West & Johnston, since last June. Mes'srs [*sic*] Evans &
Cogswell were selected as the printers, and about 50 pages had been "worked
off," when the bombardment of Charleston, necessitated the removal of the
printing presses to Columbia; where the book has remained in statu quo [*sic*],
until this week. A vexed question with reference to punctuation, and my
anxiety that the proof sheets should be correctly ready, forced me to come to
Columbia for a few days at least. Hearing that Ferguson's Battery was captured in the recent disastrous conflicts around Chickamauga, I sympathized
with you in your great anxiety concerning your son,[5] and hope most
earnestly that he escaped uninjured, and has been spared to you. In all the
views contained in your last welcome letter; I concur entirely, and there are
many topics of absorbing interest, relative to which, I should like to obtain
your opinion, but unfortunately for me, I have not the requisite leisure to
elaborate them, and must at present confine myself to a hasty and inadequate
expression of my heartfelt thanks, for all your flattering kindness and remembrance. Perils and difficulties seem thickening around our devoted young
land, and even our stoutest-hearted heroes sometimes tremble, in peering
through the gloom which like fabled Scandinavic-Ragnarok,[6] now draws its
dense folds across our sunny sky; but thank God! Justice reigns supreme,
beyond the stormy realm of our war-torn- [*sic*], battle-scarred country, and so
surely as Jehovah rules us:—"Truth crushed to earth will rise again,—The
eternal years of God are hers!"[7] In times such as these, the grand words of

Wallenstein[8] ring in my ears like a bugle's blast:—"In the night only, Friedland's stars can beam!"[9] And when I hear drooping and dejected spirits moaning over the desolation and "probable subjugation" of our beloved country, the silvery chime of George Herbert floats softly down the corridors of the past—"Faint not! For all may have, if they dare choose, a <u>glorious</u> <u>life</u>, or <u>grave</u>."[10] Amid the sombre shadows that drape the nation, the halo gleams imperishably around the ramparts of Charleston, its steady light shines like a benediction on sister states; and watching that precious beacon which Pharoslike,[11] you have kindled upon Sumter,[12] the people exclaim "<u>nil</u> <u>desperandum</u>!"[13] nerve themselves anew,—and murmur: "God bless Beauregard! and preserve him and Charleston to us." Echoing the nation's prayer for your welfare, safety and happiness I remain

Gratefully and sincerely
Your friend
Augusta J. Evans

Gen'l G. T. Beauregard
Charleston South Carolina

1. The Mordecais were a prominent family in Mobile at this time (Amos, *Cotton City*, 138), so Captain Mordecai might well be someone that AEW knows from home.

2. In 1862, Beauregard sent AEW his personal writing pen as a gesture of appreciation for her work as a volunteer nurse. See AEW to Beauregard, August 4, 1862.

3. Admiral Buchanan supervised the building of the ironclad *Tennessee* and later was her commander in the Battle of Mobile Bay, August 5, 1864, a defeat for the Confederates.

4. The book referred to is *Macaria,* which AEW worked on from June 1862 to March 1863. The publishers were West and Johnson of Richmond, Virginia, but the printing was done in Columbia, South Carolina. Due to a shortage of materials during the war, the novel was printed on coarse brown wrapping paper with wallpaper to cover the binding (Fidler, *A Biography,* 106). AEW sent one of these copies on a blockade-runner to J. C. Derby, her publisher in New York City, who arranged for the novel to be published in the North by J. B. Lippincott. When Derby heard that an unscrupulous publisher, Michael Doolady, had obtained a copy of the novel and planned to publish it without paying royalties to the author, Derby and Lippincott pressured Doolady into paying AEW royalties, which Derby held in trust for her until after the war (J. C. Derby, *Fifty Years among Authors, Books, and Publishers* [New York: G. W. Carleton, 1884], 392–94).

5. Both of Beauregard's sons survived the war (Williams, *P. G. T. Beauregard,* 323).

6. Ragnarok, according to Scandinavian myth, is the destruction of the gods and all creation in a final battle against the powers of evil.

7. William Cullen Bryant, "The Battlefield," stanza 9.

8. Albrecht Wenzel Eusebius von Wallenstein (1583–1634), an Austrian general in the Thirty Years' War. He later achieved great power and wealth under Emperor Ferdinard II, who gave him the title prince of Friedland. Ferdinand later became convinced that Wallenstein was a traitor and ordered him to be captured dead or alive. Wallenstein was murdered on February 25, 1634.

9. From *The Death of Wallenstein,* a tragedy by Friedlich Schiller, which was first performed in Germany in 1798. This line, from act III, scene X, is spoken by Wallenstein after learning that the emperor has sentenced him to death and that his regiments have deserted him. Also see AEW to Curry, December 20, 1862.

10. From *The Temple. The Church Porch,* by George Herbert (1593–1632).

11. See AEW to Victor, June 6, 1860, note 7.

12. It was Beauregard who ordered the first shots fired on Fort Sumter on April 12, 1861, an act which precipitated the Civil War. Moreover, Beauregard had twice defended Charleston from Federal attacks. See AEW to Rachel Lyons, September 12, 1863.

13. no reason to despair!

৯৻ ৯৻ ৯৻

45 / MS Library of Congress (original)
Alabama (photocopy)
Duke (photocopy)   Mobile, Jan. 27, 1864

Hon. J. L. M. Curry,
My honored friend,

Your exceedingly kind and welcome letter of the 14th reached me several days since, and I snatch the very earliest leisure half-hour to express my earnest thanks, and acknowledge its receipt. I shall not attempt to tell you how extremely gratified I am to know that my humble and crude suggestion found favor in your eyes, and that your Richmond audience manifested so cordial and flattering an appreciation of the lecture in whose success I felt scarcely less interest than yourself.[1] Forgive me if I ask, why should you withhold it from publication? The great truths embodied are surely worthy of crystallization in print, and incalculable good might result from their circulation, especially at this juncture, when public opinion seems drifting towards certain restrictions which you recommend. Buckle's[2] social and political cycles seem to some extent reproduced in the curious phases of popular opinion which now present themselves to any earnest observer. That all extremes necessitate reform is axiomatic in the science of government, and you have doubtless remarked that the most radical of quondam Jacobinical[3]—democrats are at present gravitating rapidly toward centralization, consolidation, are quite ready to anathemate [*sic*] Jefferson as the prince of sophists, and

almost prepared to yield allegiance to the dicta[4] of Hamilton.[5] Strange but
immemorial paradox! Mankind plunge into cruel wars, into internecine conflicts, in defence of principles, which during the revolution they permit to
slip through their fingers. Affrighted by the shadow of Absolutism and Abolitionism that brooded over Washington, the men of the South flew to arms;
but three years of "struggling" have singularly modified their opinions; and I
have been pained and astonished to find how many are now willing to glide
unhesitatingly into a dictatorship, a military depotism [sic],—even into a state
of colonial dependence, with gradual emancipation as a condition of foreign
intervention and protection. The original <u>casus</u> <u>belli</u>[6] has been lost sight of;
hatred of Lincoln, not love of our liberties, principles and institutions now
actuates our masses. However humiliating, this is an indisputable phase of
popular opinion, which our leaders should gravely ponder, and resolutely
oppose; and because you wield an influence so extensive, I believe that the
circulating of your lecture would be productive of great good. Discouraged
by the palpable blunders of the Administration, and the reverses superin-
duced, the people are rocking from their former firm faith in democratic
republicanism. The deplorable sequence of such infatuation, it requires
no extraordinary prescience to delineate;—tyranny, insurrection, change of
dynasty, renewed oppression, anarchy, and final disintegration of the Confederacy.[7] "Eternal vigilance" is indeed the price of Liberty! In Peace the sacred
and cherished rights of a nation are not endangered, for every whistling
happy citizen considers himself one of the band of responsible custodians,
and at the first alarm of aggression, the inroad is promptly repelled; but in the
stormy hours of revolution when the invader thunders along the frontiers,
cravens and traitors at home, lay sacreligious [sic] hands upon the palladium.[8]
Mutations of public feeling in times like these, are swift as the march of
armies, or the rush of battle and those who carefully watch the popular pulse,
counting its feverish throbs, have no leisure to fritter, to dream, or to wran-
gle away. Truely comprehending all this, do you not owe it to your country,
your principles, and your race, to diligently disseminate antidote for poison
so wide-spread? If you have inexorably resolved not to publish, will you not
at least allow me the pleasure of perusing your MS? It is scarcely problemati-
cal that the scheme of enormous taxation contemplated by Congress will
create immense dissatisfaction. Already ominous mutterings are audible, and
the spectre of individual bankruptcy haunts the land.[9] It is a curious anthro-
pological fact that men will give their sons, nay even their own bodies to
defend their homes; but ask for their property in maintenance of the conflict,
and "noli me tangere"[10] is the indignant cry. They will lay down their lives if
need be, to protect their interests, but can not appreciate the expediency or

economy of sacrificing possessions to preserve life and principles. As I am not au fait[11] in fiscal matters, I shall not presume to discuss the plans proposed, but I should suppose that some scheme similar to the real-estate banks of New-York [*sic*] might be feasible and remedial. Better that the Confederate government should own the entire real estate of the country, and redeem its currency, than suffer it to fall into the hands of Lincoln's hordes, and be parcelled out to European paupers, by a "Homestead Bill"[12] more iniquitous than the one suggested years ago by black republicans. My honored friend, I can not adequately express my regret and chagrin at the result of our State elections. I should blush for Alabama, were I not aware that her noblest, purest and most patriotic sons are breasting the storm of invasion along our borders, and that the legislature and the polls are controlled by sordid, intriguing, shallow-brained "cooperation" reconstructionists. With reference to your defeat,[13] I have heard a universal expression of sorrow and mortification and in this section it is regarded as a disgrace to the state. Yesterday Admiral Buchannan [*sic*] came out and spent the evening with me, and believe me Sir, you have in him a warm admirer and devoted friend. In recapitulating the obstacles which he was forced to overcome in constructing our very formidable gun-boat—the Tennessee, he desired me to inform you that he had made 650 applications to the Dept. at Richmond, for sailors in the army, who should be detached for naval service; and that after repeated appeals during the past twelve months, he had not yet received twenty men. He assured me that his small fleet of gun-boats in this harbor, had not more than half their quota of men, from the fact that applications for transfer were disregarded by the authorities in Richmond. The Admiral also adverted freely to the singular oversight of our Government in neglecting to furnish "prize-money"— that wonderful incentive to deeds of heroism in naval combat. He seems to attach great importance to it, and has I believe, made several unavailing attempts to convince Congress of the expediency of making such provision. The most astonishing lethargy reigns in official circles, with reference to our Naval as well as Army affairs, and Mr. Mallory[14] seems a chronic case of hopeless vis inertia.[15] God grant that Administrative "laissez nous faire" may not wreck us finally! Oh! for three months of the Consullate [*sic*] of Duilius![16] We have been anxiously watching for the completion of the Tennessee, hoping that under the command of our daring Admiral, brilliant results would gladden our hearts; consequently we regard with some impatience the procrastination of the Government in providing crew and guns. The Admiral requested me to present his kindest regards and best wishes to you Sir, and joins me in the hope that ere long we shall have the pleasure of seeing you in Mobile. Should you obtain a Staff appointment, pray contrive to be stationed near our Gulf city.[17] Mr. Curry, your letter contained a very singular expression about "fearing to annoy me." If you could realize how much enjoyment I derive from your letters, I feel assured you would not with-hold them, and thus curtail my sources of happiness. Please present my friendly remembrances to Mr. Villere and believe me Sir——

Most sincerely your friend,
Augusta J. Evans

1. See AEW to Curry, July 15, 1863, note 3.

2. Henry Thomas Buckle (1821–1862), an English historian who developed the theory that a country's character is determined by the environmental influences of geography, climate, soil, and food.

3. During the French Revolution of 1789, the Jacobins were a radical, political group espousing egalitarianism.

4. words, speeches

5. Alexander Hamilton (c. 1755–1804), a political leader (and the first secretary of the treasury) who played an influential role in getting the U.S. Constitution ratified. He supported a strong central government.

6. cause of war

7. Both AEW and Curry distrusted the power of the masses. See AEW to Curry, July 15, 1863, note 15.

8. A statue of Pallas Athena, the preservation of which was believed to ensure the safety of Troy.

9. With most of its capital tied up in land and slaves, the South was simply not able to finance the war. At first the Confederate congress tried to avoid levying taxes on its people for fear of weakening civilian morale and instead relied on bonds to raise money. When this method proved inadequate, the government turned to printing paper money, a decision that led to runaway inflation. When the government finally passed a comprehensive tax bill in 1863, it was ineffective and difficult to enforce. McPherson cites these financial problems as a major cause of the South's defeat (*The Civil War and Reconstruction,* 198–200).

10. "Do not touch me."

11. informed, in the know

12. The U.S. Homestead Act of 1862 gave 160 acres of public land to each settler who would live on the claim for five years.

13. See AEW to Curry, October 16, 1863. Curry was defeated in his re-election bid to the Confederate congress.

14. Stephen Russell Mallory, the Confederate secretary of the navy. AEW criticized his performance in other letters as well. See AEW to Beauregard, November 14, 1863.

15. inability to act

16. Duilius built Rome's first navy in three months. Also, as the Roman commander, Duilius defeated the Carthaginian fleet near Mylae (in Sicily) to win Rome's first naval victory. See AEW to Beauregard, November 14, 1863.

17. After losing his seat in the Confederate congress, Curry was given a staff position in Joseph Johnston's army, investigating charges of civilian disloyalty. Later he was given command of a regiment. At the end of the war, Curry made his way home to Talladega, Alabama and was granted parole (Rice, *J. L. M. Curry,* 46–49).

CHAPTER 5

"Mobile is safe."

46 / MS Alabama
Historic Mobile Society (typed copy)   Mobile Feb' 28th 1864

My dear Rachel,

After encountering almost as many adventures as Ulysses, I find myself once more at home, and am powerfully tempted to indite for your especial benefit, a second Odyssey. We left Columbus[1] under very unfavorable auspices, the weather was intensely cold, and <u>twice</u> we were obliged to stop, and thaw the pipes of the engine which froze stiff before we reached Opelika[2] <u>just</u> <u>in</u> <u>time</u> to make the connection. Here I found an old friend, Co'l or rather Pudge McKinstrey who offered to take charge of Ellen Muldon & myself, and consequently our escort [S——] Muldon returned to Mobile. When we arrived at Montgomery, we found that no ladies were allowed to leave that place <u>en</u> <u>route</u> for Mobile. I was fully resolved to come however at all hazards and so expressed myself to the Provost Marshal. He seemed very polite, but much puzzled, and finally gave me a pass-port to Mobile, on the express condition that as soon as I arrived, I would make <u>all</u> <u>things</u> <u>satisfactory</u> to Gen'l Maury, who had prohibited the <u>return</u> of <u>non-combatants</u>. When we reached Greenville, about half way between Montgomery and Mobile, a provost official came aboard the cars and stopped all the ladies destined for Mobile; (in accordance he said, with orders from He'dqr'ts) but when I flourished my passport under his nose, he bowed and said very blandly: "You can proceed Madam, as you have special permission." Congratulating myself on my great good fortune, I resigned my shoulder to Ellen Muldon and ears to the flowing eloquent accents of Col' McKinstrey who is a remarkably fine talker. To my supremest amazement when we arrived at <u>Pollard</u>[3] a third nuisance, yclept[4] Provost Marshal, stalked into the cars and ordered every lady out. I showed my pass which had proved "<u>open</u> <u>sesame</u>" hitherto, but here the charm ended; he declared he had received peremptory "orders" <u>to</u> <u>stop</u> <u>all</u> <u>ladies</u>. Here several gentlemen (officers) strangers to me, stepped up and urged me not to leave my seat, assuring me they would see me aboard the boat at Tensas[5] [*sic*]. To add to the troubles the proprietor of the miserable little eating house, came into the cars and advised me not to get off, as the train for Montgomery had failed to connect, and his house was over-run with passengers waiting for the next train. The Provost was obdurate and grimy as Alva,[6] and rather than have a squabble with him I picked up my satchel, and that lunch basket, and stepped off. Col McKinstrey was forced to go on, and said he would send me [a] "telegraphic pass" from Gen'l Maury. To be left over at Pollard, the travellers horror, had hung in terrorum[7] ever since the completion of that Rail Road, and now I was presented with an opportunity of testing its charms. Fancy me, dear Rachel, as the cars whistled off, leaving Ellen Muldon, Frank Crawford[8] and myself standing on the platform of the station house, at 2 oclock at night, and the ground frozen as hard as Iceland granite!! Three forlorn damsels!! But unpromising as it looked, this contre-temp[9] proved one of the pleasantest episodes of my life. A gentleman stepped up, took that basket, and "Ma's Shawl," and asked permission to show us to the only place of refuge. Of course we made a grace of necessity, and followed him into a long room lined with tables; with a huge fireplace at the end; around which clustered 15 gentlemen and 2 other forlorn ladies. Here we sat up till sun rise, when Captain Minge came down and carried us up to his house, where we remained during the rest of our impromptu visit to Pollard. I have spent many pleasant hours, but I think I never enjoyed anything more keenly than I did the conversation that took place during our sitting up. Many of the gentlemen were officers, all were intelligent, some remarkably witty. I never heard as many brilliant things said in the same length of time, and I am sure, I never laughed as much as before. The party seemed determined to make a jest of everything and everybody, and as we did not close our eyes, you can imagine how well we were entertained. I knew none of the party but they all seemed to know me, and some of the Officers who said they knew many of my friends, were remarkably kind to me. Next morning Gen'l Maury telegraphed to the Officer in command of Pollard, to "allow Miss Evans to come at once to Mobile," and I came on home by the next train. I think the alarm of an immediate attack here, is subsiding, and we expect to remain where we are. If Mobile should be invested,[10] we will move into the City, at once. The enemy shell Fort Powell[11] every-day but do no damage. Gen'l Gilmer has arrived from Charleston, and is inspecting our fortifications. Gen'l Quarles [sic] Brigade is at Camp Cunning and the Gen'l has his Hdqtrs next door to us. I can see the house from my west window. Captain Cox is quite well, and the General ditto. Both asked very kindly after you; also Capt Holland. Major Devereux left Mobile before I arrived. Dr Heustis is very well indeed. I have just received your letter and will deliver your message to him; though he has I daresay written to you before this. I looked for the cotton for you, but can find none in Mobile. Sallie says she could not find the dress you wished.[12] Ever since my return I have been trying to <u>steal</u> <u>the</u> <u>time</u> <u>to</u> write <u>to</u> <u>you</u>, but have had so much company I could not possibly do so until <u>today</u>. I am so sorry I could not see you again before you left. I looked for you all afternoon, even after dark. It was too provoking that you did not receive my note. I find many letters at home awaiting for answers. Have received a long, long letter from Col' Maclean since I returned from Columbus. How long will you remain in Columbus? My Brother Vivian has been with us for the last <u>four</u> <u>days</u> but left us yesterday to return to Talladega.[13] Today we received telegraphic dispatches from Col Jones[14] and Howard.[15] They were in the fight at Dalton, and Tom Prince also, but thanks to a Merciful God all escaped uninjured. I presume you have seen Carrie,[16] as she is in Columbus. You must really pardon this scrawl as my pen is most miserable. All your friends here seem to miss you very much indeed, and desire to be remembered kindly to you. Gen'l Quarles says you created quite a sensation the day of the <u>watch</u> <u>drill</u>. Several officers told him you were the most beautiful woman they had ever seen. The General is quite eloquent in rhapsodizing about you. He says you <u>won</u> <u>the</u> <u>house</u>. Sallie[17] says she wrote you sometime ago. Goodby my dear Rachel; and write to me often—Your friend

A Evans

1. Columbus, Georgia

2. A town in northeast Alabama.

3. A town in extreme south central Alabama, only a few miles from the Florida line.

4. Old English for "named" or "called."

5. AEW would have to cross the Tensaw River, which borders Mobile on the east.

6. The 3rd Duke of Alva (or Alba in Spanish) (1507–1582), was a Spanish general and a harsh, oppressive governor of the Netherlands, a Spanish province at the time.

7. in terror

8. A woman friend of AEW from Mobile who later married "Commodore" Cornelius Vanderbilt.

9. inopportune moment, time out of synch.

10. surrounded by troops.

11. At the mouth of Mobile Bay.

12. Beginning with the next sentence, the remainder of this letter was written in crosshatch across the text of the first page.

13. A town in east-central Alabama.

14. Colonel Bush Jones married AEW's sister Caroline after the war.

15. AEW's younger brother Howard Evans.

16. AEW's younger sister Caroline Evans.

17. AEW's younger sister Sarah Evans.

❧ ❧ ❧

47 / MS Alabama   Mobile March 18th 1864
Historic Mobile Society (typed copy)

My dear Rachel:

If you only knew how constantly I am interrupted by company, I am sure you would pardon my failure to answer your letters as promptly as they deserve. Morning noon & night my ears are greeted with the sound of "<u>Miss Gusta somebody is coming up the walk</u>." Last night there were <u>six</u> <u>gentlemen</u> here till <u>12</u> oclock, and you can readily imagine how droopy my poor eyelids were; and how <u>Sallie</u>[1] and <u>I</u> rushed to our rooms as soon as we were released. Oh! torture beyond all the refined cruelties of Torquemada[2] to be sleepy in a room full of company! Selden's Battery left Mobile some days since for Pollard, and when Mr Lovelace told me good bye, he said he expected the command would be ordered to Dalton. But I presume they will all come back to "Camp Beulah"[3] before long. I hope so at least, for I should miss Mr Lovelace very much indeed. As regards an attack here, all the symptoms have vanished; and just as I predicted Mobile is today the safest place in the Confederacy. Several days since an English Steamer ran into our harbor from Havana; and to my great surprise and inexpressible delight brought <u>me</u> a package of stockings [*sic*] handkerchiefs and a small box of champagne. "Champagne Ochiltree! Champagne!"[4] apropos! poor Dr. LeVert died two days ago. He suffered a long long time, and death must have been a welcome release. I have not yet been in to see Mrs. LeVert.[5] Tomorrow Capt Cox leaves us for a few days; he is going to Virginia, and will be absent but a short time; I expect him out this evening. By the way, Healy the Louisiana Artist has painted a <u>very</u> <u>fine</u> <u>life-size</u> <u>portrait</u> of him, which I shall take care of until the war is over and Captain Cox can send it to Washington to his Mother, for whom he had it painted. It is a very fine likeness. Healy is quite an artist, well read, humorous, an incorrigible punster and very pleasant indeed. Some days since, at his request, I accompanied Capt Cox to the Studio (at the Bishops [*sic*] residence) to be present at the last sitting. Gen'l Quarles and Major Cummings also went with me and I had a very agreeable morning I assure you. Healy and the Gen'l kept up a rapid fire of puns, until I told them they both deserved to be incarcerated in the Punjab.[6] A full length portrait of Gen'l Quarles is to be painted next week. By the By! he (the Gen'l) has been placed in command of the Post, and constantly threatened me with orders, and condign punishment, if I do not treat him with more <u>consideration</u> and <u>admiration</u>. One day last week, I was out in the front yard having some work done among my flower beds; Tennessee Johnston,[7] or rather Polk Johnston

came over from Hqtr's [Headquarters] to help me tie the vines up on my <u>tall</u>
<u>trellises</u>, and soon after Capt Cox came also. We spent the entire day, from
eleven in the morning till 4 in the afternoon in the yard, transplanting flowers, tying up vines, and saying brilliant things! which alas! for want of
a Boswell![8] will not be preserved for the kind & tender public. It was an
impromptu <u>fete champetre</u>[9] which we enjoyed vastly, and when the bell rang
for <u>dinner</u>, we obeyed the summons with great alacrity. After discussing that
crowning comfort of civilization, I took the gentlemen over to Mrs Murrills
[*sic*], and we had a charming episode, came back laden with sweet olive,
camellias and laurel, and finished the day with a cup of tea, and a pleasant
party of other gentlemen who rode out from the city. We have had delightful weather for some days past, and it is a luxury to live in the open air, under
our splendid live oak. I have bought some geraniums, "<u>they are good things</u>
<u>to have in the country</u>" videlicet[10] <u>Sparrowgrass</u>; and as it has turned very cold
today, I am exercised considerably to make room in the parlor for all the
plants. I very much fear the ground will freeze tonight, and kill all the fruit
in the interior. Tell Mrs Moses I think of her orchard whenever the wind rises
to a howl around the corners of my room. It is needless to tell <u>you</u> my
Euthiopian [*sic*] Queen,[11] that <u>I</u> <u>suffer</u> this <u>cold</u> <u>weather</u>; and bemoan the loss
of a furnace. Col Jones[12] leaves tomorrow for Selma, whither he goes to visit
his Mother, and Carrie accompanies him. After a weeks [*sic*] stay, he returns
to Dalton and she comes back to us. Since I returned to Mobile, indeed only
last week I heard from both Capt Woolley and Major Thornton; the former
was in Richmond when he wrote, and the latter at Dalton. Woolley sent me
some very elegantly written articles of his own, displaying his extraordinary
versatility of genius, and profound historic lore. Before this he has left Richmond. Major Thornton's letter was exceedingly humorous and showed him
to be in fine spirits. I believe <u>Dr Moses</u> is to be married some time this spring
and I do hope he will be as happy as he deserves—. You know how very
highly I esteem both him & Capt Holland. The latter is very well and as
pleasant and noble hearted as ever. I derive much pleasure too from the frequent visits of Major Thomas, (Genl Quarles [*sic*] nephew,) who is remark-
ably <u>witty, bright</u>, and <u>agreeable</u>. I suppose Dr. Heustis has written you <u>all the</u>
<u>particulars</u> concerning <u>his</u> <u>duel</u>, which happily resulted without bloodshed.
<u>He was not to blame</u> in the affair, and was more "sinned against than sinning."
I see him frequently, and in the absence of a <u>better likeness I gave him your</u>
<u>ambrotype</u>!!![13] He was out to see me this morning, and is very well indeed,
though of course you hear from him[14] often enough to require no such information from me. I doubt very much whether her <u>majesty of Sheba</u>[15] can decipher this scrawling chirography—but the fact is my aristocratic <u>digits</u> will not
accommodate themselves to <u>steel pens</u>. Godbrey the Captain of the "<u>Denbigh</u>"[16]

has promised to bring me the finest gold pen in Cuba and when that arrives, I promise you dear Rachel that it will require neither Champollion[17] nor B[obscured] to interpret my cunieform [sic] characters. I had intended writing you a longer and better letter but oh! uncertainty of all hours at Georgia Cottage![18] I must here close and prepare to meet company. Since I commenced this I have been forced to stop and answer a note concerning Asylum business. I "<u>make</u> <u>haste</u>" <u>continually</u>, of course, but have very little time. It is bitter cold, and my hands are almost frozen. When you write home <u>do give my love to all your family</u>. My new book will be ready for sale <u>next week</u>.[19] I hear often from Mr Evans[20] who is doing all in his power to hurry the work. Sallie and Carrie send their love. Pardon this scrawl from your [obscured]. AJE

1. AEW's younger sister, Sarah Evans.

2. Tomas de Torquemada (1420–1498), master of the Spanish Inquisition, was known for his intolerance and cruelty.

3. A hospital for Confederate troops that AEW established near her home in Mobile. See AEW to Rachel Lyons, January 22, 1862.

4. William B. Ochiltree was a delegate from Texas to the convention of the seceding Southern states, held in Montgomery in February 1861 (Clement Evans, *Confederate Military History,* 2: 22). AEW, who attended this convention, possibly heard this statement at some point of celebration during the proceedings.

5. The Le Verts were a very prominent family in Mobile. Octavia Walton Le Vert was an accomplished hostess as well as an intellectual. She wrote poetry, translated classical authors, and published her travel journal and letters (Harriet E. Amos, *Social Life in an Antebellum Cotton Port: Mobile, Alabama 1820–1860,* [Ann Arbor, Mich.: UMI, 1977], microfilm, 153–54, 156–58).

6. A region in northwestern India.

7. Tennessee Johnston distinguished himself a month later in the Battle of Mobile Bay on August 5, 1864. When Admiral Franklin Buchanan, commander of the Confederate ironclad *Tennessee,* was wounded in battle, Johnston took over his command and fought skillfully and bravely. However, the outnumbered Confederates were defeated.

8. James Boswell (1740–1795), a Scottish lawyer, is known primarily for his journals and his *The Life of Samuel Johnson,* in which he, as companion, records Johnson's activities and especially his conversations.

9. pastoral feast

10. of course

11. A reference to Rachel's Jewish background. Many ethnic groups, including Semitic ones, populate Ethiopia.

12. Colonel Bush Jones married AEW's sister Caroline (Carrie) after the war.

13. See AEW to Rachel Lyons, May 23, 1860, note 4.

14. The remainder of this letter was written in crosshatch across the text of page 1.

15. Another reference to Rachel's Jewish heritage. In the Old Testament (1 Kings 10:2), the Queen of Sheba (in southern Arabia) visits King Solomon in Jerusalem.

16. The *Denbigh,* a famous and very successful blockade-runner, traveled regularly between Mobile and Havana. After the Federals captured Mobile Bay in 1864, the *Denbigh* sailed between Galveston and Havana until the end of the war.

17. Jean-François Champollion (1790–1832), French scholar who helped to decipher ancient Egyptian writings, including the hieroglyphics on the Rosetta Stone.

18. The house near Mobile that AEW bought for her parents and siblings. See AEW to Rachel Lyons, May 27, [1859], note 1.

19. *Macaria*

20. This is probably the Mr. Evans of the firm Walker, Evans, and Cogswell of Columbia, South Carolina, which printed *Macaria.*

❧ ❧ ❧

48 / MS Alabama   Mobile May 1—1864

My dear Rachel—

What <u>do</u> <u>you</u> <u>suppose</u> I am employing my mind upon at this juncture? The Ladies of Mobile are to give a Supper for the benefit of the "Association for the Relief of Maimed Soldiers" in the Confederacy, and as I was appointed one of the Committee to make all preliminary arrangements, I am just now racking my brains to conjecture the amount of <u>cakes</u> and <u>strawberries</u> & <u>cream;</u>—the number of plates, saucers and spoons needed for a table which I expect to have charge of;—and the general appearance and appendages of the aforesaid table. To increase my tabular tribulations, my mother is now in Columbus,[1] and in her absence I have the care of home affairs and housekeeping. Really as you can readily imagine, I am not at all burdened with leisure hours hanging heavily on my hands. My correspondence is increasing every day, and I find it a difficult matter with all the company I have, to pay my epistolary debts. My new book[2] brings me many letters of congratulations, and I am very much gratified and rejoiced at the flattering criticisms upon it. Every one pronounces it superior to "<u>Beulah</u>," and I trust when you have carefully read it, you will give me your opinion <u>frankly</u> concerning its merits and defects. Dr Moses was married on Wednesday last, and will bring his bride to Mobile in a few days. Frank Crawford[3] went up to the wedding and has not yet returned. I hope dear Rachel you found less opposition at home than you <u>dreaded,</u>[4] and that all has been satisfactorily arranged. I am exceedingly glad that Dr. Heustis was able to join you so soon after your arrival at Columbia, as his presence would enable your parents to consent more readily to your wishes. I hope most sincerely that all has been <u>harmonized,</u> and that his visit to you was as pleasant as you both desired. Poor fellow!

he will feel like Adam driven out of paradise, when he starts back to Mobile, without his Eve. I trust he will come home with his heart full of happy hopes. Mobile is quite gay again, and there are a good many pleasant officers very near us now. Apropos! I wish you could see my flower garden. My roses are the admiration of all Staffs—and Generals. I enclose four dollars, as your belt only cost one. You must pardon the appearance of the money, as they were the most respectable bills I could obtain. Do give my love to your family, and also to your Uncles; and tell Ellen I will send her books by the first opportunity. As I am expecting company I have no time for more. I daresay I should be thoroughly ashamed of this scribble if I only had time to read it over but I trust to your charity for pardon for my unavoidable haste. Carrie & Sallie[5] send love. Believe me dear Rachel, your sincere friend—A.J.Evans

1. Columbus, Georgia, where several of Sarah Evans's (Augusta's mother) family members lived. AEW was born there.

2. *Macaria.*

3. Miss Frank Crawford, a friend of AEW, who later married "Commodore" Cornelius Vanderbilt.

4. Rachel Lyons, a Jew, feared that her parents would object to her engagement to Dr. Heustis, a Christian. See AEW to Rachel Lyons, March 28, 1863.

5. Caroline and Sarah, AEW's sisters.

❧ ❧ ❧

49 / MS Alabama   Mobile June 14th [1864]

My dear Rachel—

I know that when I tell you I positively have not had time to thank you for your last letter, you will at least [obscured] and not imagine that my silence implies indifference or forgetfulness. I have been literally overrun with company for some weeks past, and could not find leisure to write even to Howard,[1] as often as I wished. Morning noon and night, somebody was calling me into the parlor, and thus—but my dear Rachel, you understand it all, and I shall not longer waste time in needless explanation. Vivian[2] is married and his wife is now with us, and Sila Howard[3] has been with me for the month. Her health has improved very much since she came to Mobile. Three days since she went to Bladon,[4] but I am expecting her, and all of Col Prince's family the last of this week. Annie is in very poor health, and a physician prescribes [obscured]. Bless you dear Rachel for your kind opinion of my new book;[5] it is of course very gratifying to me to know that my friends are not only satisfied, but pleased with it. I wish I could show you some letters which I have received, from persons whose good opinion is very valuable to me, and in whose critical acumen I repose great confidence. As regards the

point you make concerning Irene, in sending for Aubrey, just before he went
into battle,[6] there is no analogy between the circumstances which surrounded
her, and those to which I objected, and still object, in "Aurora Leigh."[7] Many
years had elapsed since Romney had addressed Aurora, and in the interim he
had addressed another woman;—but Irene had concealed her own warm
affection when Aubrey declared his, and knowing that he still loves her, but
could not from her own course toward him ever allude to the subject again,
she saw fit ere bidding him a final adieu to confess her own feelings. Aurora
asked Romney to marry her. Irene assured Russell she would never be his
wife. There is not the slightest analogy in the course pursued by the two
women. I am very glad to hear that you like my Irene. She is the noblest character I ever painted, and is my ideal of perfect womanhood. Captain Woolley has been in Mobile recently and we enjoyed his visit very much. Gen'l
Buckner and Staff passed through en route from the Trans Mississippi, and
came out with all his Staff one evening to bid me good bye. They were all in
fine spirits, and we had quite a pleasant evening. Capt Holland was out yesterday morning and took breakfast with us. He comes out frequently about
7 oclock so as to make a visit, get breakfast and return before the heat of the
day. I saw Dr. Heustis two or three evenings since, when he took tea with us.
I hope all is harmonious and happy for both of you. You must make him very
happy, for he certainly deserves it, as much as any man I know. Tell me what
you think of Mrs King's new book—"Gerald Gray's Wife."[8] Do you ever see
my kind friend Mr Evans?—Give my [obscured] cousins the Mordecais. Do
not I beg of you wait as long in answering this letter as I have in writing it.
The girls[9] send love to you. Believe me dear Rachel your friend

                                                                    A.J.Evans

1. Howard Evans, AEW's brother, was serving in the 3rd Alabama Regiment.
2. Vivian Evans, AEW's brother, was in the same regiment as Howard.
3. Probably a relative since AEW's mother's maiden name was Howard.
4. Bladon Springs, a resort near Mobile.
5. *Macaria*.
6. Irene, the heroine of *Macaria,* defies her father and refuses to marry the cold,
wealthy man he had selected for her. Later Irene falls in love with Russell Aubrey, an
honorable but poor young man whom her father forbids her to marry because of his
lower-class background. Much later, Irene sends for Aubrey and tells him she will
always love him but can never marry him out of deference to her father's wishes, even
though her father is now dead. Aubrey is killed in battle the next day, and Irene
devotes herself to the arts and to good works.
7. *Aurora Leigh* (1856), by Elizabeth Barrett Browning, describes a young woman torn
between her need to be a poet and her need for love. Aurora rejects Romney Leigh, who
wants her to marry him and to work with him on his social-reform projects. Romney

later decides to marry Marian, a seamstress, to save her from a demeaning life of poverty. Their marriage plans, however, go awry. Several years later, Aurora realizes that she does love Romney after all. She reveals her feelings to him, and they agree to marry and to share their lives' work.

8. Sue Petigru King Bowen wrote *Gerald Gray's Wife,* published in 1864.

9. AEW's sisters, Caroline and Sarah.

❧ ❧ ❧

50 / MS Alabama   Mobile Sept 24th. [1864]

My dear Rachel,

After an absence of six weeks, I returned home two days ago, bringing my darling brother Howard, who has been sick for two months in Columbus.[1] He was desperately ill, having typhoid fever in addition to a very severe wound in the shoulder which <u>fractured</u> the <u>shoulder blade</u>.[2] For several days we despaired of his life, and only the mercy and goodness of God saved him. He bore the fatigue of the trip better than I expected, for he is so feeble he can not raise his head from his pillow, and we brought him home <u>on a litter</u>. His wound is in a bad condition, but thank God! he is not now considered dangerous by the Surgeon though it will be a long long time before he is able to return to duty, or even to leave his bed. I am afraid my darling you will think me negligent or indifferent in suffering so long a time to elapse without writing, but indeed if you know how <u>constantly</u> I have been occupied in nursing dear Howard, you would not blame me for a silence which was <u>unavoidable</u>. I am almost worn out with watching and anxiety, but trust the worst is over, and that our dear sufferer will rapidly improve. Doctor Heustis was out yesterday to see him and through him I learned you were well. My dear Rachel when are you coming to Mobile to live? Will you delay your marriage until the close of this seemingly endless war? You and Doctor Heustis would both be happier I should think were you married.[3] Your separation must be mutually painful. He looks very well indeed. While in Columbus, I saw your cousin R J Moses, who came to see me, and was very kind to dear Howard. We <u>of course</u> <u>spoke</u> of <u>you</u>, but he did not mention your engagement to Doctor H—and I did not allude to it. What are you doing with youself? My dear friend, it is so dark I can not see the lines and must beg you to pardon this horrible scrawl. Captain Cox was in Columbus while I was there. He has been quite sick, but is better, and is the guest of one of my cousins, Mrs Warren. He returns to his command this week. Genl Quarles is in Hoods [*sic*] army, and is as <u>witty</u> as ever. I must say good-bye—as Howard needs me. Do write to me, and believe me as ever—

Your affectionately—

A.J.Evans

1. Columbus, Georgia.

2. Howard was wounded during one of the battles around Atlanta, Georgia (Fidler, *A Biography,* 122). Atlanta fell to the Union on September 1–2, 1864, and sporadic fighting had occurred around the city for the previous two months.

3. During the war, Dr. James Heustis served as head surgeon in the army of General Braxton Bragg. On February 4, 1865, he and Rachel were married and settled in Mobile where Rachel and AEW continued their lifelong friendship. Rachel gave birth to ten children, five of whom survived to adulthood. The oldest daughter, Louise Lyons Heustis, became a critically acclaimed portrait artist in New York City (Druhan, "Louise Lyons Heustis," n.p.).

"... *all my proud fond hopes were slaughtered.*"

51 / *MS Library of Congress (original)*
Alabama (photocopy)
Duke (photocopy)   Mobile October 7th 1865

Hon' J. L. M. Curry—
My honored friend—

Although I am at present a "Martha cumbered with much serving,"[1]—and pressed with multitudinous engagements, I snatch a few moments to thank you for your kind letter, and say that I shall avail myself of your friendly offer to allow me the use of the valuable <u>congressional</u> <u>documents</u> contained in your library,—which will render me incalculable assistance,[2] when I plunge <u>in medias res</u>.[3] The truths of history crystallize slowly,—it will be a gigantic task to illuminate these from the <u>debris</u> of falsehood and exaggeration in which they are now overwhelmed, and while I am anxious to collect necessary <u>data</u>, it will be many months before I commence the <u>written</u> compilation. In the interim, as I lost my property (negroes and Confederate bonds) during that revolution, I must attend to the "question of bread and butter," and am trying to write out a novel,[4] the plan of which has been vaguely straying through my mind for some time. My history, I intend to make the <u>great end of all my labors</u> in the realm of letters, and while I gather the requisite materials, I must continue to draw a support from my inkstand. I confess my present surroundings are by no means conducive to the desired end, and I have not a doubt that a Gyges ring[5] or magical presto! would make you laugh heartily at the suggestion of <u>my devoirs</u>[6] to the Nine classic spinsters.[7] Since the advent of the Yankees, and consequent hegira of our negroes, it has been impossible to obtain servants, and as we have been obliged <u>to do our own work</u>, I have forsworn Helicon and Parnassus[8] and assumed the role of Blowselinda.[9] Fancy me with pepper cruet in one hand and with salt box in the other, deep in the mysteries of capilstade (known in proletarian parlance as <u>hash</u>) or stooping over a pot of soup as assiduously as did Medea over that celebrated Colchian[10] caldron, in which old Pelias was par-boiled![11] Lady

Mary W. Montague[12] has remarked in one of her letters, that: "to a lady of delicate sensibilities, and warm affections, the preparation of a meal for those she loves, becomes no longer mere vulgar cooking of beef and pudding, but a precious privilege of ministering to the wants of her dear ones!!"[13] Sans doute[14] this peculiarly amiable and eminently feminine theory seemed quite comme il faut,[15] when penned from the luxurious depths of her ladyship's delightful boudoir in the sublime Porte,—but I very much question the perpetuity of said culinary aesthetics when practically illustrated in a Mobile kitchen in the month of August when the temperature vividly reminds me of that volcano, in ascending which, Humboldt burnt off the soles of his boots.[16] Apropos! of Lady Mary! What do you suppose became of that same "amiable meal theory" when she and poor Pope quarreled so savagely across the Duke of Oxford's table that one or the other was forced to withdraw from the dinner that the remaining guests might enjoy the repast in comparative peace?[17] It must have been deadly ricochet firing that drove Epicurean Pope from an untasted Lucullus[18] banquet where her Ladyship victoriously held the field, and lingered over mellow walnuts and golden Amontillado.[19] You say in your letter you hoped I would now give you a recount of my trip to New York. The melancholy necessity which drove me North precluded the possibility of my deriving pleasure from the visit. The critical and worsening condition of my brother Howard who was so desperately wounded in the great battle of Atlanta, 22nd July 1864[20] and whose case seemed to baffle the skill of our surgeons forced me, in compliance with my mother's urgent request, to take him by sea, to New York, to consult one of my friends, a German physician of celebrity. Howard had lost his memory, in consequence of the wounds and terrible attack of typhoid fever, but thank God! the consultation was successful, and with a lighter, happier heart, I brought him home almost recovered. My stay in New York was very brief, (only a fortnight) and I met only such people as Ben Wood of the "Times," who had proved their detestation of the war party and policy. Some of the prominent Republican leaders wished to see me, in order (so story said) to ascertain the true condition of "affairs South" but as I knew they were well acquainted with the entire success of their infamous subjugation programme, I positively refused to see them.[21] The belief obtains among our friends North, that the entire west will repudiate the radical policy, unite with the South, and that the "Constitutional Democracy (?)" will elect the next President. Seward,[22] Raymond,[23] and Blair[24] are opposed to the darling dogma of the New England illuminatti,[25] negro suffrage, and I heard universal condemnation of the scheme as far west as St. Louis, through which I passed on my return. Mr. Ben Wood is sanguine that the "balance of power will return to the hands of the South," and urged me to tell our people so, but alas! ours is the condition of the Lombard puttarici[26] and of the nation's future I am utterly hopeless. I was surprised at the kindness and courtesy shown me wherever I went,[27] for my devotion of <u>our holy cause</u> was well known, and I freely expressed my abhorrence of the principles and people of the North. One friend on 5th Avenue invited me to accompany her to Europe and remain several years, at her expense;[28] but of course though grateful for her extreme kindness, I could not for one instant entertain the idea. I hope that you will not consider me egoistic in mentioning these personal incidents of a trip, with reference to which you expressed some curiosity. Nothing but the desire to save my brother's life would have induced me to visit a section, which it is probably unnecessary to tell you I cordially detest. I regret exceedingly, my valued friend, that you are <u>compelled to ask for pardon,</u>[29] and I hoped you would not apply for it, but first the country, which is <u>no longer our own dear sunny South,</u> our happy land of civil and religious freedom,—but a crushed, mutilated, degraded— "Niobe of Nations!" Childless and crownless in her voiceless woe!"[30] I feel that I have no country, no house, no hope in coming years, and I brood over our hallowed precious past, with its chrism of martyr blood,—knowing that like the mourning Carian Queen[31] I shall spend my life building an historic mausoleum, which will never hold the sacred ashes of the darling dead. God help me to be patient under this course of national trial! Sometimes I shudder at the bitter, bitter feelings I find smoldering in my heart. I believe I loved our cause <u>as a Jesuit his order,</u> and its utter ruin has saddened and crushed me, as no other event of my life had power to do. I fear you will dub this hasty scrawl an epistolary salmagondi[32] and a most inadequate return for your own kind and interesting letter, but indeed Mr. Curry, I throw myself on your charity, and crave forgiveness—for if I waited for time to compose and carefully pen my thousands of letters, I should throw my pen away forever and take a vow of silence. With renewed thanks for your promised contribution to materials for my history, and also for your <u>friendly words of encouragement</u> in the holy work; I am—

Most sincerely your grateful friend,
AJE

1. Martha was the harried sister who worked in the kitchen to prepare a meal for Jesus while her sister Mary sat at Jesus's feet and listened to His teachings (Luke 10:40).

2. At this point, AEW is planning to write a history of the Confederacy, a project she views as her life's work. Also see AEW to Stephens, November 29, 1865, and AEW to Beauregard, November 20, 1867.

3. in the middle of things

4. *St. Elmo,* published more than a year later in December 1866, was enormously successful.

5. Gyges, in Greek mythology, was a king of Lydia who owned a ring that made the wearer invisible (Pierre Grimal, *A Concise Dictionary of Classical Mythology*, edited by Stephen Kershaw and translated by A. R. Maxwell-Hyslop [Oxford: Basil Blackwell, 1991], 16).

6. respects, duty, compliments

7. The nine Muses. AEW is suggesting that if Curry could become invisible and observe her activities, he would be amused by the difficulties that hinder her writing.

8. Two of the mountains where the Muses lived.

9. Blowselinda is Nigel's landlady in *The Fortunes of Nigel* by Sir Walter Scott.

10. Colchis was an ancient country bordering the Black Sea.

11. In Greek mythology, Medea, in order to help Jason avenge the deaths of his parents, convinced Pelias's daughters that she could make their father young again. Following Medea's instructions, the daughters drugged Pelias, cut him into pieces, put the pieces into a pot of boiling water, and waited for Medea to work the magic that would restore him to life and youth. However, Medea disappeared, and the daughters realized with horror that they had murdered their father.

12. Lady Mary Montagu (1689–1762), English letter writer, essayist, and poet. She was at first a friend of Alexander Pope, but after an unexplained quarrel, they became bitter enemies and frequently attacked each other in their verses. Lady Mary is best known for the letters that she wrote from Italy, where she lived for twenty years after her marriage failed.

13. A rough paraphrase of a statement in a letter to the Countess of Pomfret, March 1739.

14. without doubt

15. proper

16. Alexander von Humboldt (1769–1859), German scientist, explorer, and diplomat. He climbed the Chimborazo, a mass of volcanic peaks in Ecuador, including Cotopaxi, the world's tallest active volcano, which constantly ejects hot steam.

17. This anecdote, greatly embellished with AEW's own details, was briefly reported in Samuel Johnson's *Lives of the English Poets* (vol. 2, 204). However, according to Maynard Mack, Pope's biographer, the story has no basis in fact. Lady Mary's granddaughter strongly denied it when Johnson's *Lives* was first published. Lord and Lady Oxford's daughter reputed it further by claiming that her parents would never have committed the *faux pas* of inviting Lady Mary and Pope to the same party after their quarrel (quoted in Mack, *Alexander Pope: A Life* [New York: Norton, 1985], 882n. 379).

18. A Roman general and epicure (c. 177–c. 56 B.C.E.). After retiring from the military, Lucullus lived a lavish lifestyle, patronized artists and writers, and gave extravagant, gourmet banquets.

19. a pale sherry

20. The final fall of Atlanta did not occur until September 2, 1864.

21. At a dinner party in her honor, AEW refused to meet Henry J. Raymond, editor of the *Times*, because of the vehement stand he took against the South in his editorials (Fidler, *A Biography*, 138).

22. William H. Seward, Johnson's secretary of state, urged a policy of conciliation toward the South. He was opposed to the Radical Republicans (Ben W. Griffith, "A Lady Novelist Views the Reconstruction: An Augusta Jane Evans Letter," *Georgia Historical Quarterly* 43 [fall 1959]: 109n. 29).

23. Probably a reference to Henry J. Raymond (see note 21 above).

24. Francis Preston Blair was a slaveholder who became involved in the antislavery movement and was elected to the U.S. Congress from Missouri in 1856 and 1860. He strongly opposed Negro suffrage and the Reconstruction Acts.

25. Those who claim to be especially enlightened

26. The Lombards, a barbarian tribe known for their cruelty, invaded northern Italy in 568 C.E. and dominated most of the country for the next two hundred years. AEW is comparing the condition of the South with that of a province the Lombards conquered.

27. One such kindness occurred when AEW visited her publisher, J. C. Derby. AEW and her family were poverty stricken after the war, and Mr. Derby surprised her with a large sum of money—the royalties that he and Mr. Lippincott had pressured Michael Doolady to pay her from his pirated edition of *Macaria* (Derby, *Fifty Years,* 394–95). See AEW to Beauregard, December 14, 1863, note 4.

28. According to Fidler, this friend was probably Mrs. J. C. Derby, the wife of AEW's publisher (*A Biography,* 146).

29. After the war, President Johnson offered a blanket pardon and return of property (except slaves) to all ex-Confederates who would swear allegiance to the United States. However, certain people were exempt from his pardon: high-ranking officials in the Confederate government and military, anyone who had resigned from a Federal government or military position to join the Confederacy, anyone guilty of war crimes, and anyone owning taxable property worth more than $20,000. The last provision was Johnson's attempt to humble the proud Southern aristocrats (McPherson, *The Civil War and Reconstruction,* 498). The people in these categories, however, could apply for individual pardons, which were usually granted. Once pardoned, the ex-Confederates were free to seek political office and power in their states.

30. See AEW to Curry, December 20, 1862, notes 7 and 8.

31. Caria was a division of ancient Asia Minor, located in the southwestern portion of what is now Turkey. AEW does not give enough information to identify the queen who mourned the conquest of her country, but a succession of enemies, from the Persians in 545 B.C.E. to the Romans in 129 B.C.E., conquered Caria.

32. hodgepodge (French *salmigondis*)

❧ ❧ ❧

52 / MS Emory   Mobile Nov 29 1865

Hon' A. Stephens—[1]

Dear Sir:

Permit me to tender you my most cordial thanks for your exceedingly kind, and very gratifying letter, which arrived most opportunely at a juncture, when I was seeking an excuse to recall myself to your recollection. Having met you merely par parentheses[2] during the hurried organization of our quondam government,—I feared you were too entirely engrossed by affairs of state to remember the evening I was so fortunate as to spend in your company,—and that you might deem a letter from me after the lapse of four stormy years,—an unwarrantable intrusion. In addition to the very great pleasure which I derived from Gen'l Toombs' visit,[3] I shall ever value it as a precious reminiscence affording me the long-desired opportunity of renewing an acquaintance with two Southern statesmen,[4] whom I have long regarded as our masterminds,—and to whose sage counsels I looked for national salvation, in that bloody struggle where all my proud fond hopes were slaughtered.

Frequently during the past four years, when the inexplicable policy and palpable blunders of the Aulic[5] decrees from Richmond, filled my heart with prophetic dread of the inevitable ruin that stared at us from the future,—I was powerfully tempted to write to you,—to ascertain whether you still indulged a hope of final success,—whether you could not suggest some scheme to prevent the destruction to which our executive Phaethon[6] was rapidly driving us; but the apprehension of annoying you,—or worse still—of being considered presumptuous,—discouraged the attempt which my heart dictated. Now alas! jacta est alea[7]—and—

"To bear, is to conquer our fate."[8] With reference to the history of the war, (of which Genl Toombs was so kind as to write you,) permit me to say to you candidly, that although I have been repeatedly solicited to undertake it, I doubt my intellectual credentials for this grand mission,—and am haunted by a sceptical dread that no woman is capable of the rare critical acumen in military matters,—and of the broad and lofty generalizations absolutely requisite in one who essays to become the historic custodian of our national honor,—and to set us as a people,—crowned, triumphant,—glorified,—before that august tribunal—, that immemorial and infallible assize which Clio[9] decrees for every nation that has waxed and waned since the gray dawn of time. You will I trust acquit me of the contemptible motive of mere mock humility, if I tell you honestly—I am fully—yes painfully aware that the hallowed mantle of Xenophon[10] and Tacitus[11] would not fit my shoulders,—and yet Mr Stephens, my heart vetoes the verdict of my judgment, and prompts me to offer some grateful testimonial, some tribute however inadequate, to the manes[12] of our heroes,—and above all—of our noble unknown dead who have gone down "unwept, unhonored, and unsung—"[13] in the red burial of battle. The great truths of history crystallize slowly, and it is a gigantic task to eliminate them from the debris of error and exaggeration where they now lie overwhelmed; consequently I do not purpose to write a history just

now,—but to collect at once all the data that can be rendered by the prominent actors in the bloody drama;—data which are perishable, and should
therefore be promptly and carefully garnered up, for future study and classi-
fication. Numerous books will be rapidly written on this subject, and thrown
out to the public, but only one history will live, and as two thousand years
after the events of which he wrote,—Grote has compiled the only satisfactory philosophic analysis—the truly great history of Grecian constitutions
and politics,[14]—I am encouraged to hope that by patient toil and faithful
study, I may finally accomplish something worthy of that holy cause, to
which I have been as unreservedly devoted as a Jesuit to his order. Reports of
battles, incidents of heroism, biographic materials concerning our leaders, I
can easily procure, but to you Sir, I look for that, which after all, is the only
sound and proper sub-stratum,—the secret history of the revolution; the
operations of the diplomatic machinery,—the rejected proposals of intervention, and the lost opportunities of Cabinet and Congress. Having the entree
of the diplomatic "greenroom"[15] of our government, you are thoroughly au
fait[16] in matters from which the public were debarred;—state secrets hermeti-
cally sealed by Mr Davis,—who strangled them with red-tape, and shouted
procul! oh procul este profam![17]

The information which I hope most earnestly you may find it convenient
and agreeable to give me, refers to the negotiations between Napoleon and
the Confederate Government, concerning recognition, and intervention on
the basis of gradual emancipation of slaves,[18]—and also, a correct and ample
account of all that occurred between our Peace Commissioners,—and the
Federal officials at Fortress Monroe.[19] It is believed that even so late as February last, Mr Lincoln would have allowed and protected the institution of
Slavery, had Mr Davis consented to reconstruction.[20] With regard to this on
dit,[21] and certain other rumors of favorable terms which might have been
made with France,—great diversity of opinion exists, and I hold my own in
abeyance, while ignorant of the facts. If you can furnish me the secret history
of Confederate diplomacy,—and also your views of the great fundamental
errors that compelled our ruin, you will very—very greatly oblige and assist
me. With all that transpired, I know you are conversant;—in the equity of
your judgments I have implicit faith, and what you confide to me, I assure
you shall be kept sacred, until the auspicious juncture arrives, when I can with
propriety publish a calm dispassionate, philosophic history. Personally—I have
no feuds to foster, no grievances to redress,—no favoritisms to jaundice my
vision;—the truth, the whole truth, and nothing but the truth, is now my sole
goal, and to its attainment I desire to dedicate my future years, feeling that my
life will not have been spent in vain, if I finally accomplish a historic memorabilia worthy of my matchless theme. Believe me Sir, it was not necessary

that you should thank us for sheltering and concealing <u>our</u> <u>Mirabeau</u>[22]—Genl
Toombs. My parents and I <u>regard</u> <u>it</u> <u>as</u> <u>a</u> <u>privilege</u> to claim him as our friend
and guest under all circumstances. God preserve and restore him to the coun-
try of which he is deservedly a boast and ornament.[23] With renewed thanks
for your valued letter, I am Sir

Respectfully—A. J. Evans

1. Alexander Hamilton Stephens was vice president of the Confederacy. At the
time of this letter, Stephens had just been released from Federal prison, where he was
confined after the war (William Y. Thompson, "Robert Toombs, Man without a
Country," *Georgia Historical Quarterly* 46, no. 2 [1962], 164).

2. Literally, in parentheses. Here meaning briefly or indirectly.

3. General Robert Toombs was the first Confederate secretary of state before joining the military. When the war ended, Toombs went into hiding to escape imprison-
ment, eventually making his way to Mobile, Alabama, where he was sequestered in
the home of Augusta Evans and her parents (Thompson 162–63). (Toombs was an
old friend of AEW's father.) During his stay, Toombs reportedly greatly enjoyed long
walks and conversations with AEW. In spite of her limited experience in the kitchen,
AEW cooked for Toombs and considered it a "privilege" to take care of him (Fidler,
A Biography, 119).

4. A friend of Toombs, Lieutenant Charles E. Irwin, traveled with him (Thompson 163).

5. The Aulic Council was one of the two highest courts established in the Roman
Empire.

6. In Greek mythology, Phaethon was the son of Helios, the sun god. One day
when Phaethon was driving his father's solar chariot, the horses broke free and got
too close to the earth, scorching parts of it and creating deserts.

7. The die has been cast.

8. Thomas Campbell, "Lines Written on Visiting a Scene in Argyleshire," line 36.

9. In Greek mythology, Clio was the muse of history.

10. Xenophon (431–352 B.C.E.), a Greek historian who, based on his own experiences of fighting in the army of Cyrus the Younger, wrote several books describing
Cyrus's military campaigns and ultimate defeat.

11. See AEW to Beauregard, April 29, 1863.

12. the revered spirits of the dead

13. Sir Walter Scott, "The Lay of the Last Minstrel," canto 6, stanza 1.

14. George Grote (1794–1871), a British historian, wrote the *History of Greece* in
twelve volumes, up to the time of Alexander the Great.

15. The greenroom in the theater is the common waiting room used by the actors
backstage. It is called the greenroom because the early rooms were painted green.
AEW, of course, is saying that Stephens has knowledge because of his "backstage" or
"behind-the-scenes" position.

16. in the know

17. Oh you, the profane, stay at a distance!

18. The sympathies of Napoleon III were known to lie with the Confederacy because his plan to establish a French regime in Mexico would be endangered by a Union victory. The Southern diplomats wanted to work out an agreement whereby France would recognize the Confederacy and the Confederacy would recognize Napoleon III's regime in Mexico (under the puppet Emperor Maximilian). Due to U.S. Secretary of State Seward's skillful diplomatic maneuvering and Napoleon III's fear of war with the United States, the deal fell through (McPherson, *The Civil War and Reconstruction,* 344).

19. A. H. Stephens, the addressee of this letter, led the Southern delegation to the Hampton Roads Peace Conference on February 3, 1865 (near Fort Monroe, Virginia). Negotiations broke down because neither side would compromise. Lincoln insisted on the reunion of the country and the emancipation of the slaves, and Davis insisted on Southern independence (McPherson 469).

20. AEW is misinformed about this. The emancipation of the slaves is an issue on which Lincoln would never have compromised. According to McPherson, Lincoln might have been flexible about the "timing and implementation of emancipation," but on the issue itself he was adamant. However, McPherson claims, the Union's rejection of the Confederates' terms was probably exactly what Davis anticipated and wanted, for he seemed to be "in a fog of unreality where victory still seemed possible" (469–70).

21. it is said, or hearsay

22. Honore Gabriel Riqueti Mirabeau (1749–1791), a leader and orator of the French Revolution.

23. After leaving Mobile and the home of AEW and her parents, Toombs escaped to Europe for a few years before finally returning to his home state of Georgia. He remained an "unreconstructed rebel" for the rest of his life. He refused to apply for a pardon and he refused to accept U.S. citizenship (Thompson, "Robert Toombs," 166–67).

❧ ❧ ❧

53 / MS Alabama Archives   Mobile. Feb. 3d, 1866

Mrs. J. K. Chrisman—
My dear Madame—

Permit me to tender you my cordial thanks for your very kind letter, the receipt of which I should have acknowledged more promptly, but for multitudinal and imperative engagements that precluded the possibility of my finding the requisite leisure. To know that my ill fated "<u>Macaria</u>" furnished even a modicum of consolation to your bereaved heart, is I assure you, a source of profound gratification, and richly compensates for the labor it cost me. All my hopes, aims, aspirations were bound up in the success of our holy precious cause, and its failure has bowed down and crushed my heart, as I thought nothing earthly had power to do. While the majority of persons accept with philosophic serenity the present status of the South and yield gracefully to an imperious necessity, my grief deepens day by day—grows more poignant; and I feel like Eugenie de Guerin:[1] "Oh the misery that has no good in it! The tearless dry misery that bruises the heart like a hammer." The only hope that now cheers me, is that of quitting forever that scourged, crushed, accursed country—once so irrepressibly dear to me,—now so odious and intolerable,—and finding a home in Mexico or Europe, far from the upas[2] shadow of the "Stars & Stripes." Of the future of this so-called Republic, I am hopeless,—the present does not invite contemplation,—and the past—our hallowed—past is too unutterably mournful to be dwelt upon. To a just God I commend the souls of dear dead, our martyred heroes;—and the strongest wish of my heart is, that I may live to witness, to enjoy the dire retribution,—the awful Nemesis,[3] which if God reigns in heaven, must descend upon that Synagogue of Satan.—New England. The wrongs inflicted upon us, I expect neither to forgive nor forget, until a terrible punishment overtakes the [word obscured by tear in page] branded Cain[4] that slew all our fond hopes. You tell me your noble husband fell at Vicksburg.[5] Ah my stricken friend! would you willingly recall him from the cradling arms of glory;—to live under the hated monstrous despotism which he died to avert! Oh mourn not that your darling was called to his eternal rest, before the land of his birth went down in a starless night of degradation and slavery—but rather thank God that he was spared the humiliation heaped upon us, and sigh that we could not all have perished with him. For affliction such as yours all human sympathy is inadequate and I shall attempt no words of consolation:

> "Well I know thee de profundis!
> Of your smitten spirit moan,
> When you cast your crown of sorrow
> Down before the veiled throne!"

God help you and your orphan children, and grant you the grace to be patient and brave under the great curse laid upon us all. Accept my cordial sympathy and best wishes—

Very respectfully—
Your countrywoman in captivity
Augusta J. Evans

1. Eugenie de Guerin (1805–1848), a French writer whose *Journal* was published posthumously in 1862.

2. A tree native to Asia and Africa that produces a poisonous sap.

3. In Greek mythology, the goddess of retribution.

4. The oldest son of Adam and Eve, who murdered his brother Abel. See Gen. 4:1–16.

5. Vicksburg, Mississippi, fell to the Union on July 4, 1863. See AEW to Curry, July 15, 1863, note 24.

🙣 🙣 🙣

54 / MS Library of Congress (original)
Alabama   Mobile April 15th 1866

Mr. Curry—

The enclosed article will show you that the Editors in Mobile have anticipated a letter, which I have for some days, intended writing,—but which I delayed,—simply because you have become such an <u>ignis fatuus</u>[1] that I knew not where my letter would find you; and as Carrie[2] wrote me that you intended visiting Tuskegee, I thought it advisable to defer writing, until you return to Marion. For many days past, I have been earnestly solicited by the gentlemen and ladies of Mobile, to inaugurate the movement,—with reference to which, I now take the liberty of trespassing on your time;—but a <u>dread</u> of being considered unduly forward, or desirous of thrusting myself upon the public, made me shrink from the notoriety inevitably consequent upon a compliance with these numerous petitions. But my heart turned so yearningly to the holy labor of love, that at last,—notwithstanding my many engagements—I yielded;—and the article enclosed, will fully explain the object contemplated. I believe, Mr. Curry, that you at least will not ascribe any mere contemptible vanity, to the motive which prompts me to submit the article to your perusal. The remembrance of the <u>marble</u> <u>inkstand</u> you presented to Howell Cobb,[3]— induced me to hope your acquaintance with the Talladega[4] quarries would enable you to ascertain for me, whether the accompanying design could be executed in fine white marble. The difficulty of transporting a monolith of the designated dimensions, is, I am fully aware very serious; but I should almost regard it as an <u>insult</u> to our Dead, if the cenotaph[5] raised to commemorate their devotion to our hallowed cause,— were bought in Boston,—and chiselled by hands dripping with their precious blood. I am exceedingly anxious to rear a monument of pure-polished Alabama marble, and as I am not personally acquainted with Mr Parsons, (and should dislike to apply to him, even if I were,) I felt that you Sir, would willingly aid me, by making the requisite inquiries among your numerous friends at Talladega. Will you please be so kind as to ascertain the probable cost of such a monument,—and the time required to prepare it for transportation? Had I any friends residing in Talladega, I would not trouble you, for I presume your time is fully occupied. In addition to the base and shaft, I shall need <u>eight</u> <u>square</u> <u>blocks</u> <u>of</u> <u>marble</u>, which will be carved into the same number of <u>vases</u>, <u>3</u> <u>feet</u> <u>high</u>, and placed upon the <u>8</u> <u>corners</u>. France inscribed

upon the Pantheon[6] which held the ashes of her great men, "Au grands
Hommes La Patria Reconnaissant!"[7] and under the quiet shadow of the pines
that skirt our city I want to see a Memorabilia erected to which I can go,
whenever I desire to lay a grateful offering, "memoria in aeternitate"[8] upon
the last resting place of my martyred countrymen. Such a monument shall
prove the Mecca, whither we women can turn continually, and I intend to
select some day in the year which will be reverently and tenderly consecrated
to the melancholy task of ornamenting the graves,—and pronouncing eulo-
gies upon the heroism and sublime endurance of their silent tenants. In fine,
I purpose to revive the old Hindostance[9] "Aekja," or offering of flowers, for
the repose of souls. I look forward with indescribable emotions, to the time
when the scheme so dear to my heart shall be successfully accomplished; and
when it shall be my proud privilege to watch over and keep in thorough order
that sacred spot of Gods [sic] acre,—where calmly sleep the noble standard-
bearers of a Lost Cause!

> "Where shall we lay the men whom we deplore?
> Let the voice of those they wrought for,
> And the feet of those they fought for,
> Echo round their bones for evermore!"[10]

If God spares my life, those eight vases, shall never lack their floral tributes
in summer season; nor evergreen wreaths in dun-gloomy wintry weather.
Should it prove utterly impracticable to obtain marble from Talladega, I shall
be compelled most reluctantly, to keep the matter in abeyance; and if I am
obliged to go North this summer to read proof of my new book,[11] (which I
hope to avoid, if possible,) I shall then select the most suitable monument I
can find in New York. The occasion of its erection here, will be peculiarly
solemn,—and Pericles[12]—when he stood twenty three centuries ago, in Ker-
ameikus, to deliver a funeral oration for those who were slain in the Samian
war,[13]—had not a theme half so worthy of his eloquence,—as that Southern
orator will be called on to handle, when the widows and orphans of our
slaughtered defenders cluster mournfully around their ashes, to hear their
heroic deeds recounted and extolled. But ah! the Athenian women who wept
for their dead, under the glistening olives and waving pomegranates of Ker-
ameikus,—and hushed their sobs—to listen to the silvery accents of Pericles,—
had the precious consolation of knowing that the Sacrifice was not in vain!
that the glory of their beloved Athens was untarnished! while alas! my
bereaved countrywomen who shall stand around their mouldering grey-clad
darlings,—in the day when I shall have their monument raised,—must feel
that they have laid their all on a crumbling altar, upon which God frowned!
and though their quivering lips will whisper, "Thy will be done";—their
aching hearts will echo those melancholy words:

"For the drift of the Maker is dark, an Isis[14]—
Hid by the veil!"[15]

Mr. Curry, will it be agreeable to you, to be with us on that occasion, and deliver the eulogy which I <u>know</u> your heart prompts? There are others whom I might <u>claim</u> for this hallowed task,—and who would I <u>know</u> very gladly respond;—but I turn first to you,—and should you decline, can find a substitute. Of course I can not tell how soon, I shall be able to complete the requisite preparations, but the day I trust will not be very distant, unless I am compelled to wait until I go to New York. Please furnish me as soon as possible, with the desired information concerning the Talladega quarries,— as some of my friends leave in a few days for Europe, and should you deem my present plan impracticable, I may conclude to send a different one across the Atlantic. The accompanying rude sketch is merely intended to give the <u>dimensions</u>, and I am preparing a very careful and accurate drawing, which is yet unfinished, but will be forwarded if you think it advisable, to the Talladega stone cutters. There are many things in connection with this subject which it would afford me great pleasure to discuss <u>in extenso</u>[16] with you, but the limits of a letter, peremptorily forbid. Hoping that you will pardon the trouble I have taken the liberty of giving you, I am with best wishes for your happiness and usefulness—

Most sincerely your friend & <u>compatriot</u>—

A. J. Evans

1. Literally, a flickering flame. Here, meaning someone moving around, difficult to locate.

2. AEW's younger sister, Caroline.

3. Howell Cobb was one of the Georgia delegates to the Convention of the Seceding States, which met in Montgomery, Alabama, in February 1861 following Lincoln's election as president on an antislavery platform. Curry was one of the Alabama delegates to the Montgomery convention (Rice, *J. L. M. Curry,* 37), and Howell Cobb, a Georgia delegate, was elected president of the convention (Coulter, *Confederate States of America,* 23). The inkstand that Curry presented to Cobb was made from Alabama marble. See AEW to Curry, January 1, 1902.

4. Curry's hometown in east-central Alabama.

5. A monument designed to honor an individual or a group of people whose remains are somewhere else.

6. The Pantheon was originally a temple dedicated to all the gods. Now it means a tomb or memorial to the famous deceased citizens of a nation. The one in Paris houses the remains of Voltaire and Rousseau, among others.

7. "The fatherland is grateful to its great men!"

8. "May they be remembered throughout eternity."

9. Hindustan is the Persian name for India.

10. Alfred, Lord Tennyson, "Ode on the Death of the Duke of Wellington" (1852), stanza 2. AEW changed the wording slightly. The original reads as follows: "Where shall we lay the man whom we deplore? / Here, in streaming London's central roar, / Let the sound of those he wrought for, / and the feet of those he fought for, / Echo round his bones for evermore."

11. *St. Elmo,* which was published in December 1866.

12. Pericles (ca. 495–429 B.C.E.), an Athenian statesman who helped Athens to develop both its democracy and its empire.

13. In 440 B.C.E. Samos, formerly one of Athen's staunchest allies, revolted and nearly succeeded in establishing independence. Although his army was outnumbered, Pericles quelled the insurrection.

14. Isis was an Egyptian goddess who searched throughout Egypt for the remains of her slain husband, Osiris. Also, as the goddess of magic, she was mysterious and controlled the transformation of both objects and beings.

15. Alfred, Lord Tennyson, "Maud," part 1, section 4, stanza 8, line 1.

16. at length

⁂ ⁂ ⁂

55 / MS Library of Congress (original)
Alabama (photocopy)   Mobile May 7th 1866

Mr. Curry:

"Ossa on Pelion piled,—and rolled upon Ossa, leafy Olympus!!"[1] Visitors,—work,—and heaps of unanswered and unanswerable letters;—letters begging photographs,—autographs,—letters from poor crippled soldiers, asking me to find them employment,—from Episcopal clergymen, requesting me to have them "called" to some church,—and to make up schools for their wives—letters from young gentlemen at college, praying for lists of such books as they should read in conjunction with their textbooks,—and letters plaintive, from young ladies who see from the newspapers that I am going to Europe very soon, and are in profound distress, fearing that I may be drowned in crossing the Atlantic Ocean!! "There is no rest for the wicked!"[2] Most indisputably—I have no rest, and Whateley's[3] or Mill's[4] or Aristotle's Logic will furnish the remainder of the sentence—unflattering though it may be. Up to my very lips in work, I barely have time to peep out a moment, and thank you for your letter,—which must certainly have travelled to Egypt with the Goths,[5] hunting up Algard—on the "lotus laden Nile,"—judging from the length of time it was en route. While I am sorry to learn that you deem "your education and library attainments too insignificant,["]—and consider your-self devoid of the qualifications requisite for the preparation of the oration alluded to,—I of course can not insist, or press upon you, a labor which you seem to regard as so severe. I presume your time is already fully occupied, and moreover, when I preferred my request, I assure you, the idea never once

presented itself to my mind, that you would shrink from that holy privilege,
—for fear of incurring "odium or arrest." As for my "aiding you with suggestions!" why my good friend!—I am delving in the mines of Laurium,⁶ and
have no time to go peddling "owls in Athens!"⁷ While I regret that you will
not be present, on that solemn and sacred occasion, to which I look forward
with such longing eagerness, I yield of course to your decision, and shall not
insist on a compliance with a request which I imagined would give pleasure
to your patriotic heart. Among the gentlemen you mention, I number some
very devoted friends, but my dear Sir, I do not think it obligatory upon me
to invite an Alabamian, and my most gifted friends reside in other States.
Two in Louisiana,—one, an exile from Kentucky—now in Cincinnati,—one
in South Carolina, and several in Georgia. Apropos! of dear old Mother
Georgia;—my noble, revered, and marvellously eloquent friend—Bishop
Pierce⁸—(George) told me if I would only write him the exact time of the
erection of the monument, he would come any distance to be with me. If
I send him to deliver the oration, which is possible,—how grand, how
solemn,—how replete with pathos and power,—how perfect it will be, as a
specimen of genius, eloquence, and rich ripe scholarship! Yesterday as I
looked up, into his handsome—kingly face,—my hearts verdict was, "the
noblest Roman of them all!" I understand that the Talladega quarries are
totally neglected, and fear that it will be impracticable for me to carry out my
original design. I have been offered a very handsome monument, imported
antecedent to the war, by parties, who are now impoverished, and unable to
pay even its enormous freight charges, and consequently can not erect it. I
believe it was destined for the interior, and was purchased six years ago, for
$4500; by some fond wife, who desired to raise it over the remains of her hus-
band. It was never unpacked until this week, and the Committee of gentlemen who waited upon me, with reference to the matter, belonged to one of
our military companies, who intended to purchase and erect it in honor of
their lost comrades, but finding the expense too great, are willing to yield it
to me. It is only 20 feet high, and much more ornate than I desired, for the
severe simplicity of a lofty obelisk, is certainly more appropriate for the precious and hallowed purpose—so dear to my heart. Still it is very beautiful,
and nobly proportioned, and if I decide to take it, I think now, I shall have it
raised very soon, on that large mound in the public square—in the centre of
our City where its pure marble lips will whisper to all passing strangers—Siste
viator⁹! Thank you for the touching lines on our trailing Banner, which you
were so good as to enclose in your letter. As I read them, bitter waves from
the Dead Sea Past surged and broke over my heart. I gave them to Gen'l
Beauregard, who goes to England, on pressing business for the R R of which
he is now President.¹⁰

My <u>peerless</u> <u>pearl</u> <u>Gussie</u>,[11] would no doubt send you a kiss, in return for the one you offered her, (for nature has given her a fund of <u>coquetterie</u>)—but her "<u>Auntie</u>" will not allow her, said "Auntie" being so selfish that <u>she</u> <u>keeps</u> <u>all</u> <u>Gussie's</u> <u>kisses</u> <u>for</u> <u>herself</u>. Ah! she is the loveliest darling, the sweetest cherub the Sun ever shone on! You would laugh heartily, if you could only witness her vigorous efforts to <u>scold</u> when she imagines herself slighted or injured. We are having her portrait painted <u>in</u> <u>nubibus</u>.[12] As Charles Garret says; "I have only time and space to <u>cram</u> <u>in</u>—Good-bye Sir, and God bless you."

Your friend
A.J.Evans

PS.
Please be so kind as to forward to me any information which you may receive from the <u>quarries</u>, as I do not wish to purchase the monument here if I can avoid doing so.
A.J.E.

1. Mount Pelion in the South and Mt. Ossa in the North border a chain of mountains along the Aegean Sea. According to Greek mythology, two giants determined to "pile Pelion on Ossa" and attack Olympus. However, Apollo killed them before they could carry out their plan.

2. A variation of Isaiah 48:22: "'There is no peace,' saith the Lord, 'unto the wicked.'"

3. Richard Whately (1787–1863), an English prelate, archbishop of Dublin, and a famous logician.

4. John Stuart Mill (1806–1873), an English economist and philosopher.

5. A Germanic people who overran much of the Roman Empire from the third to the sixth centuries C.E.

6. Laurium (also known as Laurion) is a Greek town near Athens. Its mines, which produced lead, manganese, cadmium, and especially silver, were exploited in the fourth century B.C.E. and finally closed, but were reopened in the nineteenth century.

7. This Greek proverb, from Aristophanes's *The Birds,* is used to suggest a condition of superfluity or overabundance. The owl is Athene's bird, so Athens would presumably have plenty of owls.

8. George Foster Pierce (1811–1884), a bishop of the Methodist Episcopal Church, South. The most prominent preacher in the Georgia Conference, Pierce was known for his oratory. He was a conservative who supported secession and after the war opposed any attempt to reunite the Northern and Southern branches of the Methodist Episcopal Church.

9. Be still, traveler!

10. After the war Beauregard came home to New Orleans impoverished but soon obtained a position with the New Orleans, Jackson, and Great Northern Railroad as chief engineer and superintendent. The directors of the railroad wanted to expand into the Ohio Valley but were hampered by a huge debt: three million dollars in

bonds held by Northern and European investors. The only hope was to convince the investors to exchange their interest coupons for second mortgage bonds. The directors made Beauregard president of the railroad and sent him to negotiate with the investors. Beauregard was successful and came home with the arrangement the directors had wanted. Everywhere Beauregard went on railroad business—in the Northern United States and in Europe—he was honored and lionized as a great military hero.

11. Little Augusta Evans, AEW's niece and namesake. She was the daughter of AEW's brother, Vivian Rutherford Evans.

12. in the clouds

13. Possibly a reference to Alexander Charles Garrett, who was born in Ireland, served as an Episcopalian missionary in British Columbia, and later became Bishop of Northern Texas.

ᕙᕗ ᕙᕗ ᕙᕗ

56 / MS Alabama Archives (original)
Historic Mobile Society (typed copy)   [May 18th 1866]

To the Hon. Mayor & Board of Aldermen
and Common Council of the City of Mobile:
Gentlemen:

In grateful commemoration of the heroism of the noble men, who fell in defense of our city, I respectfully solicit permission to erect upon the mound in the center of Bienville Square a marble monument, thirty feet in height, bearing a brief inscription in honor of the faithful standard bearers of our lost cause; "A memorabilia" whose marble lips shall whisper to every passing stranger, <u>siste</u> <u>viator</u>.[1] The distance and seclusion of the spot appropriated as the "soldiers rest," have been deemed valid objections to the erection of a monument in the city cemetery, and all who have manifested an interest in this last and most inadequate tribute to our fallen countrymen, concur in the opinion that if raised in Bienville Square it would furnish a grateful in memoriam which would ornament and hallow the site selected.

A brazen Belgique Lion on a vast pedestal of human bones, four hundred feet high, marked the Battle of Waterloo; thirty-five years ago Louis of Bavaria[2] laid near Ratisbon,[3] the corner stone of "Valhalla";[4] and upon the Pantheon at Paris, appropriated to the reception of the ashes of France's great men, are inscribed the words: "Aux Grands Hommes La Patria Reconnaissant."[5]

Shall the poor meed of a people's gratitude be withheld from the gray clad Confederate legions who now sleep unhonored on Alabama soil?

> "A people's voice! we are noble yet,
> Tho' all men else their nobler dreams forget,

We have a voice with which to pay the debt,
Of boundless love, reverence, and regret."[6]

Believing that the hallowed memories of Spanish Fort, Blakely,[7] Forts Morgan and Gaines and Powell,[8] of the Tennessee[9] and the Selma,[10] will thrill
your hearts, and plead trumpet-tongued for the privilege I request at your
hands, and that you will cordially co-operate in the attempt to rescue our
martyred defenders from oblivion[11]

I am, gentlemen, very respectfully,
Augusta J. Evans

1. Be still, traveler.

2. Louis I (1786–1868), king of Bavaria, supported German nationalism and disliked Bavaria's association with Napoleon.

3. Also known as Regensburg, a city in northern Bavaria.

4. In Scandinavian myth, Valhalla was the great hall to which the spirits of slain
warriors were admitted. Louis's monument to Bavarian soldiers is, figuratively speaking, a "Valhalla."

5. "The fatherland is grateful to its great men."

6. Lord Alfred Tennyson, "Ode on the Death of the Duke of Wellington," VII, lines
1–2, 6–7.

7. On March 17, 1865, the Union launched the Mobile Campaign, an operation
to capture Mobile. Spanish Fort, a few miles away, fell on April 8, 1865. Blakely,
Alabama, fell on April 9, the last infantry battle of the war. The Union army entered
Mobile on April 12, three days after Lee's surrender at Appomattox. However, the
Confederate Department of Alabama, Mississippi, and East Louisiana did not surren-
der until May 4, 1865.

8. The Mobile Campaign was launched from these three forts that line Mobile Bay
and that the Union had captured in the naval Battle of Mobile Bay on August 5,
1864.

9. The Tennessee, a Confederate ironclad ram, was built in Mobile and commissioned on February 6, 1864. On August 5, 1864, the Union naval forces captured it
in the Battle of Mobile Bay.

10. The Selma was a Confederate wooden gunboat that also fought in the Battle of
Mobile Bay.

11. See AEW to Curry, June 22, 1866, note 8.

❧ ❧ ❧

57 / MS Virginia   Mobile June 20th 1866

My dear kind friend[1]

Peccavi! peccavi![2] is the quivering cry of my reproachful soul, as I turn to
your letter written from Baltimore, and find how many, many weeks have
elapsed since its receipt. Again, and again I have taken up my pen to thank
you, for your friendly remembrance, and assure you of my own; but indeed

the fates seem to have conspired against our correspondence;—though believe me Sir,—not against <u>our</u> friendship, which can triumphantly defy even years of silence. If you could realize all that has engaged my time and attention since the melancholy close of a struggle, in which all my hopes were involved, and <u>crushed</u>, I feel assured you would not, you could not censure a silence—which has been unavoidable. The multitudinous engagements from which there was no escape, precluded the possibility of my finding the leisure requisite to write to my dearest and most valued relatives and friends. Recently I have been endeavoring to collect the money necessary to enclose the graves of <u>our</u> <u>Dead</u> <u>Soldiers</u>, and erect a monument commemorating their heroism and devotion in defense of Mobile.[3] In addition, I am hard at work, writing a new novel[4] which I hope to publish this fall. My book I hoped to finish long ago, but have been so constantly interrupted and retarded by visitors, that I know not exactly when I shall finish it—and oh! blessed thought! sit down—and <u>rest</u> and call my time my own. I <u>think</u> it is the best thing I have ever written, and if the public will only agree with me, I shall be <u>profoundly</u> <u>gratified</u>. Where and how is <u>your</u> <u>dear</u> <u>wife</u>? And what is your gifted Son doing? And what are your plans? And have you any fortitude—when you look back, any hope—when you look forward? I heard you were writing for some paper in Baltimore—is it true? We often speak of you, and wonder [line obscured] conversations once held at Georgia Cottage,[5] in the glorious and hallowed days of the "<u>Wearing</u> <u>of</u> <u>the</u> <u>Gray</u>." Oh Mr [obscured] my dear friend! I feel as if my heart were inurned, with my country's flag, and my people's freedom. I am not patient,—I am not reconciled, I am not philosophically, or religiously resigned—and I never shall be! My family all send kindest remembrances <u>to</u> <u>you</u> and dear Mrs. Dawson, and your son Mr. Joe. Forgive my long silence, and believe me when I assure you, that the memory of all your friendly deeds is warm in my heart. Sallie[6] sends love [line obscured] Do write me soon, and believe me as ever your sincere friend. AJEvans

1. The recipient of this letter has not been identified (also see the letter of October 23, 1866, addressed to the same person). Although Curry delivered speeches all across the United States after the war in his role as educator and minister, the recipient could not be Curry. In 1866 Curry was a widower, and he did not remarry until 1867. Also, Curry's only son was named Manly, not Joe. The Mrs. Dawson referred to at the end of the letter appears to be the recipient's wife, but there is no reference to anyone by the name of Dawson in AEW's biography.

2. See AEW to Rachel Lyons, March 20, 1863.

3. See AEW to Curry, April 15, 1866; also AEW to the Mayor, Board of Aldermen, Common Council of Mobile, May 18, 1866.

4. *St. Elmo,* a huge success, was published in December 1866.

5. The house near Mobile that AEW bought for herself and her family with

money earned from the sale of *Beulah*. See AEW to Rachel Lyons, May 27, [1859],
note 1.

    6. AEW's younger sister, Sarah Evans.

❧ ❧ ❧

58 / MS Library of Congress (original)
Alabama (photocopy)   Mobile June 22d 1866

Mr. Curry:

    I believe it was Voltaire,[1] who mournfully ejaculated in one of his letters
to Frederick the Great:[2] "<u>Negligent</u>! <u>forgetful</u> <u>of</u> <u>your</u> <u>royal</u> <u>favor</u>!! I call all
the Gods of the Pantheon to witness that I deny it!! But if your Majesty could
only dream how desperately hard I am worked, your Majesty would nobly
forgive a silence, which your Majesty's accurate knowledge of my character,
must assure your Majesty is sternly compulsory, and indescribably painful!!"
If I may be allowed a ridiculously <u>gigantic</u> illustration of a most gigantic infliction,—fancy me, at my desk, overwhelmed and struggling like
Enceladus,[3] under the crushing Sicily—of unanswered, and unanswerable
documents,—printed and unprinted,—of all imaginable, and unimaginable
styles and contents—hurled alas! not by Minerva!! Verily! verily it would
require the marvellous dexterity, and the facile pen of Giovanni Pico di
Mirandola,[4] to keep me quite clear of epistolary debts; and as parsimonious
nature denied me his gifts,—I intend to declare myself hopelessly insolvent
in epistolary matters, and take the benefit of the bankrupt act. Indeed my dear
Sir, I throw myself upon the mercy of my correspondents,—and trust that
unlike the Prussian wit, whose example I am inclined to follow, I shall not
"find their mercy more dreadful than their vengeance." While very grateful
to you, for the inquiries which you were so kind as to make for me, concerning the Ala. quarries,[5]—I was pained to ascertain the utter impracticality
of obtaining Talladega marble, and was compelled to purchase the monument
alluded to, in a former letter. The time of its erection is contingent upon several circumstances beyond my control;—1st the granite base which weighs
<u>six</u> <u>tons</u>, is now at Prairie Bluff,[6] on the river bank,—and submerged; conse-
quently can not be transported to Mobile until the subsidence of the high
water; 2nd, I have <u>petitioned</u> the City authorities for permission to raise it on
the mound in our Public Square; but <u>fear</u> my prayer will not be granted by
the Board of Councilmen & Alderman,[7] who are too cowardly to risk giving umbrage to the "powers that be."[8] <u>Nous</u> <u>verrous!</u>[9] The accompanying
papers were left in my hands for distribution, by Mr Walton—a Baptist minister of Virginia, who expressed great anxiety to enlist <u>your</u> sympathy and secure
your cooperation in his scheme. He was introduced to me by Gen'l Rosser, and

his mission is a noble one, that appeals powerfully to every <u>Southern</u> heart. At his request, I forward some of his circulars to you. During your visit to Mobile, I believe you told me you were a friend of Mr Evelyn;[10] if so, why do you not lend him a helping hand, in this hour of feeble health and sorest need? The "<u>Crescent</u>" is <u>really</u> <u>a</u> <u>good</u> <u>magazine</u>, but unless the people come to his assistance, and fill his subscription list, he will be compelled to abandon it,[11] and it will add another to the melancholy fleet of wrecks,—already drifting on the sea of Southern periodic literature. I have requested Co'l Taylor to write an essay on John Stewart Mill,[12] for the "<u>Crescent</u>," and Mr Columbus Lee, who has been studying Buckle[13] for some months past, has partially promised to prepare a review for the same magazine. Just so soon as I can possibly find the time, I intend to write for it;—and now—may I venture, may I presume, to ask, whether "your limited education, & insignificant literary attainments"————(<u>Oh</u> <u>Mr</u> <u>Curry</u>! <u>Mr</u> <u>Curry</u>!! <u>Mr</u> <u>Curry</u>!!!) will permit you to send him something? Suppose that while inspecting your "qualifications" you borrow a pair of those powerful magnifying glasses, which <u>all</u> <u>of</u> <u>your</u> <u>friends</u> are in the habit of using whenever they look at you? The "Macedonian Phantom,"[14] starts abroad and from the office of the <u>Crescent</u> rings the cry, "<u>Come</u> <u>over</u> <u>into</u> <u>Macedonia,</u> <u>and</u> <u>help</u> <u>us</u>!" Will you shut your ears my friend? Just now some of my kind friends are urging me to accompany them to Europe;—others begging me to come on at once to New York,—but I shall not leave home until I finish my new book;[15] and then unless I am obliged to go North to read proof, I shall have leisure to write for Mr Evelyns [sic] <u>Maga</u>, and hope to prepare some articles on Ruskin[16] and Jean Ingelow.[17] One of the greatest temptations of my life is now set before me; namely to throw down my pen,—leave my work, and all our sorrowful memories behind me, and rest and lose myself among the glories of Europe, with most appreciative companions. I long to touch the shores of the Old World, to rest in the awful shadow of the Alps,—

> "And write of their white raiment, the ghostly capes that
>   Screen them—
> Of the storm winds that beat them, their thunder-rents
>   And scars;—
> And the paradise of purple, and the golden slopes atween
>   Them,—
> And fields, where grow God's gentian bells, and his
>   crocus stars!"[18]

Some day—please God,—I hope to go, but not this year. Give my love to my dear Sister, and be sure you Marion people take good care of her. Mrs Chandron asks kindly after you. I write in <u>great</u> <u>haste</u>, and you must pardon any errors you may discover. I have not seen my little darling[19] for a month, as she is at Point Clear.[20] Thank God her health is much improved.

With best wishes for your happiness and usefulness, believe me

your friend AJE

1. Voltaire (1694–1778), a French author and philosopher.

2. Frederick the Great of Prussia (1712–1786), a patron of the arts, corresponded with Voltaire for forty-two years. AEW's statement appears to be a very rough paraphrase of several statements made by Voltaire in 1749, explaining delays in his correspondence.

3. In Greek mythology, Enceladus was one of the giants who revolted against the gods, even attacking them in heaven. As the giants retreated back to earth, Athena (Minerva) threw a huge missile at Enceladus that crushed him and became the island of Sicily.

4. Pico Della Mirandola, Count Giovanni (1463–1494), was an Italian humanist, philosopher, and scholar, who believed that all religions and philosophies contain elements of universal truth. He attempted, through nine hundred theses, to write a synthesis of all systems.

5. See AEW to Curry, April 15, 1866.

6. On the banks of the Alabama River, northeast of Mobile.

7. See AEW to the Board of Aldermen, May 18, 1866.

8. AEW's request was eventually granted, but according to Fidler (*A Biography*, 121), the monument was not completed until 1874, and it was erected in Magnolia Cemetery, not in Bienville Square as AEW had requested in her letter to the Aldermen and Council of May 18, 1866.

9. We are under lock and key!

10. William Evelyn, publisher of *The Crescent Monthly: A Magazine of Literature, Art, Science, and Society.*

11. *The Crescent* was published only from 1866 to 1867.

12. John Stuart Mill (1806–1873), English economist, philosopher, and social reformer, exerted a major influence on nineteenth-century thought.

13. Henry Thomas Buckle (1821–1862) was an English historian known for his environmental interpretation of history, which states that a nation's character is determined by the influence of geography, climate, soil, and food.

14. A reference to the vision that the apostle Paul experienced on his second missionary journey. A man from Macedonia appeared to Paul in a vision and said, "Come over to Macedonia and help us" (Acts 16:9). As a result of this vision, Paul changed his route and went to what later became Europe.

15. *St. Elmo,* published in late 1866.

16. John Ruskin was an English art critic and a major writer of the nineteenth century.

17. A nineteenth-century English novelist and poet. Wordsworth and Tennyson influenced her poetry.

18. Jean Ingelow, "Requiescat in Pace," lines 9–12.

19. AEW's niece and namesake, Augusta Evans.

20. A town at the mouth of Mobile Bay

CHAPTER 7

"*The aching Southern heart*"

Col' Seaver:

My dear friend:

In memory of those halcyon <u>ante</u> <u>bellum</u> days of yore, now gone forever and ever by, when you and I held our intellectual symposiums over the quiet tea table at the St Nicholas;[1]—and when you were a colloquial Coleridge, (?) nay a "Christopher North,"[2] at whose feet I sat, and listened delightedly;—in token of my grateful remembrance of all your friendship and kindness,—when I was an unknown authorling,—allow me to introduce to your acquaintance and esteem, my elegant and valued friend, Col Murrell of Mobile, who spends a few days in your city, and whom I particularly desire that you should properly appreciate. When Racine[3] was asked by a thankful young actor upon whom he had conferred some favor: "How can I prove my profound gratitude for your goodness?"—do you recollect his reply? "Introduce me to that friend whom you seem to value and regard so highly."

Believing that congenial tastes will pave the way for many pleasant hours between Col Murrell and yourself, I confidently commit him to your friendship. Meantime my dear Sir, give at least one parenthetic thought to the absent and I pray you, let me not be utterly forgotten at your favorite "teafights," or your brilliant reunions with literary esoterics at Delmonico's,[4] where when you are present, they must rival the "Blue Room" at Ambrose's in Edingburg [sic], or the Triclinium[5] at Tusculum,[6] over which Lucullus[7] presided. With best wishes for your prosperity,—and an earnest hope that God willing, we yet may renew the pleasant hours of old, I bow myself out, and leave Col Murrell to speak for himself, and show you how inadequate are my efforts to do him justice.

Gratefully your friend—

Augusta J. Evans

PS

Please present Col Murrell to Mr Derby.

1. A luxurious hotel in New York City. See AEW to Seaver, December 31, 1859, note 3.

2. An imaginary character in the "Noctes Ambrosianae," a series of articles published in *Blackwood's Edinburgh Magazine* from 1822 to 1835. Christopher North and his friends met at a tavern and discussed literary topics. See AEW to Curry, October 16, 1863, note 5.

3. Jean Baptiste Racine (1639–1699), a French dramatist known for his tragedies.

4. A famous restaurant on Fifth Avenue in New York City.

5. In Roman antiquity, a dining room with couches around a table for guests to recline as they ate.

6. A city near Rome.

7. See AEW to Curry, October 7, 1865, note 18.

❧ ❧ ❧

60 / *MS Georgia*   Mobile Oct' 23d 1866

My dear kind friend:[1]

Your welcome letter of the 12th contained the first tidings of your whereabouts, which I have received for many weeks; and you were such an <u>ignis fatuus</u>[2] that I was puzzled to know how to address my letters. I am rejoiced to learn that your dear wife is with you, as your last letter stated that she would remain in Baltimore, until her health was fully restored, and I gladly conclude that she is quite well again. But my dear Sir,—where is your son? I have such high hopes of his future, expect that brilliant intellect and brave heart of his to accomplish so much good and so much glory, both for the world, for his parents and himself,—that I do not like to lose sight of him.

Thank you my friend, for the copy of your elegant Brooklyn speech. While I do not agree with your opinion that the result of the war proved we had no right to Secede, I read your speech with great pleasure, and enjoyed its many beautiful passages and glowing metaphors. I am not surprised that the impassioned eloquence of a southern orator, should thaw and stir the frozen natures of a northern audience, and I am exceedingly glad that so soon after your arrival in New York, you had an opportunity of delivering an address which can not fail to impress the people in your favor. Still I must tell you I do not accept the conclusion of the war, as a test of its <u>legitimacy</u> or <u>expediency</u>.

<u>Might</u> often <u>crushes</u>—but never makes <u>right</u>. Today—the right of Secession is more holy than five years ago,—for now it has been sanctified—baptized anew, with the blood of our Legion of Liberty's Martyrs. Because all the reformers before Luther were crushed and destroyed,—was their right to ecclesiastical secession any less sacred than his? I shall not probably live to see it, but

> "Though the mills of God grind slowly,
> Yet they grind exceeding small,

> Though with patience he stands waiting,
> With exactness grinds he all!"[3]

I have an abiding faith that the cause for which we have suffered so much, will yet triumph, and though I shall perhaps be in my quiet grave, ere it comes, yet:

> "Truth crushed to earth will rise again.
> The eternal years of God—are hers."[4]

How long will Fanny May remain in New York? Please give my warm love and all kindly greetings to her.

Is not my friend Mr. Derby,[5] a noble true man? I know you will estimate him properly, when you know him well. Tell my kind and accomplished publisher, G W Carleton,[6] 413 Broadway, to be sure to give you an early copy of "St. Elmo."[7] If you don't really and sincerely like it better than all my other books put together,—why—I think I shall take a spell of pouting that shall last at least for a week!

Give my love to your dear wife, and present my regards to Mr. Joe. Mother and all the family send love to yourself and Mrs. Dawson. Believe me

Sincerely your friend—A. J. Evans

Send me your address as I direct this at random.

1. Unknown recipient. See letter of June 20, 1866, also addressed to "My dear kind friend."

2. Literally a flickering flame. Here meaning someone who is moving about or difficult to locate.

3. Henry Wadsworth Longfellow, "Retribution," from *Sinngedichte of Friedrich von Logau* (translated by Longfellow).

4. William Cullen Bryant, "The Battlefield," stanza 9.

5. J. C. Derby, of the firm Derby and Jackson, was the publisher who accepted AEW's novel *Beulah* (1859). Derby and AEW remained lifelong friends.

6. Carleton acquired Derby's share of the publishing firm and published several of AEW's novels, beginning with *St. Elmo* in 1866 (Fidler, *A Biography,* 127).

7. *St. Elmo* was published in December 1866, two months after this letter.

❧ ❧ ❧

61 / MS Library of Congress (original)
Alabama (photocopy)   Mobile Oct 30th 1866

Mr. J E. Cooke:[1]
My dear Sir:

I feel assured your generous heart will kindly accord me pardon, for my seeming negligence in failing to acknowledge more promptly your very flattering letters,—when I plead in extenuation of my silence, the melancholy fact that sickness and death have brooded heavily—mournfully over my home and heart. Moreover, it was impossible for me to decide with reference to the subject of our correspondence, until I had conferred with Gen'l Beauregard. Yesterday he acquainted me with his conclusion concerning the matter, and I hasten to transmit his decision. I regret to inform you that he is unwilling to allow her (Mrs B)[2] to fill a niche in your temple of glory,[3] for the reason that she was a confirmed invalid,—unable to labor in any way for the advancement of our sacred cause. He says: "Her last words were indeed worthy of a Roman matron,[4] but what are <u>words</u> to the acts of those noble-hearted women, who devoted their time and labor to assisting and caring for the sick and wounded, besides encouraging the faint-hearted, who almost despaired of the Republic." He desires me to express to you his most sincere and cordial thanks, for your kind desire to publish a sketch of his wife, but thinks it best, and <u>prefers</u> <u>that</u> <u>her</u> <u>name</u> <u>should</u> <u>not</u> <u>be</u> <u>mentioned</u>. While I regret his <u>decision</u>, and think that some tribute of gratitude is due to his suffering and heroic wife, still I feel that it is a subject of peculiar delicacy, and <u>his</u> <u>wishes</u> must of course govern us in this matter. He fully appreciates your interest, and is grateful for your kindness. Hoping your pardon for my long and unavoidable silence, and tendering my <u>earnest</u> <u>thanks</u> for the friendly words of encouragement which you so generously bestow on my little books, I am, with best wishes for the speedy advent and prosperous career of your new work, destined to commemorate our noble countrywomen——

Very respectfully
Augusta J. Evans

1. John Esten Cooke was a prolific Southern novelist and poet. His war romance, *Surry of Eagle's Nest* (1865), was so popular that seven editions quickly sold out.

2. Beauregard's first wife, and the mother of his children, died in 1850 after giving birth to a daughter. Beauregard's second wife, Caroline, is referred to here. Caroline died in 1864 after a two-year illness. Because she lived in New Orleans, a city occupied by Federal troops, Beauregard had not seen her during the two years prior to her death.

3. Cooke was contemplating a book of sketches of some of the Southern women who had worked and sacrificed on behalf of the Confederacy. The book was apparently never written.

4. Beauregard *imagined* what Caroline's last words *might* have been. When he was informed by letter of her death, he wrote to her sister: "My poor Caroline must have often asked herself on her bed of pain if she would ever see me again. . . . I well know that her beautiful soul, her generous and patriotic heart preferred the salvation of the country to the joy of seeing me. She must have said, 'The country comes before

me'—sublime words which I desire that you have carved on her tomb" (quoted in Williams, *P. G. T. Beauregard,* 204).

❧ ❧ ❧

62 / MS Library of Congress (original)
Alabama (photocopy)   At Home Sunday morning. [1866]

Mr Curry—
My dear Sir:

   I believe it was Madame de Deffand[1] who once said to the witty master of "Strawberry Hill,"[2]—after an epistolary <u>imbroglio</u>: "the writing of notes is the beginning of mischief—and sows discord among friends;"—and as your Sphinx No 2, is quite as obstinate as its predecessor, I shall not attempt to discuss, [*sic*]—what you evidently do not wish me to understand. I enclose two ambrotypes—, (the best I can obtain here,) and send <u>both</u> that you may select the one you prefer. When you have determined which you will retain, I must beg you to carry the other to my Sister Carrie. Neither of the pictures are <u>good</u> <u>likenesses</u>, but they resemble me rather more, than the photograph which I requested you to return, and which I <u>was</u> unwilling you should keep, because it always reminds me most ludicrously of those poor little fish in Mammoth Cave,[3] whose eyes are never developed. <u>Thank</u> <u>you</u> my dear friend for the photograph of yourself, which although I can not say it does you even justice,—I shall <u>always</u> preserve and value; and only regret that the face wears an expression so stern and unlike yours. . . . As I told you—Mr. Curry—two days ago, when you mentioned your sermon to me,[4]—"my presuming to offer you suggestions would be only carrying coals to Newcastle,"[5]—but nevertheless, although I know you <u>do</u> <u>not</u> <u>need</u>, and <u>will</u> <u>not</u> use them, I hand you a few coals that I find burning in my memory. Perhaps I might recall others had I leisure, but until quite late last night I had company—and have now no time for more. I daresay you will <u>laugh</u> <u>heartily</u> at my presumption and credulity, in sending anything. As our darling little Gussie[6] is much better, I shall stay in town tonight, to hear you preach. But oh my friend! . . . .

> "<u>If</u> <u>thou</u> <u>should'st</u> <u>never</u> <u>see</u> <u>my</u> <u>face</u> <u>again</u>,
> <u>Pray</u> <u>for</u> <u>my</u> <u>Soul</u>! <u>More</u> <u>things</u> <u>are</u> <u>wrought</u> <u>by</u> <u>prayer</u>,
> <u>Than</u> <u>this</u> <u>world</u> <u>dreams</u> <u>of</u>. <u>Wherefore</u>, <u>let</u> <u>thy</u> <u>voice</u>
> <u>Rise</u> <u>like</u> <u>a</u> <u>fountain</u> <u>for</u> <u>me</u>, <u>night</u> <u>and</u> <u>day</u>![7]

   May God strengthen and guide and sanctify you for your holy work, and fill your hands with golden fruitage of precious rescued souls,—is the earnest prayer of—

                                        Augusta Evans

1. Madame du Deffand (née Marie de Vichy-Chamrond) a socialite and friend of Horace Walpole. They corresponded for many years, and Walpole occasionally visited her in Paris. At the time that he knew her, Madame de Deffand was elderly and blind, but still witty and vivacious. She corresponded with Walpole by dictating letters to her secretary. See Austin Dobson, *Horace Walpole: A Memoir,* 4th ed. (Freeport, N.Y.: Books for Libraries, 1971), 200–203.

2. Strawberry Hill was Walpole's home.

3. Mammoth Cave, the world's longest cave system, is located in south-central Kentucky.

4. Trained as an orator and lawyer, Curry was also an active member of the Baptist Church and frequently preached as a layman.

5. Newcastle, a seaport in northeast England on the Tyne River, is a major center of the coal industry. Therefore, to carry coals to Newcastle is to do what is superfluous. The phrase originated with James Melville in his *Autobiography* in 1583.

6. Gussie is Augusta Evans, the infant daughter of AEW's brother Vivian Rutherford Evans. See AEW to Curry, January 9, 1867.

7. Alfred, Lord Tennyson, "The Passing of Arthur," *Idylls of the King,* lines 414–23.

❧ ❧ ❧

63 / MS Library of Congress (original)
Alabama (photocopy)   Mobile Jan' 9th 1867

Mr Curry:

Although I have barely time to write these hurried lines, I feel that I must turn from urgent and numerous engagements, to express my profound and <u>grateful</u> <u>appreciation</u> of your two very kind letters; especially the last, which contained your glowing and eloquent eulogy on my little book. Indeed my dear Sir, I am <u>inexpressibly</u> <u>gratified</u> that you esteem "<u>St</u> <u>Elmo</u>"[1] so highly; and I trust that with the blessing of God, my "labor will not be in vain,"— that I may be the humble instrument of doing <u>some</u> <u>good</u>, of leading some soul safely to Christ. The universal verdict seems to be, that "<u>St</u> <u>Elmo</u>" is far superior to my other works, and I have received some noble and precious commendations from those whose good opinion I value most. I would have answered your first letter, some time since, but hesitated—and delayed doing so, because—since my darling Gussie died,[2] I have been so sad, so hopeless, that I knew my letters could give pleasure to no one. Oh Mr Curry! I do not become at all accustomed to my loss; I feel it more bitterly every day, and the grave of my beautiful idol is the dearest spot earth holds for me. Is it not a little strange that there should now be <u>two</u> golden haired cherubic Augusta Evan's [*sic*] in heaven? One my precious niece,—the other—a little child whom I never saw, but whose father and mother (a Mr & Mrs Evans of

Northern Georgia) named their first daughter for "the woman who wrote Beulah."[3] Thank you most cordially my dear Sir, for your kind and generous words of praise, and accept the assurance that your flattering opinion of my little book, is very gratefully appreciated by—

Your sincere friend
Augusta J. Evans.

PS.
Please bring my Sister Carrie with you, when you come to Mobile in March.
        A.J.E.

1. *St. Elmo* was published in December 1866.
2. Gussie was little Augusta Evans, the daughter of AEW's brother Vivian Evans. She was twenty-two months old when she died (Fidler, *A Biography,* 147).
3. AEW's second novel, published in 1859.

❧ ❧ ❧

64 / MS Alabama   Mobile Jan' 13th 1867

Col' Seaver:
My dear Sir—
Accept my most cordial thanks for your exceedingly kind and welcome letter, the receipt of which, I should have promptly acknowledged, had not pressing and multitudinous engagements prevented my following the dictates of my heart. An unusual amount of sickness among the members of my family circle, has kept me closely occupied, and precluded the possibility of my paying my epistolary debts. I write now, in great haste, but wish to explain some circumstances, which doubtless surprised you, but which I trust gave no serious offense. A few days since, I was informed by a friend, that Judge Busteed[1] desired to call and present the letter of introduction, which you gave him some time ago; but having on all previous occasions declined to receive the visits of Federal Officers, I found it impossible to make an exception in this instance. Officers of high rank have brought me letters of introduction, but I have invariably refused to receive the bearers, and have assigned as my reason for doing so, a determination to hold no social intercourse with persons who drew their swords against a cause,—for which, I would gladly have sacrificed my life. Having been an ardent and conscientious Secessionist, and indulging still, an unwavering faith in the justice and sanctity of the principles for which we fought and prayed so devotedly, I of course could not find it agreeable to associate with those, who were arrayed in arms against my own section and people. Consequently I could not deviate from my fixed rule of conduct, even when the gentleman was Judge Busteed, and the letter of

introduction from a friend so esteemed and valued as yourself. Believe me my dear Sir, I do <u>most</u> <u>sincerely</u> <u>regret</u> that Judge Busteed's position in the Federal army renders it impossible for me to extend the hospitalities of my home to him,[2] for aside from the fact that as <u>your</u> <u>friend</u> I should like to know him,—I feel that I am indebted to his brilliant and elegant pen, for one of the <u>most</u> <u>beautiful</u> <u>and</u> <u>gratifying</u> critiques of "<u>St Elmo</u>",[3] which it has been my good fortune to receive. Feeling inexpressibly grateful for his kind and eloquent eulogy of my little <u>brow-beaten</u> <u>book</u>,[4] I am exceedingly pained to have to debar myself from <u>the</u> <u>pleasure</u> <u>of</u> <u>thanking</u> <u>him</u> <u>in</u> <u>person</u>; and I hope most earnestly that you will fully explain to him, the reasons which control my conduct, and my most grateful appreciation of his kindness and courtesy. If you do not promptly write me, I shall fear that you are <u>displeased</u> <u>with</u> <u>me</u>, and indeed my dear Sir, it would deeply grieve me to lose your friendship, or alienate your sympathy. Hoping [for] your pardon for pursuing a course, dictated by <u>mournful</u> <u>memories</u> <u>of</u> <u>my</u> <u>dead</u>, I am dear Sir,

Very sincerely your friend
A.J. Evans

1. Richard Busteed of New York served as a brigadier general in the Federal army during the war. Afterward, he became a judge in the United States District Court for the district of Alabama.

2. In addition to resenting Judge Busteed's position in the Federal army, AEW might also have considered him a carpetbagger—one of the many Northerners who came to the South during the Reconstruction era and obtained controlling positions in state and local governments. Their name was derived from the fact that they carried their belongings in a type of luggage called a "carpetbag."

3. Judge Busteed's review of *St. Elmo* has not been located. It could have been published anonymously, as many articles of that time were.

4. *St. Elmo* was a huge success with the public and became one of the best-selling books of the nineteenth century. However, some critics attacked AEW's overuse of allusions and her pretentious, erudite style. Charles Henry Webb, a New York humorist, wrote a parody of the novel titled *St. Twel'mo, or the Cuneiform Cyclopedist of Chattanooga*. Webb claimed that the author (AEW) had inadvertently swallowed a dictionary as a child, hence her pedantic style of writing.

✣ ✣ ✣

65 / MS Duke[1]　　　　　　　　　　　　　　Mobile March 30th [1867][2]

Gen'l Beauregard:

Your very kind letter of the 27th reached me yesterday, and I welcomed it cordially, as a testimonial of the pleasant fact that you had not <u>entirely</u> <u>forgotten</u> your friend and quondam correspondent. Since I saw you last,—

momentous events have followed each other in such rapid and startling succession, that I frequently ask myself, if some hideous incubus is not brooding
over our hearts and minds, and if it be indeed possible that the destiny of this
vast continent has been committed by God to the sacrilegious hands of the
insensate Jacobins[3] who now rule as ruthlessly at Washington,—as did the
"Council of Ten,"[4] in those fearful days when "Lion's Mouths" yawned at the
street corners in Venice. More pitiable than Poland or Hungary,[5] and quite as
helpless as were the Asia Minor provinces when governed by the Persian
Satraps,[6] we of the pseudo "territories," sit like Israel in the captivity; biding
the day of retribution,—the Dies Irae,[7] that must surely dawn in blood upon
the nation that oppresses us. Trusting to their honor (!) to maintain invio-
late the terms of the capitulation, and having laid down our arms,—we are
pinioned, and while our hands are tied, our cheeks are smitten; but please
God! If Astrea[8] has left the earth,—Nemesis[9] gory-handed yet lingers, and the
manes of our slaughtered legions have yet to be appeased. What will you
think of me,—if I tell you candidly that I exult at the rapidly increasing
demoralization of American society? Business with my publisher called me
recently to New York, and while there, I looked closely at the strange Social
phases that confronted me. The men are effeminate, selfish, most unscrupulously
grasping, and utterly devoid of national pride, or disinterested patriotism;—
the women are masculine, Amazonian,—"strong-minded" (?), imbued with
heinous heresies, both social and religious;—the children—heaven help
them! are not children, but miniature women of fashion and "progress,"—and
pitiable manikins already chanting paeans to the Golden Calf.[10] Northern
society is more corrupt today, than was that of Paris antecedent to the Revolution, and in the realm of morals as well as physics, only a terrific tempest
can purify the tainted and noxious atmosphere. If the analogy of the past
twenty centuries be worth the paper on which the most important epochs
are recorded,—then beyond all peradventure, we are on the eve of a mighty
convulsion, which will swing this "cradle of liberty"—(heaven save the mark!
this guillotine of liberty), as it was never rocked before, since that luckless Friday, on which America was discovered. There is no record of the successful
perpetuity of a revolutionary currency, and the grim fate of Assignats[11] must
overtake the buoyant Greenback shams[12] that now flood the country,—and
let us hope—like fiscal ignes fatui[13] lure the masses to utter ruin. Notwithstanding the vast resources of the nation, the mantle of Colbert[14] or Sully[15]
found no worthy shoulders on which to fall, at Washington, and the dancing
green bubble must be pricked ere long; then in the financial crash the
Eumenides[16] will hold their hideous assize,—and God grant I may live to witness the retributory decrees. Perhaps you will consider me too vindictive,—
but mark you! did Jehovah enjoin upon the Israelites in bondage, the duty of

loving or forgiving their task-masters? Like the Hebrews, we asked only to be allowed an Exodus; like them we were forcibly detained under a rule we abhorred; and like them our motto and policy should be, "spoil the Egyptians."[17] The Pharoahs at Washington have "hardened their hearts," and <u>the day of their plagues</u> can not be distant; neither that Red Sea of Blood, through whose waves we are to pass from the land of bondage to the Canaen [sic] of Liberty. Even <u>now</u>, our Moses may be a pampered pet in the house of Pharoah. Ah my dear Sir!:

> "Though the mills of God grind slowly,
> Yet they grind exceedingly small,
> Though with patience he stands waiting,
> <u>With exactness grinds he all</u>!"[18]

So far from "incurring my displeasure" by your published letter, I assure you I entirely concur with the sentiments which you expressed; and think your words of advice the best that could have been uttered.[19] At present, necessity bends our necks to a galling yoke, but let us not <u>perjure ourselves</u>,—neither barter our birthright for a mess of miserable political pottage. I confess I am rejoiced at the aspect of national affairs, for I hold to the infallibility of <u>history</u>, and the cosmopolitan and immemorial selfishness and recklessness of all Radicalism,—whether in politics, sociology or religion; and my reading of the mouldering past is,—that all governments oscillate, swing like a pendulum between the two extremes of absolute despotism, and rabid democracy, or red republicanism. Extreme measures necessitate reform, and the rebound is invariably equal to the pressure, or as physical philosophy proves,—<u>the angle of reflection is always equal to the angle of incidence</u>.[20] Doubtless you recollect De Stael's admirable definition of the Russian government? "<u>A despotism tempered by assassination</u>;"[21] and sometimes I am reminded of the <u>dictum, in watching the programme of Stevens,</u>[22] Boutwell,[23] and Butler,[24] <u>par nobile fratrum</u>![25] After all—Gen'l Beauregard, if the Buckle[26] theory of historic cycles be true, (and we can doubt it?) let us hope, <u>let us pray</u> that Coleridge was correct in declaring that the cycle <u>was a spiral</u>.[27] I am sorry that you wrote at all, but since the importunity of your friends required a compliance with their wishes, I am very glad that your [public] letter is just what I find it,—brave, wise, manly, and prudent. There are many things of which I should like to write you, but in these <u>uncertain times</u>, it is perhaps best to be reticent. Permit me in conclusion to refer to a matter which has given me some annoyance. I have been informed by a gentleman in Washington, that some of my letters written to you during the War, <u>are now on file in the War Office</u>; and I presume they were stolen from your baggage, which was "conquered"—after the capitulation. Of course my letters were intended for <u>no</u> <u>eyes</u> but <u>yours</u>, and if practicable, I wish them withdrawn from the scrutiny of curious strangers, and yankee [*sic*] "Jerkins." Will you please be so good as to advise me whether you deem it best that <u>I</u> should apply for them, or expedient that the matter be left in <u>your</u> hands? I <u>think</u> I can obtain them, through the agency of Mr Seward's private secretary, whom I met in New York; and who, <u>mirabile dictu</u>![28] seems to have become a very firm friend of mine, despite my hate of his master;[29] but I shall hold the affair in abeyance, until you acquaint me with your wishes. What imaginable value can a woman's <u>causerie</u>[30] trifling letters, possess, to entitle them to a nook in the archives of the Federal War Office? <u>Ohe jam satis</u>![31] Appropos of letters! The Register & Advertiser[32] has been unaccountably severe in animadverting upon your letter, published in New Orleans; and in order to correct false impressions, I showed your <u>note of the 27th</u>[33] to Mr. Forsyth, the editor of the paper. Accept—dear Sir my best wishes for your health and happiness, and believe me ever,

Sincerely your friend &
Grateful countrywoman—
Augusta J. Evans

General Beauregard

1. This letter is housed in the Special Collections Department of the William R. Perkins Library, Duke University. It was also published with editorial notes by Ben W. Griffith. See "A Lady Novelist Views the Reconstruction: An Augusta Jane Evans Letter," *Georgia Historical Quarterly* 43.1 (1959): 103–9.

2. At the top of this page is a notation in a different handwriting, presumably General Beauregard's, which states: "Ansd. April 6 / 67."

3. The Jacobins were a political group that supported total equalitarianism and helped initiate the Reign of Terror during the French Revolution (1793–1794).

4. The Council of Ten, established in 1311 in Venice as a check on other functions of government, had unlimited authority and became despotic and oppressive (John Addington Symonds, *Renaissance in Italy* [New York: Modern Library, 1935], 111).

5. Poland had become a province of Russia in 1863 and had lost the power of self-government. Although Hungary had a provincial government, conditions there were improving with a new constitution soon to be adopted (Griffith, "A Lady Novelist Views the Reconstruction," 105n. 8).

6. A satrap was the governor of a satrapy, or province of the Persian Empire.

7. Day of Wrath (Griffith, "A Lady Novelist Views the Reconstruction," 105n. 10).

8. In Greek mythology, Astrea is the goddess of justice.

9. Nemesis in Greek mythology is the goddess of retribution who tries to restore order in human affairs by taking action against wrongdoers.

10. The Golden Calf, described in Exodus 32, was the false god worshipped by the children of Israel while Moses was on Mt. Sinai receiving the Ten Commandments from God.

11. Assignats were a form of paper money issued during the French Revolution that led to severe inflation.

12. The federal government had recently passed laws, backed by Radical Republicans such as Thaddeus Stevens, for the issuing of paper money, or greenbacks, a plan that AEW distrusted.

13. Literally, flickering flames. Here meaning unstable or not trustworthy.

14. Jean Baptiste Colbert (1619–1683), as the first controller general of France (under Louis XIV), initiated a program of economic reform that transformed France into a dominant power among European countries.

15. Maximilien de Bethune Sully (1560–1641), French statesman under King Henry IV who helped rehabilitate France after the Wars of Religion (1562–1598).

16. In Greek mythology the Eumenides were the avenging goddesses, or Furies.

17. "And they spoiled the Egyptians" (Exod. 12:36).

18. Henry Wadsworth Longfellow, "Retribution," from the *Sinngedichte of Friedrich von Logau* (translated by Longfellow).

19. In March 1867, the Radical Republicans passed a law to enforce Negro suffrage. When many Southerners considered resistance, Beauregard wrote a public letter, which was published in newspapers throughout the United States, urging Southerners to accept the situation. He explained, "The Negro is Southern born; with a little education and some property qualifications he can be made to take sufficient interest in the affairs and prosperity of the South to insure an intelligent vote." By managing Negro voters, the South could regain its former influence in the nation, thus beating the Radicals at their own game (quoted in Williams, *P. G. T. Beauregard,* 266–67). Also see *The New York Tribune,* April 1, 1867. However, in a personal letter to AEW, dated March 27, 1867, (quoted in Williams 267), Beauregard took a much more vengeful tone toward the North—this is the letter that AEW favors.

20. The Law of Plane Reflections (Griffith, "A Lady Novelist Views the Reconstruction," 107n. 20).

21. Griffith identifies this as a paraphrase of a statement by Georg Herbert, County Munster, *Political Sketches of the State of Europe, 1814–1867* (London, 1868): "An intelligent Russian once remarked to us, 'Every country has its own constitution; ours is absolutism moderated by assassination'" ("A Lady Novelist Views the Reconstruction," 107n. 21).

22. Thaddeus Stevens was a leader of the Radical Republicans. After the war, he tried unsuccessfully to have the Southern plantations confiscated and divided among the freedmen. He also strongly supported Negro suffrage.

23. George Sewall Boutwell was also a Radical and served on the joint committee of reconstruction.

24. Benjamin Franklin Butler was a member of Congress and a leader of the Radical Republicans.

25. "A noble pair of brothers." Horace *Satires* 2.3.243.

26. Henry Thomas Buckle (1821–1862), an English historian who developed the theory that a country's character is determined by the environmental influences of geography, climate, soil, and food.

27. Griffith traces this allusion to Coleridge's "Hint for a New Species of History" in *The Table Talk and Omnia of Samuel Taylor Coleridge* ("A Lady Novelist Views the Reconstruction," 108n. 27).

28. Wonderful to relate.

29. Griffith points out that AEW might have disliked Seward for his antislavery sentiments, but as Johnson's Secretary of State, he urged a policy of conciliation toward the South ("A Lady Novelist Views the Reconstruction," 109n. 29).

30. An informal talk or chat.

31. A shortened form of "Ohe! jam satis est," which means "Hold! that is enough." Horace, *Satires* 1.5.12.

32. *The Mobile Daily Advertiser and Register* (a newspaper).

33. Beauregard's personal letter to AEW (see note 19 above), in which he takes a more militant tone toward the North than the one expressed in his public letter.

❧ ❧ ❧

66 / MS Virginia   Mobile April 1st 1867

Mr H C Anderson[1]

In reply to your letter of the 22nd, I write to say that "your lady friend" must be laboring under some delusion, as I have no recollection of ever having used the word which you quote. I should be exceedingly glad to ascertain <u>how</u> and <u>where</u> and <u>from</u> <u>whom</u> she "obtained possession of a note" written by me. Say to her that she will oblige me by forwarding the note to me, and <u>if</u> <u>it</u> <u>is</u> <u>not</u> <u>a forgery</u>, I will give her all the information in my power—Pardon my haste which is unavoidable—

Very respectfully—
A.J.Evans

1. There is no indication, either in AEW's writings or in her biography, as to the identity of the recipient or the subject of this letter.

❧ ❧ ❧

67 / MS Virginia   Mobile July 29th 1867

Hon' W E Robinson:[1]
Dear Sir:

Permit me to tender you my very sincere and cordial thanks, for the great pleasure which I derived from the perusal of the eloquent and noble speech, which you did me the honor to send me. The brave utterance of sentiments so completely at variance with the policy of the "Cabal" who now dictate the destiny of the browbeaten and degraded nation,—[2] has caused a thrill of joy in the aching Southern heart,—analogous to that which must have followed the glowing phillipics that Edmund Burke[3] launched at those, who so ruthlessly trampled the sacred principles of the British constitution.[4] From the present melancholy condition of American politics, I have been able to extract a species of grim philosophy, which comforts me with the assurance that <u>extreme measures necessitate reforms</u>,—that the recoil is ever equal to the pressure, and that in political as well as natural philosophy—"<u>The angle of reflection is always equal to the angle of incidence</u>."[5] <u>We</u> of the insulted and down-trodden South, obey the old Scotch maxim: "Smile when you can not strike," and meanwhile bide our time, fully intending to adhere to the Wodehouse[6] motto: "<u>Frappez fort!</u>"[7] With reiterated thanks for your noble defense of Mobilians, and the cause of my suffering section, and the earnest hope that I may one day express my gratitude in person, I am Sir— Respectfully—AJEvans

1. William Erigena Robinson (1814–1892) was born in Ireland and immigrated to the United States at the age of twenty-two. After working as a writer and editor for several Northern newspapers, he was elected to Congress in 1867 on the Democratic ticket. While in Congress, he was mainly responsible for a bill that established the right to expatriation. Known for his espousal of the Irish cause and his hatred of England, Robinson also had some sympathy for the plight of the South.

2. After the war, the Radical Republicans, who insisted on protecting blacks' rights in the South, defeated President Johnson's more conciliatory policy toward the South. Under the Radical Reconstruction program, Southerners were required to elect new constitutional conventions and form new state governments. They were also required to ratify state constitutions that guaranteed equal rights to all citizens and gave voting rights to both blacks and whites. In addition, each state was required to ratify the Fourteenth Amendment to the Constitution, which guaranteed equality before the law to all Americans regardless of race. When these conditions were met, the Southern states were restored to normal status in the Union. Many white Southerners at the time regarded these measures as dictatorial and deeply resented the Republican governments. In addition, Southern whites blamed Republicans for the South's economic ruin after the war and for being held liable for prewar debts owed to Northerners and for back taxes that the Federal government had not been able to collect during the war years.

3. Edmund Burke (1729–1797), a British statesman who lived in an age of revolution, rejected revolutionary politics and instead stressed the need for gradual reform.

4. As a member of Parliament, Burke believed the British constitution was in danger due to the low regard with which many politicians viewed party membership. Burke argued that political parties were respectable and necessary for the performance of public duty. AEW's allusion to Burke may seem odd, given his political views against revolution. However, AEW, like most other Southerners of the time, believed that the North had violated the principles of the United States Constitution by denying the South the right of self-government (through secession).

5. The Law of Plane Reflections.

6. Bartram de Wodehouse, a Norfolk knight who, under Edward I, distinguished himself in battle against the Scots. AEW indiscriminately draws allusions from both sides of the Scottish-English dispute.

7. "Strike hard!"

✤ ✤ ✤

68 / MS Brown   Mobile Nov' 20th 1867

Gen'l Beauregard:

The letter incidentally referred to, in my conversation with Gen'l Maury,[1]—was one written immediately after the receipt of the books which you consigned to my care, on the eve of your departure for the North; and contained the request that you would instruct me what disposition I should make of your valuable military notes,[2] in the event of my leaving America, before your return to New Orleans. I enclosed the letter to Mr Proctor, urging him to forward it promptly, if it arrived after your departure, but some contra temps[3] seems to have frustrated my wishes. At the time when I wrote you, I had fully determined to cross the Atlantic in September, and spend several years in Syria, Egypt, Persia, and Northern Hindoostan,[4] [sic] consequently, I was very solicitous to commit your precious military notes and data to the custodian whom you might designate as worthy of the trust. L'homme propose, et Diem dispose,[5]—and since that letter was penned, circumstances beyond my control have peremptorily forbidden the accomplishment of my long-cherished scheme of oriental travel and study,[6]—and all my gorgeous visions of Deodunga snows,[7]—roses of Shiraz,[8] and rhododendrons of Nepaul,[9] have faded as swiftly as the fata morgana[10] of the Levant;[11]—have paled and gone down into that wide grave, where silently sleep so many noble aspirations, and fervent hopes of my Bygone. Requiescat in pace. . . . [12]

> "Cased in cedar, and shut in a sacred gloom,
> Swathed in linen, and precious unguents old,
> Painted with cinnabar, and rich with gold,
> Silent they rest, in solemn salvatory."[13]

Having learned some months since that Mr Alexander Stephens was carefully compiling a history of our struggle for freedom,[14] and feeling that it would be presumptuous indeed in me to venture to glean in a field which he deigned to labor, I humbly put my fingers on the throat of my ambitious— daring design of becoming the Confederate Xenophon, and thoroughly strangled it.[15] To Mr Stephens your notes and criticisms would be invaluable, and I retain them at present subject to your order. Had he not begun the history, I would gladly have dedicated my future years to the successful completion of a work inexpressibly dear to my heart,—but before his superior wisdom, ripe scholarship, mature experience, and profound political philosophy and acumen—I meekly lay down my feeble pen, and hoping all noble fruition for his arduous labors—in vindicating our past before the august tribunal where impartial Clio[16] reigns,—I earnestly pray that God will speed his hallowed work. To you Sir, who know something of my deathless devotion to that cause, which now seems hopeless—in its grave of gore,—I confess it cost me a severe struggle to relinquish the fond dream of weaving historic immortelles[17] for the tombs of its martyrs,—but abler hands snatched it from my weak womanly fingers, and waved me to humbler paths of labor. All that poor tortured Chopin strove to express when in his dreams of Poland he murmured [obscured][18] now and ever more shall echo for me, in that mournful word Confederacy. There are many things touching this Southern Rama,[19] which I should like to discuss with you, but why invoke visions more appalling and drear [sic] than those which Endor's Sibyl brought to bewildered Saul?[20] Can you tell me where I shall find some satisfactory account of the ministry and policy of Cavour?[21] He exerted so powerful an influence over the political philosophy of Continental Europe that I am anxious to compare his policy with that of Bismark,[22] Brougham,[23] Napoleon and Russell.[24]

Permit me once more to express my grateful appreciation of the confidence with which you have honored me, and for the great pleasure I have derived from the perusal of your military records. With cordial good wishes for your health and happiness, and many thanks for your kind letter of the 9th, I am General

Most sincerely
Your grateful friend
Augusta J. Evans

1. Major General Dabney H. Maury, who after the war authored *Recollections of a Virginian in the Mexican, Indian, and Civil Wars* (New York: Charles Scribner's Sons, 1894).

2. AEW, planning at the time to write a history of the Confederacy and the Civil War, had asked Beauregard to send her official records and documents from his military service that she could use for research. In a note dated August 14, 1867, Beauregard carefully inventoried all the "books and papers sent to Miss Augusta J. Evans." These include miscellaneous letters, telegrams, letter books, general orders, and personal reminiscences (Papers of P. G. T. Beauregard, Library of Congress).

3. bad luck, mischance

4. Hindustan is a Persian word meaning "land of the Hindus." It was formerly used to designate the subcontinent of India.

5. Man proposes and God disposes.

6. According to Fidler, AEW decided not to travel abroad because of the illness of her father. Also, while her brother, Howard Evans, had mostly recovered from his war

injuries and illnesses, he remained permanently crippled in one arm. Both father and brother needed AEW's skills as a nurse (Fidler, *A Biography*, 146–47).

7. Possibly Deogarh or Deoghar, both in east India.

8. Shiraz is a city in southwestern Iran that was often mentioned in Persian poems for its rose gardens and wine.

9. Nepal is a country in Asia between India and the Tibet region of China.

10. The fata morgana is a complex mirage that causes the horizon—coastlines and buildings—to appear as castles in the air. The phenomenon is named for Morgan Le Fay, the sorceress in the King Arthur legends. The fata morgana has been observed in the following places: the Strait of Messina, Italy; the Toyama Bay, Japan; and Lake Geneva, Switzerland.

11. The countries bordering the east Mediterranean.

12. May it rest in peace.

13. Jean Ingelow, "A Dead Year," lines 4–7.

14. Alexander Stephens was the former vice president of the Confederacy. When the war ended, AEW had planned to write a history of the Confederacy and had written Stephens to ask for his help in obtaining military records and other data. See AEW to Curry, October 7, 1865, and AEW to Stephens, November 29, 1865. AEW abandoned her plans, however, upon learning that Stephens was writing his own history. Stephen's book, *The Constitutional View of the Late War Between the States* (two volumes, 1868–1870) was, of course, a discussion of the war from the Southern point of view.

15. In discussing AEW's vacillation between traditional and nontraditional roles for women—both in her novels and in her own life—Drew Gilpin Faust refers to AEW's statements in this letter to Beauregard: "Her extraordinary letter exemplifies the fate of female ambition in the South—its transformation into coexisting docility and assertiveness, compliance and repressed rage. . . . Evans' ambition was crushed—'strangled'—only indirectly by male prerogative; the actual murder took place at her own hand. . . . she became the final victim of her own paradoxes" (Introduction to *Macaria; or Altars of Sacrifice*, by Augusta Jane Evans, edited by Drew Gilpin Faust [Baton Rouge: Louisiana State University Press, 1992], xxvi).

16. In Greek mythology, the muse of history.

17. Flowers that, when dried, retain their color; hence they are saved as mementos. Literally the word means something that is everlasting.

18. Frederic Chopin (1810–1849), a Polish-French composer and pianist, left his native Poland in 1830 for a concert tour of Europe. While he was away, the Poles revolted against Russian control of their country. Chopin's friend returned home immediately to join the struggle. Chopin, however, did not, and was tortured with feelings of guilt for not helping his country and with worry over the fate of his family. Russia crushed the rebellion within a year.

19. A Hindu deity, known for his chivalry and virtue, who was possibly based on an actual tribal hero.

20. Saul, the king of Israel, beset by many problems and feeling that God was no longer with him, asked the witch of Endor to conjure up the spirit of Samuel for him, although he himself had outlawed the practice of conjuring. When Samuel's spirit appeared, he told Saul that the Philistines would kill him and his sons in battle the next day (1 Sam. 28).

21. Count de Cavour (1810–1861), an Italian statesman, believed in democratic ideals, instituted many reforms in government, and helped unify Italy.

22. Otto von Bismarck (1815–1898), a German chancellor, unified Germany into a strong empire but at the expense of democracy.

23. Henry Peter Brougham (1778–1868), a British politician, reformed the legal system and public education and helped abolish slavery in the British Empire.

24. Lord John Russell (1792–1878), a British politician and reformer, helped write and pass the Reform Bill of 1832, which increased the power of the middle class.

69 / MS Virginia   Mobile Nov' 20th 1867

Col' Seaver:[1]

My dear friend:

Have you ever allowed your fervid and most versatile fancy to conjecture what must have been the bewildered character of the reflections of those classic prototypes of slumber-loving Sancho Panza[2]—i.e.—the "Seven Sleepers" whom Decius shut up at Ephesus,[3]—when emerging from their cave they were confronted by all the <u>novelties</u> in <u>costume</u>, which Ephesian milliners and mantaumakers [*sic*] had invented during their 187 years nap,—to drive the economical papas and spouses in Asia Minor, to the extremist verge of frenzy? If you have adequately imagined the conflicting emotions of those pitiable young gentlemen, (Kitnier included,) you can readily realize my utterly indescribable sensations, when the quiet frugality and almost ante-diluvian old fogyism of my simple "Snuggery" was suddenly invaded by that most marvelous avalanche of ultra-fashionable <u>beau-mondeism</u>[4] yclept[5] "Harper's Bazar"[6]!! Comparing my poor little plain head, (<u>vise</u> enclosed) with the tortured and ornate pericraniums <u>a</u> <u>la</u> <u>mode</u>,[7] I was forced to conclude that the architecture of my "palace" of thought was not only not a fair specimen of the "composite," but certainly belonged to some <u>Pre</u>-<u>Noahic</u> style. Laudably ambitious to improve the artistic advantages which you so kindly and considerately placed within my reach, I eagerly applied myself to the study of the technicalities of the "new styles;" but that aforesaid sleeper was not more puzzled to make the bakers in Ephesus realize that he was logically and pardonably hungry, after his long fast,—than I to comprehend the fashionable jargon of great Gotham,[8] and most humbly do I confess that after an examination of all the startling novelties and dazzling wonders, it occurred to me that after all, a single typographical blunder had marred an otherwise faultless triumph and rendered "Harper's Bazar" instead of Harper's Bizarre!!! I assure you my dear friend, I was heartily rejoiced to discover your familiar and ever welcome chirography[9] on the wrapper of the paper, and beg you to believe that I do forever gratefully appreciate your kind remembrance. Jesting aside, I have derived much pleasure, and many new ideas from the perusal of the Bizarre. How and where are you? And when are my eyes to be gladdened by one of those pleasant, sparkling "notelets," which were such welcome guests at my desk, in the blessed Bygone? Of course you have read Jean Ingelow's "Story of Doom"?[10] Then pray tell me where she finds authority for christening Noah's wife (before the flood at that) "Nilorya"? You possibly do not know;—if so ask some of the literary Sanhedrin[11] "who most do congregate" at Delmonico's[12] to enlighten my benighted mind. Intellectually as famished as Ugolino,[13]—I come a hungry Israelite to that Egypt of lore— New York, and beg of you the presiding Joseph of the royal granaries[14]— a few grains of mental pabulum. Accept reiterated thanks for your courtesy, and believe me, dear Sir,

Your sincere friend
Augusta J. Evans

1. William A. Seaver was an editor of *Harper's New Monthly Magazine* and a friend of AEW. See AEW to Seaver, December 31, 1859.

2. The peasant squire of Don Quixote in the satiric novel *Don Quixote de la Mancha* (1615) by Miguel de Cervantes.

3. According to legend, seven Christian youths of Ephesus, in order to escape persecution from the Roman consul Decius in 250 C.E., fled to a cave in Mount Celion where they fell asleep. After 230 years, they awoke but died soon thereafter. In the following lines of this letter, AEW imagines the sleepers' astonishment as they awaken and discover the new styles in clothing, just as she is astonished by the new styles, particularly in hats, displayed in the magazine that Seaver has sent her.

4. beau monde—the world of high society and fashion.

5. Old English for "named" or "called."

6. Seaver has sent AEW a copy of the first issue of *Harper's Bazar*, which appeared on November 2, 1867. Within six weeks it had a circulation of more than 100,000 copies. The Harper's publishing company, founded by the four Harper brothers, had already been successful as a publisher of books and two periodicals—*Harper's New Monthly Magazine,* for which Seaver was an editor, and *Harper's Weekly,* a newspaper. Seeking to expand their business, the brothers settled on a weekly fashion magazine based on the German periodical *Bazar,* which had been very successful in Europe. *Harper's Bazar* included pictures of the latest fashions, with cutout patterns, short stories, serialized novels, and articles of general interest for the whole family. The spelling was changed to *Bazaar* in 1913 (Exman, *The House of Harper,* 99–100, 121, 126).

7. in fashion

8. Gotham, a nickname for New York City, came from the name of a proverbial town in England that was known for the foolishness of its inhabitants.

9. handwriting

10. Jean Ingelow (1820–1897), an English poet, published *A Story of Doom and Other Poems* in 1867.

11. The supreme council and tribunal of the ancient Jewish nation.

12. A restaurant on Fifth Avenue in New York City.

13. Ugolino, one of the characters in *The Divine Comedy* (1320) by Dante Alighieri, is punished for his treachery by being confined in one of the coldest regions of hell where he spends eternity devouring the brain of his betrayer.

14. As told in Gen. 37: 39–50, Joseph was sold into slavery in Egypt by his brothers but, nevertheless, convinced the pharaoh to store grain during seven years of plenty. During the following seven years of famine, Joseph was in charge of distributing the grain—both to the Egyptians and to his own brothers who traveled from Israel to obtain it.

"... our quiet little home in Mobile."

MS 70 / Tulane   Mobile Jan' 16th 1868

Rev. E. Fontaine[1]
Dear Sir:

I trust that you will not judge of my appreciation of your exceedingly kind letter, by the unavoidable brevity of my reply; for a multiplicity of imperative claims upon my time and attention, leave me barely leisure to express my thanks for your friendly remembrance and consideration. I regret that circumstances beyond my control, render it impossible for me to gratify my long cherished desire to visit New Orleans, and it is particularly unfortunate that I am debarred this pleasure at a juncture when your city is unusually attractive.

May I beg you to be so good as to express to the proprietors of the "St James" Hotel my earnest gratitude for their courteous and very hospitable invitation, which I assure you I do most cordially appreciate? Hoping that the day is not distant when smiling fortune will permit your family to join you in New Orleans, and decree you all the comforts and amenities of affluence, I tender my grateful acknowledgments for your kind letter, and claiming your general pardon for my great haste, am

Very respectfully
A.J.Evans

1. A handwritten notation on the back of this letter reads as follows: "Autograph letter of Augusta Evans presented by Dr Fontaine."

❧ ❧ ❧

MS 71 / Historical Society of Pennsylvania   Mobile Oct' 29th [1868][1]

Mr Howland:

In compliance with your request I furnish the desired autograph, and am

Very respectfully
Augusta J. Evans

1. The year was added in a different handwriting at the top of the page.

❧ ❧ ❧

MS 72 / Detroit Public Library   At Home Dec. 1st [1868][1]

In token of my devoted love for my darling Frank,[2] I sit down one hour before my marriage, and write for the last time, my old name—

Augusta J. Evans

    1. AEW married Colonel Lorenzo Madison Wilson on December 1, 1868. (The title of Colonel was honorary.) The Wilson family lived on a large estate called Ashland, less than half a mile from Georgia Cottage, where AEW resided with her parents and siblings. In 1862 AEW had helped to nurse the first Mrs. Wilson during her final illness. During the next few years, AEW and Mr. Wilson gradually became closer. Like the heroines in most of her novels, AEW married a wealthy, older man. Mr. Wilson was sixty and she was thirty-two at the time of their marriage.
    2. Miss Frank Crawford, a friend of AEW from Mobile, who less than a year later married "Commodore" Cornelius Vanderbilt. See AEW to Rachel Lyons, February 28, 1864.

❧ ❧ ❧

MS 73 / North Carolina   Mobile August 27 [1869+][1]

My dear Rachel:
    I am <u>so</u> <u>nearly</u> <u>blind</u> from "hay fever,"[2] that I can scrawl only a line to <u>thank</u> <u>you</u> <u>most</u> <u>sincerely</u> for <u>your</u> <u>kind</u> <u>letter</u>, and loving <u>interest</u>. I have tried many inhalers, without relief, but will order the circular you are so good as to commend to me. If you could hear the <u>fugue</u> my nose plays in <u>sneezes</u>! I am driven to the use of <u>towels</u>,—with visions of <u>sheets</u> in the near future! Hoping to hear soon, that your dear mother is <u>better</u>, I am with <u>much</u> <u>love</u>

Affectionately yours A.E.W.

PS
I saw your husband last week and he looks <u>very</u> <u>well</u>.

    1. AEW signed this letter with her married initials, so the letter would have been written in 1869 or later. (The Wilsons married on December 1, 1868.)
    2. In discussing AEW's problem with hay fever, Fidler quotes from this letter and adds that the Wilsons traveled all over the country for years to find a location or climate that would relieve the allergy (*A Biography,* 173–74). AEW herself attributed the cause of her hay fever to freshly cut grass or hay, but she never found a remedy. See AEW to Rachelle, July 25, [1892].

❧ ❧ ❧

MS 74 / Detroit Public Library   Mobile Feb 9th [1870]

My darling Frank[1]

Although I have not heard from you for a week, I am well aware you are at this season <u>overwhelmed</u> with <u>social</u> and <u>domestic</u> <u>duties</u> and engagements, hence I do not wait for you. Today I have only time to send a few lines, and enclose a slip cut from the "Register"[2] of this morning, which contains many <u>astounding facts</u> about my <u>gentian-eyed</u> <u>darling</u>!! What modern Hercules will deliver us from the monstrous <u>Hydra</u>[3]—yclept[4] Reporters—and Newspaper Letter Writers? <u>Sanctity</u> of <u>home</u>, <u>reverence</u> for <u>womanhood</u>—are unknown elements in Northern Civilization. One might as well employ Argus[5] for a footman, as live in Boston or New York!! As yet have received no good tidings from Sallie Bush,[6] and can not avoid feeling much anxiety, but pray God all may be right. The weather is intensely disagreeable, and I have never known as wet and debilitating a winter. I also enclose the Report of my husband's Bond business,[7] that you may see what <u>he</u> <u>has</u> <u>accomplished</u>. With a heart<u>full</u> of love—

Your old <u>A</u>

1. Frank is Miss Frank Crawford, a friend of AEW from Mobile (see AEW to Rachel Lyons, February 28, 1864). The date of this letter is probably 1870. In 1869, Frank married "Commodore" Cornelius Vanderbilt. At the time of their marriage, Vanderbilt was 75 and Frank was 30. The marriage created a scandal and generated much gossip. Frank was regarded as a "shameless woman" who had obviously married Vanderbilt only for his money (Edwin P. Hoyt, *The Vanderbilts and Their Fortunes* [Garden City, N.Y.: Doubleday, 1962], 193). AEW and other friends, such as General Beauregard, supported Frank.

2. *The Mobile Daily Register* had reprinted an article from a Northern newspaper that was critical of Frank.

3. In Greek mythology, the second labor of Hercules was to kill the Hydra, a nine-headed creature. This was a difficult task because, when one head was chopped off, two grew to take its place.

4. Old English for "named" or "called."

5. In Greek mythology, Argus was a creature with one hundred eyes. Since all of the eyes did not sleep at the same time, Argus made an excellent guard or watchman.

6. Sallie Bush was AEW's sister, Sarah "Sallie" Evans, who married Colonel J. W. Bush of Birmingham, Alabama (Fidler, *A Biography,* 209). The cause of AEW's concern on this occasion has not been identified.

7. Mr. Wilson was an officer and director of a prominent bank in Mobile, a director of the Mobile and Montgomery Railroad, and the principal stockholder of a streetcar line that ran from Spring Hill to Mobile. In addition, his investments outside

the South left him, unlike most Southerners, financially comfortable after the fall of the Confederacy (Fidler 150).

❧ ❧ ❧

MS 75 / Detroit Public Library   Mobile May 25th [1871]

My dear Frank—I enclose a letter for your perusal, and also transcribe literally my answer as follows.
Copy
Mobile May 25th
Mr. Andrew Dunn:[1]
Dear Sir—

In reply to your letter of the 20th, permit me to say: 1st Mrs Vanderbilt's maiden name was Frank Armstrong Crawford. 2nd She is a Southern woman, and of the best blood. 3rd She is a zealous Methodist, and an earnest, devout faithful Christian. 4th She is, always has been, and always will be a true and devoted Southern woman, cherishing as sacred the memory of our "Lost Cause." 5th She is now about 33 years old, and has no children. 6th She was married two years since, to Commodore Vanderbilt, who is a distant relative of her mother. It is proper that I should add,—that I shall forward your letter to Mrs Vanderbilt, with whom I correspond.

Very respectfully—
AJEvans Wilson

Now I put all this matter in your hands—A week ago I wrote you a long letter, and have only time to say—give love to all and may God bless you— Yours ever—A

1. There is no record as to the identity of Andrew Dunn or the reason for his request for information regarding Frank Crawford Vanderbilt. Mrs. Vanderbilt was, of course, an object of curiosity and criticism from the time of her marriage to Cornelius Vanderbilt in 1869 until her own death at the age of forty-six in 1885.

❧ ❧ ❧

MS 76 / Virginia   Mobile March 20th [1875][1]

My dear Col' Seaver:
Before the arrival of your welcome and valued letter, which reached me only yesterday, I had received the copy of the "Bazar,"[2] which exhaled such delicious incense around the altar of my amour propre;[3] and although entirely ignorant of the fact that your occasional raids into Bohemia carried you into the august realm of Harper's vast Trimurti[4] i.e. "Magazine, Weekly and Bazar,"[5] —my subtle instincts recognized the friendly hand that swung the fragrant

censer, and some wise familiar, infallible as Socrates' "Suset,"[6] assured me that
your kind fingers penned the pleasant notice.[7] For it, for your kind letter, and
especially for the <u>excellent</u> <u>photograph</u>, which so vividly and agreeably recall
happy <u>ante</u> <u>bellum</u> days in Gotham,[8] please accept my sincere and most cordial thanks. The Wilkie Collins' "Breakfast"![9] what classic fumes, what
immortal ghosts of <u>jeu</u> <u>d'</u> <u>esprit</u>[10] the bare mention evokes? Indeed, I doubt
whether the banquet that Lucullus[11] held in the "Appollo" at Tusculum[12] were
half as pleasant, as that, where my valued old friend reigned in all the glory
of incomparable <u>Symposiarch</u>![13] Why did not you after the similitude of
"<u>Noctes</u> <u>Ambrosianae</u>,"[14] provide a second "Ears of Dionysius,"[15] wherein
safely screened from the blaze of wit, some meek "Gurney, the short-haun
[sic] writer,"[16] might have gathered and preserved the sacred crumbs, the crystal drippings, from that "feast of reason and flow of soul"? How many charming, gifted cultivated spirits New York can furnish for such occasions?
Sometimes in thinking of the Astor Library, the Galleries, and the Artists'
Receptions which I once enjoyed so keenly, I feel disposed to question
whether any other spot in America constitutes such an intellectual hot-bed.
In Boston a chronic East-wind chilled me perpetually, even in the sunshine
of Longfellow's presence, but Gotham—glorious Gotham is the tropic realm
for shivering genius, and ambitious authorlings. Had we indeed that reputed
"Bank" whereof you wrote, New York would often sun me in its genial literary glow, but <u>minus</u> that apochryphal "Bank," my husband's interests anchor
him here, and even the witchery of Gotham though dear to my soul, has not
induced me to leave him, since my marriage. Do you ever see Mr Carleton,[17]
or has he drifted away to Caracas, as he threatened, until these "ides of
March" are safely over? When you meet "Rutledge" (Mrs Harris)[18] present to
her the affectionate remembrance of one, who holds her in undiminished
admiration. Apropos! what of her new book, "A Perfect Adonis"?[19] Is her
noble-looking husband the hero? Circumstances <u>may</u> pave the way for a visit
to New York next winter, and should kind fate so ordain, I shall anticipate no
greater pleasure than that of seeing you once more, and making the acquaintance of your wife, whom I have always desired to know. Then should the
critic <u>horde</u> raise the war whoop with which they invariably welcome me,
and fall upon me, "foot, horse, and dragoon,"[20] will not your glittering "Excali-
bar" leap from its scabbard in defence of that injured innocence, whose scalp
has often dangled in imagination from the gory pens, ambushed in the Sanctum of the "Tribune," or the "Times?" With renewed thanks, and fervent
good wishes, ever gratefully-AJEWilson

1. The novel *A Perfect Adonis,* mentioned in note 19, was published in 1875.
2. *Harper's Bazar* (later spelled *Bazaar*).
3. vanity

4. In the Hindu religion, a trinity composed of Brahma the Creator, Vishnu the Preserver, and Shiva the Destroyer.

5. The three periodicals published by the Harper brothers: *Harper's New Monthly Magazine, Harper's Weekly* (a newspaper), and *Harper's Bazar* (a weekly fashion magazine).

6. Possibly a reference to the "voice" that Socrates supposedly heard throughout his life and which advised him not to do certain things.

7. Seaver had written a favorable review of *Infelice,* AEW's sixth novel, which had just been published.

8. A nickname for New York City, based on a fictitious town in England that was known for the folly of its inhabitants.

9. Wilkie Collins (1824–1889) was a British writer and the father of the modern detective novel. His best-known novels were *The Woman in White* (1860) and *The Moonstone* (1868). From 1873 to 1874 Collins made a reading tour of the United States. The breakfast in Collins's honor, mentioned in this letter and attended by Seaver and his friends, apparently occurred at some point during this tour.

10. a game of wit

11. See AEW to Curry, October 7, 1865, note 18.

12. An ancient city of Latium, south of Rome.

13. One who directs or presides over a symposium.

14. See AEW to Curry, October 16, 1863, note 5.

15. In classical mythology, Dionysus was the god of wine and inspiration. From the revels associated with his worship evolved comedy, tragedy, and satiric drama.

16. See AEW to Seaver, December 31, 1859.

17. AEW's publisher.

18. Miriam Cole Harris wrote *Rutledge,* her first novel, in 1860.

19. Another novel by Harris, published in 1875.

20. AEW is, of course, referring to the negative reviews that her novels frequently received from the critics.

❧ ❧ ❧

MS 77 / Virginia   Mobile Sept. 20th [1875]

Miss Alice Jacobson:

I am sorry you suffered so much annoyance with reference to your former letter to me, for I certainly never received one from you until yesterday, and hasten to comply with your request. Hoping that you will like "<u>Infelice</u>,"[1] as well as my other books, of which you speak so kindly, I am,

Very respectfully
Augusta Evans Wilson

1. *Infelice* was published in 1875.

ॐ ॐ ॐ

MS 78 / Virginia   Mobile June 10th [no year]

Miss Harriet Jacobson

Your kind note of the 23d has been forwarded by my publisher, and tendering my sincere thanks for the friendly professions it contained, I furnish
the desired autograph.

Very respectfully
Augusta Evans Wilson

ॐ ॐ ॐ

MS 79 / Virginia   Mobile Nov' 8th 1875

Col W A Seaver:
My dear friend:

Having read with much interest and pleasure the sketch of "the melancholy man" of Harper's "D[obscured] contained in the Boston "Gazette," I
write to thank you very sincerely for your kind remembrance and to express
my great regret that during my brief visit to New York I saw you only once,
and under such unsatisfactory circumstances that a thousand things which I
wished to speak of must be left unsaid. In one of Mrs Vanderbilt's letters she
gave me a very pleasant account of your visit with her and if you knew how
happily she spoke of that occasion, I feel assured you would call frequently at
10 Washington Place. <u>Hers</u> is one of the loveliest Christian characters it has
been my good fortune to know intimately, and I hope that a further acquaintance will cement your friendship for one who is very dear to me. Now having sacrificed upon the altar of very earnest friendship, permit a scanty
libation before the fetich of Self! Boston "dealt with you kindly," gives you
your dues, for which indeed, I am truly glad,—but me that modern Areo-
pagus[1] soon inclined to prick to death with venomous pen points! Is Mr
Horace Seaver of the "Investigator"[2] even a distant relative [line obscured]. If
he is not then I shall declare boldly that the name of his paper is a misnomer,
and support my assertion by the grim and barbarous fact that he has grossly
misquoted and travestied "Macaria," and savagely criticized my new book
"<u>Infelice</u>,"[3] before a page had been printed! If <u>au</u> <u>contraire</u> he is so supremely
fortunate and happy as to <u>call</u> <u>you</u> <u>relative</u>,—then indeed,—I will only say
that being of kinhood to you, I shall return good for evil, and if "Infelice"
luckily survives his maledictions, I will dedicate a portion of the proceeds
thereof to the purchase of one of those "terra cotta busts of Horace Seaver"
which are advertised in the "Investigator"!!! Can human magnanimity soar
beyond this! Where will you spend your winter? Need I assure you how glad
we should be to welcome you and Mrs Seaver to our quiet little home in

Mobile? Could I tempt your wife with the promise of a bouquet of lovely white camellias every morning at her breakfast plate? Will it avail to offer you the finest oranges you ever dreamed of, gathered from our trees, whose golden treasures hang in full view as I write? What meager attractions (!) in comparison with the wits of the "Union"[4] and all the varied charms of most bewitching Gotham,—which certainly served me as the flesh pots of Egypt did the far distant journeying Jews! With a very cordial hope that you may never fall into the claws of the "Investigator" and with best wishes for life-long happiness and prosperity [obscured]

Your friend
AJEWilson

1. The highest council in ancient Athens.
2. *The Boston Investigator,* a weekly newspaper, was published from 1831 to 1901.
3. Published in the spring of 1875.
4. A social club for men in New York City.

⁂ ⁂ ⁂

MS 80 / Virginia   Mobile April 3d 1876

Editors of "American Cyclopaedia"[1]
Gentlemen:
   In reply to your kind note of the 28th, permit me to say, that I was born on the 8th of May 1835, in Columbus Georgia. My books are as follows: "Inez," "Beulah," "Macaria," "St Elmo," "Vashti," "Infelice." "Inez" was published by the Harpers in 1856, "Beulah" by Mr James C Derby in 1859, and the remainder by Mr G W Carleton since the war. My maiden name was Augusta J Evans.

Very respectfully
Augusta Evans Wilson

   1. Appleton and Company published the *New American Cyclopaedia,* a popular dictionary of general knowledge, from 1858 to 1863. Later editions were called *The American Cyclopaedia.*

⁂ ⁂ ⁂

MS 81 / Virginia   Mobile Sept 7th [1876]

Col W A Seaver:
My dear friend:
   Across the waste of 17 years,—over the bloody chasm of the late war,—high above the smoke and thunder of battle—float to me this autumn morning the memories of a day,—a sunny summer day in 1859,—when you, Mr. Milburn,

"Kervian" and I all sat in the Harper sanctum and talked with Mr. Fletcher Harper[1] and other members of the firm, of the immense establishment we had been visiting and admiring.[2] What a huge engine of possible good! Because I remember that day, and believing you to be not only a christian [*sic*] gentleman, but one whose patriotism means something more than grateful devotion for favors received—or ardent expectation of preferment yet to come, from political potentates,—I enclose an article cut from the "Mobile Register" of Sept. 5th,[3] and beg that you will call the attention of the Mess'rs Harper to this expression of sentiments which are very general at the South. By whom the extract was written, I know not, but it correctly reflects public opinion. While the mere business aspect of the matter may be quite unimportant, as the Mess'rs Harper can doubtless smile and afford to incur the loss of Southern patronage for their periodicals,—there are principles involved, for which dollars and cents furnish no standard, and do these gentlemen realize the amount of positive injury, the flagrant injustice they are now inflicting upon their innocent and unfortunate country men? Claiming preeminence, as journalists par excellence of "Civilization" organs,—how can they deliberately and systematically pursue a policy[4] which arouses and fosters the most barbarous sentiment in a large class of American citizens, who are but a few removes from brutal savages? The aim of the Harper periodicals is to inflame and array the negroes against the whites, not from philanthropic love of the former, but solely to sow dissension that will favor the election of a Republican ticket next November, and in endeavoring to accomplish this object, libel, vituperation, and satire are exhausted. Are these the tactics of Civilized Journalism? Does adherence to the Republican Party require so fearful an oblation of all genuine patriotism, and necessitate the sacrifice of every conscientious scruple? Have ten years of serfdom to Radical rule and proscription entitled the Southern States to no sympathy;—or do the Mess'rs Harper hate us so intensely, so unrelentingly, so everlastingly—that they merge all other aims in that of maligning,—caricaturing and persecuting their white countrymen, who are willing for all men to vote legally, but prefer to cast their own [vote] for men who promise something better, wiser, and purer than the Republicans have given them for the last 8 years? Is this bitter and revengeful crusade worthy of christian [*sic*] gentlemen and of publishers of influence and distinction, who emulating the light bearing example of Lucifer, seem in danger of forgetting the sequel of that brilliant career? Pointing to the myriad graves of our Confederate dead, we ask only for that Peace, which was promised Lee, when he unbuckled and laid down his sword, ten long years ago, but today every rail way train that rushes South bears the anathema-maranatha[5] of the Messr's Harper—"There is no Race!" Devoting their energies, talents, and wealth to the promotion of bitterness, sectional strife, and social hatred,—resorting to every expedient to goad their countrymen into a war of races, do they indeed utterly forget that <u>final</u> <u>assize</u>—where preferment no longer bribes, and the God of Peace-Makers reigns? As a Southern woman who has outlived the impetuosity of youth,— who has no political aspirations, but an ardent love of <u>justice</u> and truth; I would respectfully ask the gentlemen who are responsible for the publication and circulation of the social and political libels prepared by Mr Nast,[6]— to pause, and gravely inquire of their own souls, how they shall one day answer—for the cruel mischief they are trying to accomplish? Perish all the candidates, and abolish the offices that entice them, rather than rekindle the fires of hate among the people of the two sections. Feeling my dear friend, that you who have known me so long will fully appreciate the motive that prompts these lines, I trust you will show them to the Mess'rs Harper, who in days past were my first publishers and literary sponsors. When will "Daniel Deronda"[7] be completed? The next generation of Jews will rejoice in the name of Deronda. I know of one already in New Orleans. When you have nothing more important or pleasant to occupy your valuable time, be pleased to write as of yore, to

Your sincere friend
Augusta Evans Wilson

1. One of the four Harper brothers who established the Harper publishing company in 1817.

2. The Harpers had published AEW's first novel, *Inez,* in 1855.

3. AEW does not give enough information to identify the article she is sending Colonel Seaver. However, the September 5th issue of *The Mobile Daily Register* reveals Mobile to be a troubled city in 1876. One article, "That Circular Letter," reprints instructions from the secretary of war to the U.S. Marshals, reminding them of their duty to protect the voting rights of all people and to protect them from reprisals for voting.

An article titled "The Radical Programme" reported a legal case against Mr. J. T. May, assistant registrar, who was charged with making blacks wait in line for several hours to register to vote, a delay that prevented many of them from getting registered. White voters, on the other hand, were admitted into the courthouse by a different door and were registered quickly. One of May's accusers, a black man named Alfred Campbell, apparently retracted his previous testimony and claimed at the trial that he had never attempted to register. U.S. Commissioner Hunter, however, found May guilty of "preventing Alfred Campbell from registering." The newspaper, ignoring the other evidence against May, ridiculed the guilty verdict in light of Campbell's testimony.

Another article, "Radical Persecution," reprinted from the *Richmond Enquirer* (Virginia), described the plight of a black man, J. W. Dungee, who had registered as a Democrat. Because of his political convictions, members of his own race harassed and threatened him with physical harm. The article claimed that the Radical Republicans would have protected Dungee if he had registered as a Republican and if whites had threatened him. The writer ends by condemning the Radicals and carpetbaggers in general for their lack of principles.

4. From the beginning of the Civil War, the Harper periodicals had supported the Union cause, the abolition of slavery, and the Radical Republicans.

5. The maranatha is the phrase, "O Lord, come," which was used as an invocation (1 Cor. 16:22). AEW's coupling of this word with *anathema* is, of course, to suggest that the slogan or philosophy of the Harper periodicals is evil.

6. Thomas Nast, a political cartoonist for *Harper's Weekly* (a newspaper), supported the Radical Republicans.

7. A novel by George Eliot, published in 1876.

❧ ❧ ❧

MS 82 / Virginia   Mobile Feb 8th 1877

Col' Seaver
My dear Sir:

Why did not you arrange your programme so as to be present at "Mardi Gras" in New Orleans? Or have you enjoyed the Carnival so intensely in Rome and Naples, that American shadowy imitations offer no attraction? I shall be exceedingly glad to see you, and to make the acquaintance of your wife, and as I do not reside in the city, you must be sure to send me your card through PO Box 833 as soon as you reach the Battle House, (the best hotel in Mobile), and I will immediately present myself in the gracious guise and pleasant light of welcome! Hoping that <u>Mrs</u> Seaver's health will be improved by the journey, I am as ever

Sincerely your friend
Augusta Evans Wilson

PS.
Can not you find time to call on Mr Derby at Appletons, and <u>persuade</u> <u>him</u> to come South with you? He has promised for fifteen years to make me a visit, but thus far, has kept Punic faith with me.

❧ ❧ ❧

MS 83 / Virginia   Mobile March 10th [1878][1]

Col Seaver:
My dear Friend:

Positively and actually, (not metaphorically) sitting under my own vine and fig tree (Scuppernong arbor) warily keeping <u>one eye</u> on an errant white turkey hen, who with as many adroit maneuvers as Talleyrand,[2] is cautiously meandering towards her nest, (which I must discover in order to save the precious

eggs from marauding dogs,) I essay to divide my thoughts, my vision, and my
affection between this snowy cunning fowl of my watchful care, and thank a
valued friend in New York, whose recent welcome letter was not needed to
ensure his being remembered <u>by</u> <u>all</u> at "Ashland." Behold the insufficiency of
the most exalted bucolic beatitude! Even in the midst of my country home,
with whitening dogwoods, fringy wild cherry trees, gorgeous yellow jasmine,
and trailing dewberries all starred with blossoms greeting me on every side;
with a tender sky blue as Capri, and a soft fragrant gulf breeze whispering of
the <u>far</u> south it has just left;—with white geese, white guineas, white turkeys,
and white game chickens cackling and gobbling all about me,[3]—while the
Jersey and Ayrshire cows stand near, in the shade of the crape myrtle trees,
and chew the cud of contentment, watching me with their soft solemn eyes,
as I scribble this eclogue (?) to you,—and a pretty young calf only ten days
old timidly makes acquaintance with my little Skye terrier,—even now I say,—
surrounded by all the Lares and Penates[4] of the farm "Ashland," my truant
fancy wanders (like my tormenting turkey hen) to that "<u>Dinner</u> <u>at</u> <u>the</u> <u>Union</u>
<u>Club</u>,"[5] where for <u>five</u> blissful hours,—

> "How pheasant heads with cost collected,
> And phenicopters stood neglected,
> To laugh at <u>Seaver's</u> lucky hit,
> Brady's bon mot, or <u>Barger's</u> <u>wit</u>!
> Intemperance listening to the tale,
> Forgot the turbot growing stale,
> And admiration balanced hung,—
> 'Twixt peacock's brains, and Godwin's tongue!"

Ah! What a necromancer is the menu card! conjuring up that "Union" Symposium, in comparison with which, Lucullus'[6] little tame tea fights in the
"Apollo" at Tusculum,[7] fade into insignificance! As I gaze at the lovely illustrations that adorn it, I am reminded of those banquets in the Farnesina,[8]
when Chigi[9] entertained Leo X,[10] and gold and silver dishes consecrated by
the touch of the honored and gifted guests, were immediately after the feast,
thrown into the Tiber.[11] That you my dear Sir, reigned as <u>Symposiarch</u>[12] of
the assembled wits, I feel assured, and knowing what a "feast of reason" you
must have enjoyed at that veritable one of the "Noctes Ambrosianae"[13] I only
wish I could have stolen into the sacred "<u>Ear</u> <u>of</u> <u>Dionysius</u>," (vide "Noctes
Ambrosianae") and heard the bursts of eloquence that————!! <u>just</u> <u>here</u>
patience receives her glorious reward, for my <u>turkey</u> <u>hen</u> rashly concluding
that I am too much engrossed by my letter, to keep up my Argus[14] watch
upon her movements, has finally darted into a cluster of dewberry vines, and
settled herself comfortably upon the nest! Behold then recompense of faithful strategy!

I was sincerely glad to receive your friendly letter;—and for your kindly expressed goodwill for my husband's successful commissionship, please accept our united thanks. I opposed and regretted his appointment to the guardianship of the troublesome elephant yclept "Municipal Bankruptcy" but since he has been installed Chairman of the Committee,[15] I most earnestly and conscientiously hope that the brilliant success of his efforts to galvanize the corpse of public credit, will leave me so vanquished by wifely pride in his triumph, that I shall gladly forego the precious feminine privilege and prerogative (which since the days of Cassandra[16] all wives have so dearly prized!) of solemnly whispering in the conjugal ear—"I told you so!"

Do you still contemplate for the ensuing summer, the European tour, of which you spoke when I saw you last in New York? Present my kindest regards and best wishes to your wife, whose health is I trust, fully restored, and believe me

Very sincerely
Your friend

Augusta E Wilson

PS

When you have the requisite leisure, I should be glad to have you call on Mrs Commodore Vanderbilt,[17] and ask her to show you a certain paper I wrote concerning Judge Black's shameful attack upon her.

      AEW.

1. Judge Black's criticism of Frank Crawford Vanderbilt, referred to at the end of this letter, apparently occurred in the autumn of 1878. Beauregard mentions the incident in a letter he wrote to AEW on November 26, 1878 (housed in the Detroit Public Library).

2. Prince de Talleyrand (1754–1838), a French diplomat who managed, through many changes of government, to continually rise in power and influence.

3. The Wilsons' house, Ashland, was known for its beautiful gardens, varieties of flowers, and lawns. Many different types of fowl were allowed to wander about freely on the lawns. All domestic fowl, such as turkeys, geese, leghorns, and guineas, were white because the Wilsons enjoyed the artistic effect of the white birds against the green lawns (Fidler, *A Biography,* 154).

4. In Roman religion, the benevolent spirits and gods that watched over a household.

5. The Union Club, founded in 1836, was one of the oldest men's social clubs in New York City.

6. See AEW to Curry, October 7, 1865, note 18.

7. An ancient city of Latium, south of Rome.

8. The Villa Farnesina was the luxurious home built by Agostino the Magnificent (c. 1465–1520), who became an extremely successful banker, lived a lavish lifestyle, and patronized writers and artists.

9. The family name of Agostino the Magnificent (see note 8 above). The Chigis, members of the Italian nobility, produced famous bankers, ecclesiastics, and patrons of the church.

10. Leo X (1475–1521) served as pope from 1513 to 1521.

11. A river in central Italy that runs through Rome.

12. The director or master of an ancient Greek symposium.

13. See AEW to Curry, October 16, 1863, note 5.

14. In classical mythology, Argus had one hundred eyes in his head and never closed more than two of them at a time, even in sleep. He, therefore, made an excellent watchman.

15. The records of Mr. Wilson's business dealings have not survived. At the time of his marriage to AEW, he was wealthy due to business investments outside the South. He was also the director of Mobile's leading bank, a director in the Mobile and Montgomery Railroad, and the chief stockholder in the Spring Hill and Mobile streetcar line. Concerning Mr. Wilson's later business dealings, Fidler writes only that "Mr. Wilson's business interests were expanding in the seventies, and a dutiful wife could not choose but hear about them and share the necessary anxieties" (181).

16. See AEW to Curry, July 15, 1863, note 16.

17. AEW's friend, Miss Frank Crawford, married Cornelius "Commodore" Vanderbilt in 1869 when she was thirty and he was seventy-five. The marriage created a great deal of negative comment about Frank, who, it was assumed, had married Vanderbilt only for his money. Vanderbilt died in 1877 at the age of 83. Judge Black's criticism of Mrs. Vanderbilt has not been located. However, in a letter dated November 26, 1878 (housed in the Detroit Public Library), General Beauregard refers to a newspaper article about Judge Black's attack on Mrs. Vanderbilt. Beauregard claims that Judge Black, in an attempt to besmirch Mrs. Vanderbilt's reputation, "has only destroyed his own."

❧ ❧ ❧

MS 84 / Virginia   Mobile Sept' 28th 78

Mr E Lane:
Dear Sir:
    In compliance with the request contained in your letter of the 25th, I furnish the desired autograph, and am

> Very respectfully
> Augusta Evans Wilson

❧ ❧ ❧

MS 85 / Historical Society of Mobile   At Home Dec. 24th [no year]

My dear Randolph:[1]
    If you had searched all the stores in Mobile, you could not have bought a present which would have been as acceptable to me as your <u>dear</u> <u>letter</u> which

has just reached me. I am sure that Santa Claus will generously provide for a little boy who stands head of all his classes, and who is so obedient and affectionate to his parents. It gives me great pleasure to hear you are so studious, and I am building high hopes of your future. If you will only study faithfully, you can be anything you choose, and make me very proud of you. Thanking you my dear Randolph for your welcome letter,

    I am

Most Lovingly—
Aunt A.

1. Randolph's relationship to AEW has not been traced. AEW had a younger brother named Randolph, but his children were Augusta and Clarence. T. C. DeLeon, in his "Biographical Reminiscences," mentions the children of several of AEW's siblings, but no Randolph. Also, Mrs. Virginia Barrett, of Jacksonville, Florida, a distant relative of AEW, consulted a family history, *Nehemiah Howard and His Family* (by Rebecca Echols Terry, 1983), but found the listing of the children of AEW's siblings to be incomplete. There was no mention of a child named Randolph.

❧ ❧ ❧

MS 86 / Barnard College Library   Mobile June 25th [1880+][1]

My dear Mr Carleton:[2]

Accept my thanks for your kind letter relative to the dramatization of "Infelice."[3] May I trouble you to hand the enclosed letter to Mr Hall of your house; and to address one to "Rutledge,"[4] which I have left unsealed for your perusal? As I was quite dubious about Mrs Harris' correct address, I hope you will supply it. And now my dear Sir, can you possibly goad your imagination to conjecture what prosaic memory flutters through my brain at the approach of the 1st of July? Pray do not deem me hopelessly mercenary and ignobly avaricious, because I carry the virtue of punctuality to the infallible perfection of never forgetting when payments of "filthy lucre" are due.[5] The height of my ambition, (as regards sublunary matters) is to attain that sublime niche in financial architecture where I can with supreme contempt banish every thought of the existence of the 1st of July!! . . . I saw from the papers that Mrs Holmes[6] had gone to Europe for quite an extended tour. Happy Mrs. Holmes! I sincerely hope she will enjoy her foreign travel more than "Marion Harland"[7] seems to have done, judging from the savage bitterness of the book "Loiterings in Pleasant Paths."[8] Mrs. Terhune is usually so genial, I was surprised at her last crusade. I am sincerely glad to learn your summer programme is so charming,—and equally sincere in thanking you for your kind invitation to join the party,—mais Helas![9] the grim fates are not propitious.

With much love to your dear wife and daughters, and kind regards to Mr Dillingham[10] and Mr Hall, believe me

Gratefully your friend
Augusta E Wilson

1. The novel *Loiterings in Pleasant Paths,* referred to in note 8 below, was published in 1880.

2. G. W. Carleton published several of AEW's novels, beginning with *St. Elmo* in 1866. Carleton bought out J. C. Derby, AEW's previous publisher and friend.

3. *Infelice,* AEW's sixth and most melodramatic novel, was published in 1875. In 1878, Wisner Gillette Scott wrote a dramatic version of the novel, but there is no indication that the play was ever performed (Fidler, *A Biography,* 182–83).

4. To the author of *Rutledge,* Miriam Coles Harris, an American novelist. *Rutledge* was her first novel, published in 1860. Carleton was also Harris's publisher.

5. It was customary to pay royalties to authors every six months. This is apparently the payment to which AEW is referring.

6. Mary Jane Hawes Holmes (1825–1907) was a popular American novelist, some of whose books Carleton published.

7. Marion Harland was the pen name of Mary Virginia Hawes Terhune, a popular nineteenth-century novelist, whose books Carleton also published.

8. Marion Harland, or Mrs. Terhune, published *Loiterings in Pleasant Paths* in 1880.

9. but alas!

10. A member of the publishing firm who later succeeded Carleton as head.

❧ ❧ ❧

MS 87 / Historic Mobile Society   At Home December 10th [1886]

Dr Mastin:[1]
Dear Sir:

I were indeed a hopeless victim of pseudoblepsis[2],—if, in addition to the very valuable information contained in your exceedingly kind note of the 9th, I failed to discern vividly the generous courtesy which prompted your friendly consent, and eminently successful effort to enlighten my ignorance. The technicalities of ophthalmology constitute a terra incognito, which I am not sufficiently daring to explore; but a slight abstract speculation relative to pseudoblepsis,—or pseudopia rendered me very curious to peer at least across the boundary lines, and trace the vagaries of distorted vision. Accept my sincere thanks for your courtesy, which I assure you I cordially appreciate, and believe me

Gratefully your friend
Augusta Evans Wilson

1. Dr. Mastin was AEW's physician in Mobile. He and his wife were close friends of hers.

2. Pseudoblepsis, or pseudoblepsia, is visual hallucination (E. L. Becker, et al., *International Dictionary of Medicine and Biology* [New York: Wiley, 1986]). AEW made use of this information while writing *At the Mercy of Tiberius* (1887). After Lennox Dunbar, the prosecuting attorney, becomes convinced of Beryl's innocence, he compares his earlier misconceptions about her guilt to those of a person suffering from pseudoblepsis. He explains to the jury: "Professors of ophthalmology in a diagnosis of optical diseases, tell us of a symptom of infirmity which they call pseudoblepsis or 'false sight.' Legal vision exhibits, now and then, a corresponding phase of unconscious perversion of sight. . . ." (Wilson, *Tiberius,* 257).

೩ೕಲ ೩ೕಲ ೩ೕಲ

MS 88 / Historical Society of Pennsylvania   Mobile April 8th 1887

My dearest Friend:[1]

Your <u>kind</u> <u>loving</u> letter, relative to Florrie's questions about my life, reached me yesterday, and my heart <u>swells</u> with gratitude for your tender interest in me. Since my own precious Mother and my darling Frank are together in our Father's Mansion of rest,[2] I seem to cling closer to my Frank's mother, <u>than</u> <u>ever</u> <u>before</u>; and your love is very comforting, very dear to me. This is Good Friday;—but without it,—no blessed Easter Dawn,—no hope of the reunion with our beloved dead—sleeping in Jesus. One of the book marks in my bible is an Easter card, with a cluster of flowers,—and only the words—"Augusta darling"—in my Frankincense's[3] handwriting. . . . Of myself, what can I tell you? You know all my busy life; its many mercies from God,—its many trials; its fierce storms of heartbreaking sorrow, as one by one my idols have been taken away. I thank my God for <u>so</u> <u>much</u> and my <u>dear</u> <u>husband</u> <u>has</u> <u>been</u> <u>spared</u>. If you say anything for me let it be, that I owe in a peculiar degree,—all that by God's mercy I have tried to accomplish, to my blessed <u>father</u> and <u>mother</u>. Never was child so crowned with parental love and care as I have been. Oh the unuttered patience and tenderness of my sainted father and mother! What did they not deny themselves—to guide me aright! If only I could cover their sacred names with some deathless light! <u>You</u> <u>know</u> <u>all</u> <u>they</u> <u>were</u> <u>to</u> <u>me</u> . . . .

Do write me you are better. I long to know you have escaped from the prison of a sick room. God bless and invigorate you—prays

Your Loving

Old <u>A</u>.

1. This letter is addressed to Mrs. Crawford, the mother of Frank Crawford Vanderbilt.

2. AEW's mother died in 1878. Frank Crawford died in 1885 at the age of 46. She survived her husband, Cornelius Vanderbilt, by eight years. (Mr. Vanderbilt died in 1877 at the age of 83.)

3. A pet name for Frank.

🙦 🙦 🙦

MS 89 / Historical Society of Pennsylvania   Mobile July 25th [1887][1]

Mr W J Bok:
Manager Literary Bureau[2]
Dear Sir:

Accept my thanks for your very kind letter of the 23d, and in reply, permit me to refer you to my publisher George W Dillingham, 33—West 23d St New York, who will give you the desired information relative to my new book "<u>At</u> the <u>Mercy</u> <u>of</u> <u>Tiberius</u>," which is now in press. It is <u>not</u> a historical novel, and has no connection with the <u>era</u> of the Roman Emperor, though the title involves his name, and only a perusal of the book will explain the relevancy of the title.[3] Please present my kindest regards to Mrs. Holloway, and also to Mrs Terhune.[4] Hoping that your mother will extend her friendship for my earlier works, to my new book, which I trust will prove the most useful and acceptable of my lifelong labors, I am, with renewed thanks for your courtesy

Very respectfully
Augusta Evans Wilson

1. 1887 is the year of publication for AEW's novel *At the Mercy of Tiberius* (mentioned below).

2. The American Literary Bureau was a publishing company in New York City. In addition, in a publication of its "season 1879–80" it advertised itself as "an agency for lecturers, readers, soloists, concert and opera companies, and other first class entertainments."

3. In the novel, when the heroine, Beryl, is falsely accused of murdering her grandfather, she feels that she is at the mercy of the prosecuting attorney, Lennox Dunbar, a seemingly hard, cold man who reminds her of the cruel Roman Emperor Tiberius.

4. Mary Virginia Hawes Terhune (1830–1922), under the pen name of Marion Harland, authored several novels and also books and articles on household management.

🙦 🙦 🙦

MS 90 / Columbia   Mobile October 20th [1887–1890][1]

Editors[2] of "Library of American Literature":

Having received from my publisher, Mr G W Dillingham, your application for permission to insert selections from my writings in your "Library of

American Literature,"³ I desire to express my thanks for your courteous remembrance, and deem it a <u>privilege</u> to comply with your complimentary request.

The place and date of my birth will be found in the accompanying sketch.⁴

Very respectfully

Augusta Evans Wilson

1. *A Library of American Literature: from the earliest settlement to the present time* (referred to in note 3 below) was published in eleven volumes during this time period.

2. The editor was Edmund Clarence Stedman.

3. An excerpt from *Beulah* (Guy's proposal to Beulah) is included in volume 9 of Stedman's collection.

4. See the following manuscript (Memorandum, 1887).

❧ ❧ ❧

MS 91 / Historical Society of Pennsylvania   [1887]¹

Memorandum²

I was born at Columbus GA May 8th 1835. Moved to Texas where we lived three years. Came to Mobile when I was scarcely 14. Was the oldest of 9 children. My Mothers [*sic*] maiden name was Sarah L. Howard. My fathers [*sic*] Matt Ryan Evans. My books were "Inez," "Beulah," "Macaria," "St. Elmo," "Vashti," "Infelice"—written in the order named, and I hope to publish my new novel this fall—DV.³ I was married Dec 2nd 1868.⁴ My books continue to sell surprisingly; and during the last two years, the sales have <u>steadily</u> increased. A new edition of "Beulah" will soon be issued. Have been a member of the Methodist Church since I was <u>eleven years old</u>.

1. 1887 was the date for the publication of "the new novel" (*At the Mercy of Tiberius*) referred to in the letter.

2. The word *Memorandum* was added in a different handwriting. This is possibly "the accompanying sketch" referred to in the previous letter to the Editors of the "Library of American Literature." However, the two manuscripts are housed in different libraries.

3. Deo volente (Latin), meaning God willing.

4. In a letter written to Frank Crawford and dated December 1, [1868], AEW identified this day as her wedding day.

❧ ❧ ❧

MS 92 / Historic Mobile Society   [Nov. 14, 1887]¹

Belfords Magazine²
June 1888
Vol. 1 No. 1

Complete in this Number
Old Man Gilbert[3]
By Elizabeth W. Bellamy[4]
Preface by Augusta Evans Wilson[5]
Preface.

Mrs. Bellamy has allowed me the privilege of reading her MS., "Old Man Gilbert," and I am anxious to see it in print, as I feel assured it will prove a literary success as decided as that of any genre work of this era. Her skillful etchings of Florida life, her peculiarly happy delineations of negro types, of Southern provincialisms in dialect and characterization, are as admirable as any portraiture Miss Murphee has painted of Tennessee manners;[6] and in some respects the careful work in dialect surpasses much that is found in "Uncle Remus."[7] The description of Old Gilbert in his cabin, of the kitchen at "Thorn Hill," and of Missy sprawled face downward on the piazza with Amity toiling to put on her shoes, are as life like and as artistically true and fine as a group by Teniers,[8] or one of Van Ostade's[9] Dutch interiors. What Miss S. O. Jewett[10] has done for placid New England life dear Mrs. Bellamy has certainly achieved most successfully for Florida. There is less descriptive work as regards scenery, than in Miss Woolson's "East Angels"[11] but the type drawing is equally fine, and the delicate distinctions in dialect will impress Southerners as infinitely superior.

Hoping that your opinion will coincide with the views I have taken the liberty of expressing, I am dear friend,

Always gratefully,
Augusta Evans Wilson

Mobile Nov. 14

1. AEW added the date, November 14, at the end of this letter. The year must have been 1887 because the preface was published the following June in 1888.
2. AEW's Preface was published in the first issue of *Belford's Magazine,* which appeared in June 1888.
3. This was Mrs. Bellamy's third novel, published in 1888 but set in 1857 in Tallahassee, Florida. The central character, Gilbert, is a charming, humorous black man.
4. Elizabeth Whitfield Crown Bellamy (1837–1900) was born in Florida but moved to Mobile in 1863 after the death of her husband in the war. She taught school in Mobile for the rest of her life and also published four novels. She was a close friend of AEW. See AEW to Dr. Wyman, December 12, [1887], note 4.
5. The Historic Preservation Society of Mobile houses a typed copy of this "letter." The location of the original is unknown. The information in the first seven lines of the letter was likely added at a later date by someone else. At the time of this letter, November 14, [1887], AEW has read only Elizabeth Bellamy's *manuscript*. The book was published in 1888.

6. Mary Noailles Murfree (1850–1922), a novelist and short story writer, was born in Murfreesboro, Tennessee. Her stories about Tennessee life were published in *Lippincott's Magazine* and the *Atlantic*. In 1884, a collection of her short stories, *In the Tennessee Mountains,* won critical acclaim.

7. Joel Chandler Harris, a journalist and native of Georgia, wrote *Uncle Remus: His Songs and His Sayings* in 1880. The book is a collection of animal tales and folktales written in the black dialect of middle Georgia.

8. David Teniers, the Younger (1610–1690), a Flemish painter known for his portrayal of peasant life and landscapes.

9. Adriaen van Ostade (1610–1685), a Dutch painter known for his humorous portrayal of peasant life.

10. Sarah Orne Jewett (1849–1909) wrote short stories and novels about life in rural New England. She is best known for *The Country of the Pointed Firs* (1896).

11. Constance Fenimore Woolson (1840–1894) wrote both short stories and novels. *East Angels* (1886) was a regional novel set in St. Augustine, Florida.

❧ ❧ ❧

MS 93 / Emory   Mobile December 12 [1887]

<u>Personal</u>
Dr. W S Wyman:[1]
Dear Sir:

Having been informed by the Mess'rs Nunnellee & Sons and also by Mrs. Bryce, that I am indebted to your courtesy and good opinion for the brilliant defence of my books, which the Tuskaloosa "Gazette" has published in reply to the persistent philippics of the Montgomery "Advertiser"[2]—I can not refrain from offering you my sincere thanks, for this manifestation of your flattering estimate of my work. Anent[3] the "harsh criticisms"—which in some quarters have assailed "At the Mercy of Tiberius,"[4]—permit me to say that I feel assured the vast body of American readers are sufficiently enlightened and just to discriminate between coarse abuse, vulgar sneers and flippant jeering—and that dispassionate, impersonal faithful analysis of literary work—which renders genuine criticism as unlike much newspaper "reviewing," as the subtle satire of Hogarth[5] differs from the broad caricature of Nast[6] or Dr. Maurier.[7] If the universally acknowledged masterpieces of fiction from Bulwer,[8] Thackeray,[9] Victor Hugo[10] or Tolstoi[11] were subjected to similar treatment, what a grotesque array of "encyclopedia lore" and "dictionary scraps" might be presented as verbal scare-crows to frighten the masses? Would not an intelligent public pillory the "reviewer" who offered as specimens of George Eliot's "highfalutin style" the two "thundering words" picked as pedantic plums from one of her books—"<u>Magicodumbras</u>," and "<u>Zuzumotzis</u>"?[12]

Is it not rather unfortunate that all the amenities of critical controversy which should characterize the knights of culture, have been exchanged for rude personalities, and coarse vituperation? How marked is the contrast presented by the genial tolerance, the generous catholicity of spirit that breathes throughout the recent admirable review of "Realism and Romance" contributed by Andrew Lang to the "Contemporary"?[13] "Why should the friends of one kind of diversion quarrel with the lovers of another kind? That is good which is good for each of us; and shall we 'crab' and underrate any genre because it chances not to be that which we are best fitted to admire? The pretension that all modern novels should be composed in this genre, (Realism) and that all others are of the nature of original sin, seems to be an impossible pretension. One only begins to object if it is asserted that this genre of fiction is the only permissible genre, and that nothing else is of the nature of Art."[14]

To even my most malevolent "critics" I desire to be just,—and it is my unalterable conviction that under the pressure of "overwork" they have been unable to really read my new book,—and haunted by the unlaid ghost of "Lempriere's Dictionary"[15] (a volume I am so unfortunate as never to have even seen,) have merely run their noses through the pages of "At the mercy [sic] of Tiberius," snuffing for "classical mythology" and "far-fetched learning"— exactly as some English animals are trained to hunt truffles,[16]—and as certain other creatures in continental Europe search for the same dainty vegetable. These busy hunters see no flowers,—inhale no perfume,—have no perception of golden harvest,—but true to their training are intent solely on scenting truffles. I have become accustomed to the tinsel and jingle of those "critics" who wear the cap and bells of Caricature, and my bona fide readers will readily understand that truffle hunters rarely avoid bespattering their game. If they could be persuaded to cease snarling, and lift their heads long enough to listen, I might feel tempted to soothe them, by repeating the comforting exhortation of Thomas Carlyle: "Of no given book, not even of a fashionable novel, can you predicate with certainty that its vacuity is absolute; that there are not other vacuities which shall partially replenish themselves therefrom, and esteem it a plenum.[17] How knowest thou,—may the distressed Novelwright exclaim,—that I, here where I sit,—am the foolishest of existing mortals;—that this my "Long Ear of a Fictitious Biography shall not find one and the other, into whose still longer ears it may be the means, under Providence—of instilling some good? We answer, none can certainly know; therefore write on Brother, even as thou canst, even as it has been given thee."[18]

I confess, I am very proud of the championship of Tuskaloosa,—the acknowledged seat of culture and classical learning in Alabama,—the University city where the light of thorough education shines so generously that the rawhead and bloody-bones of the decrepit ogre "Encyclopedia & Dictionary" has long ceased to frighten even timid readers. Although a stranger, you courteously lifted your polished, brilliant pen in behalf of my new book, and for your kind words and complimentary estimate of my work, please accept my sincere thanks.

Very respectfully.
Augusta Evans Wilson.

1. Dr. Wyman was a professor of Greek and Latin and later president of the University of Alabama.

2. Wyman had answered an article that appeared in the *Montgomery Advertiser* on November 26, 1887, attacking AEW's novels for their lack of realism and their pedantic vocabulary. In his rebuttal, which appeared in the *Tuscaloosa Gazette* on December 8, 1887, Wyman claimed that novelists and other artists should seek to portray ideal truths, not aim for verisimilitude. Moreover, he found AEW's liberal use of quotations and her elevated style to be admirable qualities that would help to educate and uplift her readers. See Fidler, *A Biography,* 192–93.

3. Concerning

4. AEW's seventh novel, published in 1887. Although *At the Mercy of Tiberius* has many passages written in AEW's pedantic, elevated style, it also is more realistic than her previous novels, particularly in its settings and conversations. In writing the realistic details and dialogue of this novel, AEW was advised by her close friend, Mrs. E. W. Bellamy, who wrote short stories and novels in black dialect (Fidler 186–87). See also AEW to *Belford's Magazine* of November 14, 1887.

5. William Hogarth (1697–1764), an English artist known for his satiric paintings that depicted the manners of his time.

6. Thomas Nast (1840–1902), an illustrator and political cartoonist who worked for *Harper's Weekly,* a newspaper. Through his drawings, he helped break up the Tweed Ring in New York, and he created the elephant and the donkey as symbols of the Republican and Democratic parties, respectively (Exman, *The House of Harper,* 87–89).

7. George du Maurier (1834–1896), a British caricaturist who drew illustrations for *Punch.*

8. Edward George Earle Lytton Bulwer (1803–1873), a British author and statesman, known especially for his scholarly historical novels.

9. William Makepeace Thackeray (1811–1863), an English writer known for his satiric novels and essays.

10. Victor Hugo (1802–1885), French poet, novelist, and playwright, and a major figure in the French romantic movement, author of *The Hunchback of Notre Dame* and *Les Miserables.*

11. Count Leo Tolstoy (1828–1910), Russian novelist and social reformer, author of *War and Peace.*

12. Eliot's reputation declined in the late nineteenth and early twentieth centuries when her novels were criticized as being too didactic and scholarly (Janet Mullane and Robert Thomas Wilson, eds., *Nineteenth-Century Literature Criticism* [Detroit, Mich.: Gale Research, 1989], 23: 48). Critic R. R. Bowker wrote in 1877 that readers of Eliot's novel *Daniel Deronda* constantly had to consult a dictionary as they read (quoted in Mullane and Wilson 4: 68–76).

13. Andrew Lang (1844–1912) was a British author, poet, and translator of Greek texts. As one of the leaders in the rebellion against realism and naturalism, Lang advocated a revival of romantic fiction. AEW, whose novels were frequently criticized for their unrealistic plots and dialogues, would have agreed with Lang.

14. AEW has put together sentences from two different paragraphs from page 685 of Lang's essay "Realism and Romance," which was published in the *Contemporary Review* of November 1887.

15. John Lempriere (c.1765–1824) wrote *Lempriere's Classical Dictionary of Proper Names mentioned in ancient authors with chronological table* (Reading, Berkshire: T. Caddell, 1788).

16. The truffle is a potato-like underground fungus that is regarded as a delicacy and is located by its odor with the help of swine or dogs.

17. a complete entity

18. From Carlyle's essay "Biography," first published in 1832.

❧ ❧ ❧

MS 94 / Yale, Beinecke Library

Selected from
"At the mercy [*sic*] of Tiberius."

"Like oceanic streams meeting, running side by side, freighted with cold for the equatorial caldrons, with heat for the poles,—are not the divinely appointed currents of mercy and of affliction God's agents of compensation, to equalize the destinies of humanity?"[1]

Augusta Evans Wilson

Mobile Feb 16th 1888

1. This quotation, from chapter 33 of *At the Mercy of Tiberius,* was apparently written in response to a request for an autograph.

" . . . *a heart so sad and lonely*"

MS 95 / Emory   Mobile March 26 [1888][1]

My dear General Beauregard:

Tonight as I opened the "Picayune"[2] of today, my eyes fell upon the sad and startling announcement of the death of your darling Lilian,[3] the beautiful sunbeam who kept your heart warm, when her own young mother[4] was blighted by the untimely frost;—and <u>before</u> <u>I</u> <u>sleep</u>, I feel impelled to express briefly my very sincere sympathy in the keen distress that now overwhelms you. Bitter experience has taught me the utter futility of all human attempts to comfort, and none knows more sorrowfully than I, how empty and mocking are words of condolence to an aching heart, bruised by that <u>awful</u> <u>blow</u> which only the divine hand that inflicted can possibly heal. Sympathy is the sole balm friendship is privileged to offer, while pointing to the Eternal Home where broken household bonds <u>are</u> <u>reunited</u> in everlasting circles of blessedness in <u>our</u> <u>Father's</u> <u>house</u>.

Peculiarly mournful for you, must be the sudden loss of the bright angel of your fireside, who twined her baby fingers about your heart strings, and made music in your lonely home, but dear friend, in the midst of your desolation, <u>try</u> <u>to</u> <u>remember</u>:—

> "We see but dimly through the mists and vapors,
>   Amid these earthly damps.
> What seem to us but sad funereal tapers,
>   May be heaven's distant lamps.
> She is not dead,—the child of our affection,—
>   But gone unto that school
> Where she no longer needs our poor protection,
>   And Christ himself doth rule."[5]

Because I realize how precious your beloved grand daughter was to you, I have yielded to the impulse to <u>offer</u> <u>you</u> <u>the</u> <u>assurance</u> <u>of</u> <u>my</u> <u>profound</u> <u>and</u> <u>earnest</u> <u>sympathy</u> in your great bereavement, and am, with kindest wishes, in which my husband unites,—Your sincere friend

A. E. Wilson

1. In pencil at the top of this letter is the following note, presumably in Beauregard's handwriting: "Ans. March 29 / 88."

2. *The New Orleans Picayune.* Beauregard and his family lived near New Orleans.

3. Lilian was the child of Beauregard's beloved daughter Laure.

4. Three years before Lilian's death, Laure had died giving birth to a second daughter. Each death was a devastating blow to Beauregard (Williams, *P. G. T. Beauregard,* 324–25).

5. Henry Wadsworth Longfellow, "Resignation," stanzas 4, 6. From *The Seaside and the Fireside* (1849).

❧ ❧ ❧

MS 96 / Historic Mobile Society   At Home
Feb' 20th [1890][1]

Dear Mrs. McCoy:

I have just returned from the funeral of my sister's child, and find your kind note awaiting me. I expect D̲ V̲[2] to spend tomorrow (Saturday) at home, and it will give me pleasure to receive your relatives and yourself at any hour between 1̲0̲ A. & 3̲ PM. Hoping to welcome you to Ashland, I am,

Very respectfully,
A. E. Wilson.

1. This letter was transcribed from a typed copy housed by the Historic Preservation Society of Mobile. The location of the original is unknown. At the top of the letter was this typed note: "Copy of letter from Mrs. Augusta Evans Wilson to Mrs. F. J. McCoy, Government Street." Since AEW was still living at Ashland, this letter would have been written before 1891, the year of Mr. Wilson's death.

2. Deo Volente (Latin), meaning "God willing."

❧ ❧ ❧

MS 97 / Historic Mobile Society   Mobile July 22d [1891+][1]

My dear Friend:[2]

I am quite sure I am indebted to you and to your good husband for the box of beautiful pears which came in perfect order yesterday, and proved a <u>fruitful</u> source of delightful surprise. Please accept the assurance of my most grateful appreciation of your kind and generous remembrance, which is very precious to a heart so sad and lonely as mine. Recently a telegram called me to Birmingham to nurse my sister, Mrs. Bush,[3] who was quite ill for some days and when, returning home last week, I passed "<u>Wilson</u>,"[4] I leaned longingly out of the car window, hoping to catch a glimpse of <u>some</u>—who honor and cherish my precious husband's name. Tell Mr McCoy I went today to say good bye to dear Bishop Wilmer,[5] who is so feeble that his son <u>Dr</u> Wilmer has come to carry him to Virginia, and <u>I</u> <u>fear</u> he may not live to come home. With renewed thanks for the beautiful pears, and hoping you may all enjoy a charming summer I am

Always Affectionately
Your Friend
A. E. Wilson

PS
Kiss my dear namesake for me.

1. This letter was written some time after the death of AEW's husband, which occurred in 1891. The Historic Preservation Society of Mobile holds a typed copy of this letter. The location of the original is unknown. At the top of the letter was this typed note: "Copy of letter from Mrs. Augusta Evans Wilson to Mrs. F. J. McCoy, Wilson Station, Alabama, via L & N R. R."

2. Mrs. Frank J. McCoy, identified by Fidler as a close friend of AEW in her later years (*A Biography*, 212–13).

3. AEW's younger sister Sarah Evans, who married Colonel J. W. Bush of Birmingham.

4. Wilson Station, Alabama, on the L & N Railroad line.

5. Bishop Richard H. Wilmer, a close friend of AEW for many years, was the head of the Mobile diocese of the Episcopal Church. Fidler points to AEW's friendships with Wilmer, Rachel Lyons Heustis (Jewish), and Mother Stanislaus (Catholic) as evidence of a religious tolerance AEW acquired as an adult, in contrast to her harsh criticism of the Catholic Church that she expressed in *Inez,* her first novel, written at the age of fifteen (185).

❧ ❧ ❧

MS / 98 Alabama
Historic Mobile Society (typed copy)   <u>1917</u> Park Avenue
Birmingham July 25 [1892][1]

My dear Rachelle [*sic*]:[2]

An hour ago I received your kind letter, and behold the promptness of my reply! Before I left New York my "hay-fever" returned with such severity that my eyes are so weakened and inflamed I can not write legibly,—still I am unwilling to delay an expression of my thanks for your <u>loving</u> <u>interest</u> and <u>tender</u> <u>sympathy</u>. Certainly if anything could attract me to Spring Hill,[3] it would be <u>your</u> <u>dear</u> <u>presence</u>; but I dread any <u>country</u> place where <u>grass</u> <u>abounds</u>, as at "Spring Hill," because my suffering in New York was caused entirely by a visit to the "Metropolitan Museum of Art" in Central Park, where the lawn grass had been mown the day previous, and raked into small piles. While I should <u>enjoy</u> <u>being</u> <u>with</u> <u>you</u>, and would doubtless find the Hotel much cooler than the city, I dread a renewal of my great suffering and think it safe to return to Mrs Fosdicks[4] [*sic*]. Were it not for this <u>grassphobia</u> I should go to my own precious home,[5] for a couple of months. I am <u>so</u> <u>rejoiced</u> to learn <u>you</u> are <u>better</u>, for I was very wretched about you dear. Sallie sends more love than the U S mail can carry! When I see you, I have <u>much</u> <u>to</u> <u>say</u> that I am unwilling to write. I presume Maddie[6] has written Mabel[7] about her beau, and his recent visit to New York? Give my love to Mabel and to Rose. Hoping to see you soon, and find you well,

<u>Lovingly</u> <u>yours</u>

A.

1. Mr. Wilson died in 1891. This letter, on black-bordered mourning paper, appears to have been written the following summer.

2. Rachel Heustis.

3. Spring Hill, where Rachel was apparently visiting, is located a few miles west of Mobile. A note on the typed copy of this letter, housed in the Historic Mobile Preservation Society Archives, lists the addressee as Mrs. J. F. Heustis, in care of Mrs. Fern, Spring Hill Hotel, Spring Hill, Alabama.

4. For the first few months after her husband's death, AEW lived in Mobile in the home of her friend, Mrs. Anna M. Fosdick.

5. Ashland, the home AEW had shared with her husband. She did not sell their estate until a year after Mr. Wilson's death.

6. Miss Madison Wilson, Mr. Wilson's granddaughter, who later married S. Palmer Gaillard.

7. Rachel's daughter.

❧ ❧ ❧

MS 99 / Buffalo Public Library   [1891+]

... and as the picture is a mere caricature, I have no desire to possess the volume that contains it.[1]

Very respectfully

Augusta Evans Wilson

1. Only the last page of this letter, written on mourning stationery, survives. The stationery suggests that the letter would have been written after 1891, the year of Mr. Wilson's death. The curator of the Rare Book Room of the Buffalo and Erie County Public Library (New York), William H. Loos, offered this explanation: "We have only the last leaf of a letter by Augusta Evans Wilson. It was apparently preserved as a specimen of her signature" (July 6, 1994).

❧ ❧ ❧

MS 100:Alabama
Historic Mobile Society (typed copy)   <u>304</u> Joachin St.[1]
August 8th [1892–1894]

My dear Rachelle:[2]

A <u>thousand</u> <u>thanks</u> for your kind and valued notes—which I hope to answer in person as soon as possible. Having promised a friend to see her <u>any</u> <u>morning</u> <u>this</u> <u>week</u>, I can scarcely go out on the car you mention, until <u>after</u> her visit, but hope to ride out some afternoon soon, on the 5 oclock train. I am rejoiced to learn you have improved so rapidly, and I long for a <u>good</u> <u>old</u> <u>fashioned</u> face-to-face talk. As soon as weather permits I hope to come out. "Hay-fever" has left me so blind I can not write <u>legibly,</u> but I feel assured you will generously condone <u>all</u> <u>defects</u>. Love to Mabel[3] and your precious self.

Always Affectionately yours—

A.E. Wilson

1. This letter was written on black-bordered mourning paper. Following the death of her husband in 1891, AEW felt that she could no longer live at Ashland, the home the two of them had shared. She spent a few months with a friend and then moved in with her sister, Mrs. Virginia Bragg, at this address. (Virginia was married to Braxton Bragg, Jr., the nephew of General Braxton Bragg, whom AEW had maligned in several of her wartime letters.) In 1894, AEW bought the house at 930 Government Street and lived there until her death.

2. Rachel Lyons Heustis.

3. Mabel was Rachel Heustis's daughter.

❧ ❧ ❧

MS 101 / Alabama   Mobile Sept' 3d [1894][1]

Mr Norfleet Harris:
U S Consul, Leeds[2]
Dear Sir:

I am so nearly blind from a severe attack of "hay-fever," that at present I can attempt merely a very brief expression of my thanks for your courteous letter of the 20th. When "At the Mercy of Tiberius"[3] was published the newspaper reviewers ridiculed and sneered at the "<u>preposterous</u> <u>and</u>[4]

1. The year, 1894, was added in brackets in a different handwriting under the date. The letter was written on mourning paper, so it would have been written after 1891, the year Mr. Wilson died.

2. The envelope accompanying this letter was addressed to Mr. Norfleet Harris, United States Consul, Leeds, England.

3. AEW's seventh novel, published in 1887.

4. Only the first page of this letter is now extant. However, Fidler, writing in 1951, saw the complete letter and referred to it in his biography of AEW. In the subsequent pages of the letter, AEW told Mr. Harris that the critics had ridiculed *At the Mercy of Tiberius* for its improbable plot. In the novel, the heroine, Beryl, is accused of murdering her grandfather, but refuses to defend herself for fear of implicating her brother. However, both Beryl and her brother are absolved of the crime by a "lightning photograph" that had been imprinted on a windowpane, revealing that a bolt of lightning had killed the grandfather. In the now missing pages of this letter, AEW assured Mr. Harris that, before writing the novel, she had carefully researched the phenomenon of "electrical photography" and had found several "authenticated instances of faces photographed on window panes by flashes of lightning" (quoted in Fidler, *A Biography,* 189).

❧ ❧ ❧

MS 102 / Historical Society of Pennsylvania
Mobile October 21st [1894+][1]

Gen'l James Grant Wilson[2]
Dear Sir:

The enclosed note, relative to the Thackeray[3] drawing, explains my inability to forward it.[4] Should Mrs Johnstone succeed in finding it, you shall receive it without delay. I do not know whether any member of Mrs LeVert's[5] family survives. Having lost her social prestige in consequence of her pronounced sympathy with the Union army, during and subsequent to the Civil war, she found Mobile an unpleasant place of residence and removed to the North.

Hoping the desired drawing will be added to your Thackery collection

Very respectfully
Augusta Evans Wilson

930 Government St.

1. This letter was written on black-bordered mourning paper. AEW purchased the house at 930 Government Street (see address at bottom of letter) in 1894, three years after Mr. Wilson's death. This letter, therefore, would have been written in 1894 or later.

2. James Grant Wilson (1832–1914), no relation to AEW, served in the Union army during the war and later worked as an editor and author in New York City. He co-edited *Appletons' Cyclopaedia of American Biography* (1886–1889) and wrote biographies of military figures and authors. His book *Thackeray in the United States, 1852–53, 1855–56* was published in 1904 and described two lecture tours Thackeray made to this country. Perhaps Wilson's attempt to locate the Thackeray drawing mentioned in this letter was in preparation for his book on Thackeray.

3. William Makepeace Thackeray (1811–1863) was an English novelist and illustrator. Some of his drawings were published in *Vanity Fair,* and he also drew caricatures to illustrate some of his own novels.

4. There is no indication in AEW's biography or in her writings as to the subject of this letter.

5. Octavia Walton Le Vert, wife of Dr. Henry Le Vert, was at one time Mobile's most prominent hostess. Fluent in six languages, she wrote poetry, translated classical authors, and published her travel journal and letters. Her weekly receptions attracted the most fashionable guests, including actors, actresses, writers, and politicians (Amos, *Cotton City,* 65–67; Amos, *Social Life,* 153, 156–57). There is no evidence, however, that AEW ever attended one of the Le Verts' social events. After the fall of Mobile in 1865, Octavia Le Vert invited Union officers to her weekly receptions—an unforgivable sin in AEW's eyes (Fidler, *A Biography,* 46).

❧ ❧ ❧

MS 103 / North Carolina   [1897][1]
Mobile Feb' 10th

My dear Lou:

May I trouble you to aid me in answering the enclosed letters which explain themselves? Every thing connected with the memory of dear cousin John[2] is so sacred that if possible I should like to identify the ring hallowed by his blood. Never having known his middle name, I feel assured you can give me the desired information. Hoping that the celebration of your "Silver wedding" proved as successful and happy as its <u>raison d'etre</u>,[3] and that it may furnish a sheaf of precious reminiscences for a "golden" future, I am, dear cousin

Lovingly yours
Augusta E. Wilson

930 Government St

1. A note, written in pencil at the top of the page, identifies the date as 1897 and the addressee as Mrs. Samuel Spencer. The letter was written on mourning paper, and AEW's address indicates that the letter would have been written after 1894.

2. "Cousin John" is most likely Colonel John W. Jones of Columbus, Georgia, who traveled with AEW to New York in 1859 so she could try to sell her manuscript of *Beulah* to a publisher. J. C. Derby of Derby and Jackson accepted the book. Jones, described by Derby as "a fiery young Southerner," had planned to throw a book at Derby's head if he rejected AEW's novel. Jones was killed four years later in the Battle of Gettysburg (Fidler 68–69).

3. reason for being

❧ ❧ ❧

MS 104 / Library of Congress (original)
Alabama (photocopy)   Mobile Oct' 24th [1898][1]

My Dear Lettie:[2]

   Although I have not heard from you since my last hurried scribble—in the midst of fumigation,—I must send you a line, to assure you of my tender and unfailing remembrance. There has been no more diphtheria on my lot, but brother Howard[3] was sick with severe cold, and I—?—well,—at least I contrive to keep out of bed. We are all distressed at the illness of Mr Frank Clark, which is reported hopeless, but I trust he will be spared to his helpless boys. Hitherto, I have avoided going to your house, fearing the germs of contagion might cling about my clothing, but as all danger is now over, I hope to see Ellen and Gaylord[4] as soon as I am able to leave home. I gave your address to George Cox, and requested him and Ernest to call upon you. Have you abandoned the contemplated trip to New York? Should you accomplish it, please see my dear child Fannie,[5] who remains at <u>182</u> <u>West</u> <u>75th</u> st for another year. I hope your summer has been agreeable in all respects, and that you have resumed interest in cultivating the <u>artistic</u> <u>talent</u> God gave you so abundantly. With <u>earnest</u> <u>and</u> <u>tender</u> <u>love</u>, for my darling friend, I am always <u>Faithfully</u> <u>yours</u> A.E.W.

   1. On the original of this letter, housed at the Library of Congress, the date was added in parentheses in a different handwriting at the top of this page, along with the note: "Augusta Evans Wilson author of 'St. Elmo.'"

   2. Mrs. Gaylord Clark. The Clarks were close friends of AEW, especially in her later years. Gaylord Clark was her lawyer (Fidler, *A Biography,* 212). A handwritten note accompanying this letter at the Library of Congress explains, "This is from Augusta Evans Wilson, who wrote *St. Elmo and Beulah*—To Mrs. Gaylord Clark—the wife of the present Mobile lawyer." The envelope with the letter is addressed to Mrs. Gaylord B. Clark at 1528 "I" Street NW in Washington, D.C. The Clarks were apparently in Washington temporarily since AEW writes in this letter about going to their house in Mobile.

   3. Howard Evans, AEW's younger brother. After the death of Mr. Wilson, Howard lived with AEW in her house on Government Street until his death in 1908.

   4. Probably the son and daughter-in-law of Mrs. Clark.

   5. Fannie (Frances) Wilson Jordan was Mr. Wilson's youngest daughter. Fannie, who was thirteen at the time of her father's marriage to AEW, developed a close relationship with her stepmother (Fidler 151).

❧ ❧ ❧

MS 105 / Emory   Mobile May 14th [1900][1]

Dear Bishop Candler:[2]

Today's mail brought me the dainty volume—"<u>Christus Auctor</u>"[3] which I owe to your very kind remembrance, and I am unwilling to delay an expression of my cordial thanks for your courtesy. Anticipating both pleasure and profit from the perusal of your book, I am, with best wishes for your family and yourself,

Gratefully yours
Augusta Evans Wilson

1. This letter was written on black-bordered mourning paper although AEW's husband had been dead for nine years. See AEW to Mrs. George, July 6, 1903, note 1.

2. Warren Akin Candler (1857–1941) was president of Emory College in Oxford, Georgia, from 1888 to 1898 and became bishop of the Methodist Church. He was instrumental in founding a school of theology at Emory and served as its first chancellor from 1914 to 1922. He was the author of fifteen books and numerous articles (Kenneth Coleman and Charles S. Gurr, *Dictionary of Georgia Biography* [Athens: University of Georgia Press, 1983]).

3. *Christus Auctor; A Manual of Christian Evidences* was published in 1900. It is a book of "proofs" to support the claims of Christianity.

❧ ❧ ❧

MS 106 / Virginia   Mobile October 31st [1900][1]

<u>Personal</u>
Professor H T Peck:[2]
Editor of "The Bookman"
Dear Sir:

On page 212 of "Chronicle and Comment" in the November "Bookman" I find the following: "The central episode (in "The Circular Study")[3] is in a measure an obvious imitation of an incident in Mrs Augusta J Evan's 'St. Elmo.' <u>Of</u> <u>course, it is very likely that Mrs Wilson took it from some one else, who in turn had filched it</u> from an earlier story-teller." For forty years numerous persons have attacked my books in various ways, but this is the first time the charge of theft has been brought against me,[4] and I very respectfully request that the gratuitous accusation of dishonesty published in the "Bookman" be proved distinctly, or else withdrawn. Where and from whom did I "filch" the incident in "St. Elmo?" If the truth of the charge can be established it is obligatory on the writer to do so promptly; if not, simple justice demands a retraction.[5] Legitimate criticism, however hostile, is so thoroughly equipped for attack that the aid of calumny need not be invoked, and "filching" is an accusation every honest author must challenge.[6] Because I do not know who conducts the departments of "Chronicle and Comment," I have taken the liberty of addressing this remonstrance to you, feeling assured you will at least courteously consider it.

Very respectfully
Augusta Evans Wilson

930 Government St.[7]   Mobile

1. *The Circular Study,* referred to in note 3 below, was published in 1900.

2. Harry Thurston Peck (1856–1914) was a distinguished professor of Latin at Columbia University for many years. From 1895 to 1902 he was editor-in-chief of *The Bookman,* a literary monthly magazine published by Dodd, Mead, and Company.

3. A novel published in 1900 by the American author Anna Katherine Green (1846–1935). The article in *The Bookman* stated, "The central episode in the feud between the Cadwaladers and John Poindexter which directly led to the crime is not only utterly extravagant and ridiculous, but is in a measure an obvious imitation of an incident in Mrs. Augusta J. Evan's *St. Elmo.*" (In *St. Elmo,* the leading character, St. Elmo Murray, deeply resents the members of the Hammond family after discovering that his best friend, Murray Hammond, had stolen his fiancée.)

4. This statement is not entirely true. At least one critic in 1859 charged that *Beulah,* AEW's second novel, was but a poor imitation of *Jane Eyre* (quoted in Fidler, *A Biography,* 80). Furthermore, when *St. Elmo* was published in 1866, some critics claimed that Mr. Rochester in *Jane Eyre* had influenced the portrayal of the leading man, St. Elmo Murray (Fidler 133–34).

5. Peck did indeed apologize to AEW in the January 1901 issue of *The Bookman.* He claimed, in part, that his remarks had been "unfortunately worded" and he had only meant to suggest "that perhaps the general plot of this very popular book [*St. Elmo*] was vaguely suggested by other works that had gone before. Our general thesis was that almost every work of fiction has both ancestors and descendants" (447).

6. AEW spoke out against false charges of plagiarism in *Macaria* (1864). In that novel, Russell Aubrey informs Electra that he had seen a painting in Europe of the Erythroean Sibyl that was very similar to one of Electra's paintings. Electra worries that the critics will think she had copied the other painting. Russell reassures her that the charge of plagiarism has been falsely pressed against many honest writers and artists and that remarkable coincidences can and do occur (Evans, *Macaria,* [Baton Rouge: Louisiana State University Press, 1992], 206–7).

7. This letter was written on black-bordered paper from the house where AEW lived as a widow.

❧ ❧ ❧

MS 107 / Duke   Mobile January 1st 1902

My Dear Mr Curry:

Very frequently during the last decade I have desired and intended to express my grateful appreciation of your kind courtesy in sending me several pamphlets and addresses, but feeble health vetoed my purpose, and recently a severe injury to my right hand makes it very difficult for me to <u>write</u> <u>legibly</u>. Through the medium of the press I have kept in touch with your educational campaign[1], and on this first day of the new year I wish to congratulate you most cordially upon the honor conferred in the special mission to Madrid[2]— a national recognition of your brilliant diplomatic career[3] which is peculiarly gratifying to the South. <u>Forty</u> <u>one</u> <u>years</u> ago, I listened to the speech you delivered in the "Confederacy Congress" at Montgomery when presenting to Howell Cobb an inkstand of Talladega marble.[4] How many who heard you then, survive today to congratulate you on this latest laurel wreath earned by your successful service? Hoping that 1902 comes freighted with blessings for you and your wife, and soliciting your general indulgence for this ugly scrawl, believe me—as of yore,

Your sincere, unreconstructed rebel friend,

Augusta Evans Wilson

1. For several years after the war, Curry served as president of Howard College, a Baptist college in Alabama. He campaigned tirelessly to attract both students and funding for the college. Later, from 1880 to 1885, he was the general agent for the Peabody Education Fund, an educational foundation that George Peabody established in 1867 with a two-million-dollar endowment for the purpose of assisting schools in the South. In this position, Curry became something of an educational reformer, campaigning for public schools in the South and for educational opportunities for blacks and women (Rice, *J. L. M. Curry,* 53–55, 85–98, 111–12).

2. Curry had recently been appointed U. S. Special Envoy to Spain for the celebration of the Coming of Age of King Alphonso XIII. Curry had been present at the king's birth sixteen years earlier (Rice 176). See note 3 below.

3. In 1885, President Cleveland offered Curry the U. S. Mission to Spain. Curry served in this capacity for three years, living in Madrid with his wife. In 1886 Curry, along with other dignitaries, had been invited to wait at the palace for the birth of the queen's baby. Shortly after his birth, the baby Alphonso XIII was presented to the dignitaries (Rice 121–27).

4. In February 1861, the convention of the seceding states met in Montgomery, Alabama, to draft a provisional constitution and to elect a provisional president (Jefferson

Davis). Curry, as one of the Alabama delegates, presented Howell Cobb, a delegate from Georgia and president of the convention, with an inkstand made from marble quarried in Talladega, Curry's hometown in east-central Alabama. See AEW to Curry, April 15, 1866.

✣ ✣ ✣

MS 108 / Barnard College Library   Mobile, August 21st 1902

Dr Charles E Rice:
Dear Sir:
 While I had seen the perfunctory criticism in "Public Opinion,"[1] I desire to thank you most cordially for your exceedingly kind letter which gives me sincere pleasure. Among my very loyal and valued friends, I remember some in the north and the far west, whose courteous remembrance and complimentary good opinion I gratefully appreciate. A severe injury to my right hand and wrist makes it painful and quite difficult for me to write legibly, hence I ask your generous indulgence for this cramped and ugly scrawl. Hoping that should you revisit Mobile you will afford me an opportunity of expressing in person my earnest thanks for your friendly interest,—and trusting [that] you will not be disappointed in "A Speckled Bird," I am

Very respectfully
Augusta Evans Wilson

930 Government St.[2]

 1. *A Speckled Bird,* AEW's eighth novel, was published in the late summer of 1902. Although the novel was very successful with the public, critics attacked it, as they had AEW's previous novels, for its pedantic style and unnatural dialogue (Fidler, *A Biography,* 208–9).
 2. This letter was written on black-bordered paper from the house where AEW lived as a widow.

✣ ✣ ✣

MS 109 / Alabama Archives   Mobile July 6th [1903][1]

My Dear Mrs. George:[2]
 Your Postal card and the box of jonquil bulbs have just reached me, and I scrawl my most cordial thanks to yourself and daughter for your kindness and generosity. For three weeks I have suffered terribly from a severe attack of inflammatory rheumatism which leaves me very helpless, and my hands are so stiff and swollen I can scarcely grasp my pen, hence I ask your generous indulgence for this <u>ugly</u> <u>scribble</u>. Please accept for your daughter and yourself

the assurance of my most grateful appreciation of the bulbs so kindly sent, and believe me with earnest good wishes,

Affectionately your friend
Augusta Evans Wilson

1. The envelope accompanying this letter was postmarked July 7, 1903. This letter was written on black-bordered mourning paper although Mr. Wilson had been dead for twelve years and there had been no other deaths of family members during the intervening time. Fidler points out that after her husband's death, AEW, following Victorian standards, cherished her widowhood to an extent that was almost morbid. For years after Mr. Wilson's death, she wrote her letters on black-bordered stationery (198–99).

2. The name on the envelope with this letter was Mrs. L. A. George of Demopolis, Alabama.

❧ ❧ ❧

MS 110 / Emory   Mobile October 12 [1905]

Miss M Rutherford:[1]
Dear Madam:

I trust that you will accept an apology for my seeming neglect, in failing to acknowledge more promptly the receipt of your very kind letter of August last,—and I feel assured you would generously grant me absolution, could you realize the complete physical prostration which my annual attacks of "Hay Fever" entail. I have been, in consequence, so nearly blind that all correspondence was for a time impossible, and although I am growing stronger with the approach of cool weather my feeble eyes admonish me that I must even now be very brief. The accompanying photograph is the best I can at present command, but the face is much <u>too large</u> and the cheeks <u>far too full</u>. The most accurate sketch of my early life will be found in "Women of the South," by Mary Forest—published in 1860.[2] Mr. James C. Derby's "Fifty Years with Authors and Publishers"[3] contains a chapter relative to my literary career when "Beulah" was . . .[4] and Mrs. Holloway's [The] Woman's Story by T[wenty] American Women"[5]. . . biographical sketch of. . . . Recently an article descri[ptive] of my home life has b[een] prepared by a Georgia lady at . . . the request of a New York editor, and when it appears in print I will send you a copy. Should you intend to make quotations from my novels—permit me to suggest that some passages in "Vashti,"[6] "Infelice"[7] and especially in my last and . . . "At the Mercy of [Tiberius][8] would represent . . . [m]ost finished literary. . . . One month ago, [p]ublisher wrote me that . . . sale of my novels in America amounted to—<u>425,000</u> copies, irrespective of foreign reprints. With very sincere thanks for your kindness and courtesy, which I cordially appreciate, I am

Very respectfully
Augusta Evans Wilson

1. Mildred Lewis Rutherford, a noted teacher and writer of Athens, Georgia. Miss Rutherford was teacher, principal, and president in a forty-year career at the Lucy Cobb Institute, a girls' school that achieved national prominence (Coleman and Gurr, *Dictionary of Georgia Biography*). She was also the author of ten books. In this letter, AEW is providing information about herself to be included in Rutherford's upcoming book, *The South in History and Literature: A Hand-Book of Southern Authors from the Settlement of Jamestown, 1607, to Living Writers,* published in 1906.

2. Derby and Jackson published *Women of the South: Distinguished in Literature,* by Mary Forrest, in 1860. The chapter on AEW consists of a photograph, a biographical sketch of several pages, and excerpts from *Beulah.*

3. Derby's *Fifty Years among Authors, Books, and Publishers,* published by G. W. Carleton in 1884, includes a chapter on Derby's professional relationship with AEW.

4. When this letter was folded, the upper right-hand corners were torn from pages 3 and 4. These tears obliterated several words from the following sentences.

5. *The Woman's Story as Told by Twenty American Women (with Portraits and Sketches of the Authors)* was compiled by Laura C. Holloway and published by John B. Alden in 1889. For the chapter on AEW, Holloway reprinted a section from *At the Mercy of Tiberius,* titled "The Trial of Beryl." The book also contains excerpts from the writings of nineteen other American women authors, including Harriet Beecher Stowe, Rebecca Harding Davis, Mary J. Holmes, Marion Harland, Louisa May Alcott, Ella Wheeler Wilcox, and several obscure authors.

6. Published in 1869.

7. Published in 1875.

8. Published in 1887.

✢ ✢ ✢

MS 111 / Dartmouth   Mobile November 8th [1905+?]

Mr Harrold Goddard Rugg:[1]

If you are so fortunate as to possess brothers and sisters, I feel assured you can realize my maternal reluctance to express favoritism regarding my literary progeny, because doubtless you share my belief that parents should be impartial. Nevertheless even just mothers often indulge a peculiar tenderness for the <u>baby</u> of their family.[2] With best wishes for your success,

Very sincerely
Augusta Evans Wilson

1. According to a letter written to the author by Philip N. Cronenwett, curator of manuscripts and chief of special collections at Dartmouth College, this letter by AEW is "from an autograph collection by Goddard Rugg, Dartmouth Class of 1905, and a librarian at the College for many years" (July 21, 1994).

2. Presumably Mr. Rugg created this autograph collection while working as a librarian at Dartmouth, in which case this letter would have been written after 1905 and AEW would have been claiming as her favorite book either *A Speckled Bird,* published in 1902, or *Devota,* published in 1907.

❧ ❧ ❧

MS 112 / Emory   July 26 [1906]

Dear Miss Rutherford:[1]

Although I am so nearly blind from "hay fever" that I can not attempt a letter—I am unwilling to delay an expression of my <u>sincere</u> <u>thanks</u> for all the kind and friendly things you have so gracefully said of me and my writing—in your new book which has just reached me. At present, the condition of my eyes renders it impossible for me to read the volume <u>as I desire</u>, but until I can do so, I shall place it in the hands of several literary friends of whose critical appreciation I feel assured. I will also call attention to its great value as a compend for the use of literary classes—several of which exist in Mobile during the winter and spring. As a textbook I should think it would prove invaluable, and I certainly hope to interest some of the teachers here who must feel the need of such a book. The copy you so kindly sent me, shall be circulated where it can accomplish most good as an advertisement. Accept the assurance of my cordial appreciation of your exceedingly complimentary sketch of my little books, and believe me—with warm good wishes,

Gratefully yours
Augusta E Wilson

PS
Pray pardon this ugly scrawl, which I have accomplished with <u>difficulty</u>.

1. See AEW to Miss M Rutherford, October 12, [1905]. Accompanying this letter in the Emory University file is a handwritten note by an unknown author: "Enclosed is the letter of thanks for the chapter about her written in The South In History and Literature by Mildred Lewis Rutherford—page 568. The author Augusta Evans Wilson's best known books—are Beulah—St.Elmo—Vashti—At the Mercy of Tiberius—etc. She received $15,000 for 'Vashti' before it went to press. In her day she was considered the most brilliant novelist in the South."

Appendix

CONTRACT BETWEEN AUGUSTA EVANS AND HARPER AND BROTHERS

113 / Columbia

Memorandum of an Agreement made this First Day of November, 1854 between Miss Augusta Jane Evans of Mobile and Harper & Brothers, Publishers, of New York:

Miss Evans being the Author & Proprietor of a work entitled "Inez, a Tale of the Alamo," grants to Harper & Brothers the exclusive right to publish the same during the terms of copyright.

Harper & Brothers agree to publish the said work in good style and to keep the market fairly supplied—and, in consideration of the right herein granted, farther [*sic*] agree to pay to the said Miss A. J. Evans, or her legal representatives, semi-annually, ten per cent, on their trade-list price for each copy sold by them over and above one thousand.

Dated at New York, the day and year above mentioned.

Augusta Jane Evans
Harper & Brothers

Bibliography

PRIMARY SOURCES

Alcott, Louisa May. *The Selected Letters of Louisa May Alcott.* Edited by Joel Myerson and Daniel Shealy. Athens: University of Georgia Press, 1995.

Barrett, Virginia. Telephone interview by author. 4 August 1997.

Beauregard, P. G. T. Letters. Manuscript Division. Library of Congress.

Bianchi, Martha Dickinson. *The Life and Letters of Emily Dickinson.* Boston: Houghton Mifflin, 1924.

Bulwer-Lytton, Edward Robert. *Lucille.* New York: Caldwell, n.d.

Carlyle, Thomas. *Sartor Resartus.* New York: Clarke, Given, & Hooper, n.d.

"Chronicle and Comment." *The Bookman,* Nov. 1900, 212.

Cooper, Anna Julia. *The Voice of Anna Julia Cooper: Including A Voice from the South and Other Important Essays, Papers, and Letters.* Edited by Charles Lemert and Esme Bhan. Lanham, Md.: Rowman & Littlefield, 1998.

Derby, J. C. *Fifty Years among Authors, Books, and Publishers.* New York: G. W. Carleton, 1884.

Dickinson, Emily. *The Letters of Emily Dickinson.* Edited by Thomas H. Johnson. Cambridge, Mass.: The Belknap Press of Harvard University Press, 1960.

————. *Letters of Emily Dickinson.* Edited by Mabel Loomis Todd. Cleveland, Ohio: World, 1951.

————. *Open Me Carefully: Emily Dickinson's Intimate Letters to Susan Huntington Dickinson.* Edited by Ellen Louise Hart and Martha Nell Smith. Ashfield, Mass.: Paris Press, 1998.

Evans, Augusta J. *Beulah.* New York: Derby & Jackson, 1859.

————. *Inez; a Tale of the Alamo.* New York: Harper & Bros., 1855.

————. *Macaria; or, Altars of Sacrifice.* Richmond, Va.: West & Johnson, 1864.

————. *Macaria; or, Altars of Sacrifice.* 1864. Reprint, with an introduction by Drew Gilpin Faust. Library of Southern Civilization. Baton Rouge: Louisiana University Press, 1992.

————. "The Mutilation of the Hermae." *Gulf City Home Journal,* 9 Nov. 1862.

————. "Northern Literature." *Mobile Advertiser,* 16 Oct. 1859.

————. "Southern Literature." *Mobile Advertiser,* 30 Oct., 6 Nov. 1859.

————. *St. Elmo.* New York: G. W. Carleton, 1866.

————. "To John Lothrop Motley, Historian of the Dutch Republic and United Netherlands." *Mobile Advertiser and Register,* 21 Aug. 1861.

————. *Vashti; or, Until Death Us Do Part.* New York: G. W. Carleton, 1869.

Fergusson, Robert. *The Poems of Robert Fergusson.* Edited by Matthew P. McDiarmid. 2 vols. Edinburgh and London: Blackwood, 1956.

Freeman, Mary E. Wilkins. *Infant Sphinx: The Collected Letters of Mary E. Wilkins Freeman.* Edited by Brent L. Kendrick. Metuchen, N.J.: Scarecrow, 1985.

Fuller, Margaret. *The Letters of Margaret Fuller.* Edited by Robert N. Hudspeth. 6 vols. Ithaca, N.Y.: Cornell University Press, 1983-94.

Gilman, Charlotte Perkins. *A Journey from Within: The Love Letters of Charlotte Perkins Gilman, 1897–1900.* Edited by Mary A. Hill. Lewisburg, Pa.: Bucknell University Press, 1995.

Grimké, Sarah. *Letters on the Equality of the Sexes and Other Essays.* New Haven, Conn.: Yale University Press, 1988.

Hosmer, Harriet. *Letters and Memories.* Edited by Cornelia Carr. London: Lane, 1913.

Jewett, Sarah Orne. *The Letters of Sarah Orne Jewett, 1849–1909.* Edited by Annie Fields. Boston: Houghton Mifflin, 1911. Irvine, Calif.: Reprint Services, 1994.

Lang, Andrew. "Realism and Romance." *Contemporary Review* 52 (July–Dec. 1887): 683–93.

Loos, William H. Letter to author. 6 July 1994.

"Radical Law." *Mobile Daily Register,* 5 Sept. 1876, 2.

"Radical Persecution." *Mobile Daily Register,* 5 Sept. 1876, 2.

"The Radical Programme." *Mobile Daily Register,* 5 Sept. 1876, 2.

Roberts, Joyce. "Letters of Caroline Kirkland." Ph.D. diss., University of Wisconsin, Madison, 1976.

Stanton, Elizabeth Cady. *Elizabeth Cady Stanton as Revealed in Her Letters, Diary, and Reminiscences.* Edited by Harriet Stanton Blatch. 1897. New York: Harper, 1975.

Swisshelm, Jane Grey Cannon. *Letters to Country Girls.* New York: J. C. Riker, 1853.

"That Circular Letter." *Mobile Daily Register,* 5 Sept. 1876, 1.

Timrod, Henry. *The Poems of Henry Timrod: With Memoir and Portrait.* Boston: Houghton Mifflin, 1899.

Torrey, Charles J. Letter to the author. 24 July 1994.

Walpole, Horace. *Journal of the Printing-Office at Strawberry Hill.* London: Cheswick, 1923.

Weld, Theodore Dwight. *The Letters of Theodore Dwight Weld, Angelina Grimké Weld, and Sarah Grimké, 1822–1844.* 1934. Edited by Gilbert H. Barnes and Dwight L. Dumond. 2 vols. New York: Da Capo, 1970.

Wilson, Augusta Evans. *At the Mercy of Tiberius.* New York: G. W. Dillingham, 1887.

———. *Devota.* New York: G. W. Dillingham, 1907.

———. *Infelice.* New York: G. W. Dillingham, 1875.

———. *A Speckled Bird.* New York: G. W. Dillingham, 1902.

SECONDARY SOURCES

Alderman, Edwin Anderson, and Armistead Churchill Gordon. *J. L. M. Curry: A Biography.* New York: Macmillan, 1911.

Alexander, J. H. "Literary Criticism in the Later 'Noctes Ambrosianae.'" *The Year-book of English Studies* 16 (1986): 17–31.

Altick, Richard D. *Victorian People and Ideas.* New York: Norton, 1973.

Amos, Harriet E. *Cotton City: Urban Development in Antebellum Mobile.* Tuscaloosa: University of Alabama Press, 1985.

———. *Social Life in an Antebellum Cotton Port: Mobile, Alabama 1820–1860.* Ann Arbor, Mich.: UMI, 1977. Microfilm.

"Augusta Evans Wilson: Confederate Propagandist." *The Alabama Confederate Reader.* 2nd ed. Edited by Malcolm C. McMillan. Tuscaloosa: University of Alabama Press, 1991. 352–55.

"Augusta J. Evans on Secession." *Alabama Historical Quarterly* 3, no. 1 (1941): 65–67.

Bakker, Jan. "Overlooked Progenitors: Independent Women and Southern Renaissance in Augusta Jane Evans Wilson's *Macaria; or, Altars of Sacrifice.*" *The Southern Quarterly: A Journal of the Arts in the South* 25, no. 2 (winter 1987): 131–42.

Baym, Nina. *Woman's Fiction: A Guide to Novels by and about Women in America, 1820–70.* Ithaca, N.Y.: Cornell University Press, 1978.

Becker, E. Lovell, Sidney I. Landau, and Alexandre Manuila. *International Dictionary of Medicine and Biology.* 3 vols. New York: Wiley, 1986.

Buttrick, George Arthur, et al., eds. *The Interpreters' Dictionary of the Bible.* 4 vols. New York: Abingdon, 1962.

Carlebach, Michael L. *The Origins of Photojournalism in America.* New York: Smithsonian Institute, 1992.

Coleman, Kenneth, and Charles S. Gurr. *Dictionary of Georgia Biography.* Athens: University of Georgia Press, 1983.

Cott, Nancy. *The Bonds of Womanhood: Woman's Sphere in New England, 1780–1835.* New Haven, Conn.: Yale University Press, 1977.

Coulter, E. Merton. *The Confederate States of America 1861–1865.* A History of the South, vol. 7. Baton Rouge: Louisiana State University Press, 1950.

Davidson, Cathy N. *Revolution and the Word: The Rise of the Novel in America.* New York: Oxford University Press, 1986.

Day, Karen. "From Dependency to Self-Reliance: The Phenomenology of Feminism in Augusta Evans Wilson's *Beulah.*" *Mount Olive Review* 8 (winter/spring, 1995–96): 56–62.

DeLeon, T. C. "Biographical Reminiscences." In *Devota,* by Augusta Evans Wilson. Chicago: M. A. Donohue, 1913.

Dobson, Austin. *Horace Walpole: A Memoir.* 4th ed. Freeport, N.Y.: Books for Libraries, 1971.

Druhan, Catherine L. "Louise Lyons Heustis: Southern Artist." *The Vulcan Historical Review* 4 (2000); http://www.sbs.uab.edu/history/varticles/Louisely.htm (accessed 10 December 2001).

Evans, Clement A., ed. *Confederate Military History.* 12 vols. New York: Yoseloff, 1962.

Exman, Eugene. *The House of Harper: One Hundred and Fifty Years of Publishing.* New York: Harper & Row, 1967.

Faust, Drew Gilpin. Introduction to *Macaria; or Altars of Sacrifice,* by Augusta Jane Evans. Edited by Drew Gilpin Faust. Library of Southern Civilization. Baton Rouge: Louisiana State University Press, 1992.

―――. *Mothers of Invention: Women of the Slaveholding South in the American Civil War.* Chapel Hill: University of North Carolina Press, 1996.

Fidler, William Perry. *Augusta Evans Wilson, 1835–1909: A Biography.* Tuscaloosa: University of Alabama Press, 1951.

Forrest, Mary. *Women of the South Distinguished in Literature.* New York: Derby & Jackson, 1860.

Foster, Susan Lynch. "Making Utopia Home: Domestic Discourse and Radical Politics in Nineteenth-Century American Women's Writing." Ph.D. diss., Cornell University, 1997.

Fox-Genovese, Elizabeth. Introduction to *Beulah,* by Augusta Jane Evans. Edited by Elizabeth Fox-Genovese. Library of Southern Civilization. Baton Rouge: Louisiana State University Press, 1992.

Freibert, Lucy M., and Barbara A. White, eds. *Hidden Hands: An Anthology of American Women Writers, 1790–1870.* New Brunswick, N.J.: Rutgers University Press, 1985.

Fryer, Judith. *The Faces of Eve: Women in the Nineteenth-Century American Novel.* New York: Oxford University Press, 1976.

Goshgarian, G. M. *To Kiss the Chastening Rod: Domestic Fiction and Ideology in the American Renaissance.* Ithaca, N.Y.: Cornell University Press, 1992.

Griffith, Ben W. "The Lady Novelist and the General: An Unpublished Letter from Augusta Evans to P. G. T. Beauregard." *Mississippi Quarterly* 10 (summer 1957): 97–106.

―――. "A Lady Novelist Views the Reconstruction: An Augusta Jane Evans Letter." *Georgia Historical Quarterly* 43, no. 1 (1959): 103–9.

Grimal, Pierre. *A Concise Dictionary of Classical Mythology.* Edited by Stephen Kershaw and translated by A. R. Maxwell-Hyslop. Oxford: Basil Blackwell, 1991.

Hamilton, Edith. *Mythology: Timeless Tales of Gods and Heroes.* New York: Mentor, 1962.

Hecht, N. S., et al., eds. *An Introduction to the History and Sources of Jewish Law.* Oxford: Clarendon Press, 1996.

Holstein, Suzy Clarkston. "'Offering Up Her Life': Confident Women on the Altars of Sacrifice." *Southern Studies: An Interdisciplinary Journal of the South* 2, no. 2 (summer 1991): 113–30.

Hoyt, Edwin P. *The Vanderbilts and Their Fortunes.* Garden City, N.Y.: Doubleday, 1962.

Hubbell, Jay B. *The South in American Literature: 1607–1900.* Durham, N.C.: Duke University Press, 1954.

"Introduction." *The Poems of Henry Timrod: With Memoir and Portrait.* Boston: Houghton, Mifflin, 1899.

Jin, Li. "Between Mary and Eve: American Women Writers and Their Heroines in the Mid-Nineteenth Century." Ph.D. diss., Texas Christian University, 1993.

Johnson, Samuel. *Lives of the English Poets.* 1779. 2 vols. New York: E. P. Dutton, 1954.

Jones, Anne Goodwyn. *Tomorrow Is Another Day: The Woman Writer in the South, 1859–1936.* Baton Rouge: Louisiana State University Press, 1981.

Kelley, Mary. *Private Woman, Public Stage: Literary Domesticity in Nineteenth-Century America.* New York: Oxford University Press, 1984.

Lane, Bessie Mell. "Rutherford, Mildred Lewis ('Millie')." *Dictionary of Georgia Biography.* Edited by Kenneth Coleman and Charles Stephen Gurr. Athens: University of Georgia Press, 1983.

Lauter, Paul. "Teaching Nineteenth-Century Women Writers." *The (Other) American Traditions: Nineteenth-Century Women Writers.* Edited by Joyce W. Warren. New Brunswick, N.J.: Rutgers University Press, 1993. 280–301.

Link, Samuel Albert. *Pioneers of Southern Literature.* 2 vols. Nashville, Tenn.: Church, South, 1900.

Lofts, Norah. *Queens of England.* Garden City, N.Y.: Doubleday, 1977.

Lucas, E. V. *The Life of Charles Lamb.* 4th ed. London: Methuen, 1907.

Macdonald, Linda Roberts. "The Discarded Daughters of the American Revolution: Catharine Sedgwick, E. D. E. N. Southworth, and Augusta Evans Wilson." Ph.D. diss., University of Colorado, Boulder, 1993.

Mack, Maynard. *Alexander Pope: A Life.* New York: Norton, 1985.

Matthews, Irene. "Women Writing and War." Ph.D. diss., University of California, Davis, 1990.

McCandless, Amy Thompson. "Concepts of Patriarchy in the Popular Novels of Antebellum Southern Women." *Studies in Popular Culture* 10, no. 2 (1987): 1–16.

McKay, Ernest A. *The Civil War and New York City.* Syracuse, N.Y.: Syracuse University Press, 1990.

McPherson, James M. *Ordeal by Fire: The Civil War and Reconstruction.* New York: Knopf, 1982.

Mencken, H. L., ed. *A New Dictionary of Quotations on Historical Principles from Ancient and Modern Sources.* New York: A. A. Knopf, 1942.

Moss, Elizabeth. *Domestic Novelists in the Old South: Defenders of Southern Culture.* Baton Rouge: Louisiana State University Press, 1992.

Mullane, Janet, and Robert Thomas Wilson, eds. *Nineteenth-Century Literature Criticism.* Vol. 23. Detroit, Mich.: Gale Research, 1989.

Olsen, Kirstin. *Chronology of Women's History.* Westport, Conn.: Greenwood, 1994.

Owsley, Frank Lawrence. *King Cotton Diplomacy: Foreign Relations of the Confederate States of America.* 2nd ed. Chicago: University of Chicago Press, 1959.

Papashvily, Helen. *All the Happy Endings; A Study of the Domestic Novel in America, the Women who Wrote it, the Women who Read it, in the Nineteenth Century.* New York: Harper & Bros., 1956.

Petter, Henri. *The Early American Novel.* Columbus: Ohio State University Press, 1971.

Pickett, LaSalle Corbell. *Literary Hearthstones of Dixie.* Philadelphia: J. B. Lippincott, 1912.

Rable, George C. *Civil Wars: Women and the Crisis of Southern Nationalism.* Urbana: University of Illinois Press, 1991.

Reynolds, David. *Beneath the American Renaissance: The Subversive Imagination in the Age of Emerson and Melville.* New York: Knopf, 1988.

Rice, Jessie Pearl. *J. L. M. Curry: Southerner, Statesman and Educator.* New York: King's Crown Press, 1949.

Roberts, Diane. Introduction to *St. Elmo,* by Augusta Jane Evans. Tuscaloosa: University of Alabama Press, 1992.

Roland, Charles P. *An American Iliad: The Story of the Civil War.* Lexington: University Press of Kentucky, 1991.

Rutherford, Mildred Lewis. *The South in History and Literature.* Atlanta, Ga.: Franklin-Turner, 1906.

Smith-Rosenberg, Carroll. "The Female World of Love and Ritual: Relations between Women in Nineteenth-Century America." *Signs: Journal of Women in Culture and Society* 1 (1975): 1–29.

Stanesa, Jamie Lynne. "Slavery and the Politics of Domestic Identities: Ideology, Theology, and Religion in American Women Writers, 1850–1860." Ph.D. diss., Emory University, 1993.

Stayton, Susan Dean. "From Rowson to Chopin: Radical Compromise." Ph.D. diss., University of Texas, 1992.

Symonds, John Addington. *Renaissance in Italy.* New York: Modern Library, 1935.

Thompson, William Y. "Robert Toombs, Man without a Country." *Georgia Historical Quarterly* 46, no. 2 (1962): 162–68.

Tracey, Karen Kaiser. "Reconcilable Differences: Double Proposals and the Renegotiation of Marriage in American Women's Fiction, 1850–1890." Ph.D. diss., University of Illinois, 1994.

Trachtenberg, Joshua. *Jewish Magic and Superstition: A Study in Folk Religion.* New York: Atheneum, 1977.

United States Department of the Navy. Naval History Division. *Civil War Chronology, 1861–1865.* Washington, D.C.: Government Printing Office, 1971.

Wasserstrom, William. *Heiress of All the Ages: Sex and Sentiment in the Genteel Tradition.* Minneapolis: University of Minnesota Press, 1959.

Welter, Barbara. *Dimity Convictions: The American Woman in the Nineteenth Century.* Athens: Ohio University Press, 1976.

Williams, T. Harry. *P. G. T. Beauregard: Napoleon in Gray.* Baton Rouge: Louisiana State University Press, 1955.

Yearns, Wilfred Buck. *The Confederate Congress.* Athens: University of Georgia Press, 1960.

Young, Bette Roth. *Emma Lazarus in Her World: Life and Letters.* Philadelphia: Jewish Publication Society, 1995.

Index

R